The Sense of Film Narration

D1795918

Edinburgh Studies in Film
Series editors: Martine Beugnet and Kriss Ravetto-Biagioli
Founding editor: John Orr

Advisory board
Duncan Petrie (University of Auckland)
John Caughie (University of Glasgow)
Dina Iordanova (University of St Andrews)
Elizabeth Ezra (University of Stirling)
Gina Marchetti (University of Hong Kong)
Jolyon Mitchell (University of Edinburgh)
Judith Mayne (The Ohio State University)
Dominique Bluher (Harvard University)

Titles in the series include:

Romantics and Modernists in British Cinema
John Orr

Framing Pictures: Film and the Visual Arts
Steven Jacobs

The Sense of Film Narration
Ian Garwood

www.euppublishing.com/series/esif

The Sense of Film Narration

Ian Garwood

EDINBURGH
University Press

Edinburgh University Press Ltd
The Tun – Holyrood Road
12 (2f) Jackson's Entry
Edinburgh EH8 8PJ
www.euppublishing.com

First published in hardback by Edinburgh University Press 2013

Typeset in Garamond MT Pro by
Servis Filmsetting Ltd, Stockport, Cheshire,
and printed and bound in Great Britain by
CPI Group (UK) Ltd, Croydon CR0 4YY

A CIP record for this book is available from the British Library

ISBN 978 0 7486 4072 0 (hardback)
ISBN 978 1 4744 0278 1 (paperback)
ISBN 978 0 7486 7839 6 (webready PDF)
ISBN 978 0 7486 7841 9 (epub)

Contents

List of Illustrations

Acknowledgements

I would like to thank the series editors, Martine Beugnet, Kriss Ravetto-Biagioli and the late John Orr for commissioning this monograph, and for their invaluable support and patience through the writing process. I also want to thank Vicki Donald, Esmé Watson and Gillian Leslie, successive editors at Edinburgh University Press, who were extremely helpful and accommodating. My colleagues at University of Glasgow were always on hand to give advice and were very thoughtful in reorganising my other work commitments to give me space to write the book. A research trip to the Lux experimental film archives in London was funded by a grant from the Carnegie Trust, and I received support from the school's research committee to attend conferences in Nottingham, London and Cluj-Napoca to present papers that helped me develop my ideas. I also benefited from testing my work on postgraduate students at University of St Andrews and University of Oxford at the invitation of David Martin-Jones and Andrew Klevan respectively. At extremely short notice, Lucy Fife Donaldson and Tim Barker kindly supplied me with (at the time) unpublished research of theirs which helped greatly in the writing of my conclusion. Many of the ideas in the book were first mooted and discussed in teaching situations, so I would like to thank all my students, especially those on the various versions of my postgraduate course on Multi-Strand Narratives in the Fiction Film.

My parents have always been an immense source of support to me and I would like to apologise to my mother for cutting her conversation short on the phone when I was up against my final deadline. My partner Karen was extremely supportive throughout, helping to create the space and time for me to write the book and acting as an incredibly effective proofreader in the latter stages.

Finally, I dedicate *The Sense of Film Narration* to my children, Alec and Carys, positive hindrances to the process of writing this book but enrichments to my life in every other way.

Introduction

The cover image of this book is extracted from *Double Take* (Grimonprez, 2009), a film that, as I will explore in Chapter 3, features a complex juxtaposition of different kinds of images: archive news recordings pitched against excerpts from Alfred Hitchcock's feature films; original digital footage presented in grainy monochrome that cedes to specially shot images which are marked by lustrous colour; a series of coffee commercials from different eras that chart visual developments in television advertising.

The hybrid nature of *Double Take*'s image system and the playful character of its visual combinations constitute an aesthetic that is at some distance from the seamlessness associated with many forms of mainstream cinema.[1] In keeping with a number of artists' films that rework the televisual and/ or cinematic archives, the experience *Double Take* offers the viewer is one involving a self-conscious apprehension of the formal distinctions between different types of images, and of the methods used to join them together: the seams are deliberately highlighted rather than obfuscated.

In the flaunting of its seams, the cover image is symptomatic of this aesthetic. The shot features Hitchcock passing himself on the street and this impossible event is manufactured by compositing together two of the director's cameo performances from his own films. The Hitchcock further back in the frame was first seen in *Stage Fright* (1950) while the more youthful figure in front made his debut in *Foreign Correspondent* (1940). The image bears the marks of collage in a variety of ways. The *Stage Fright* Hitchcock appears as an oversized cut-out figure behind the shoulder of his *Foreign Correspondent* alter ego rather than as a character represented through a naturalistic sense of perspective. The focus of the shot operates on a principle of alternation rather than taking the much more common option of either creating an evenly focused space (through the use of deep focus) or clearly separating foreground from background (through the use of shallow focus): *Foreign Correspondent* Hitch, closest to the camera, is slightly out of focus; *Stage Fright* Hitch behind him is the element within the frame in clearest focus; the woman in middle distance is the most indistinct figure, with the bus at the very back of the frame somewhat clearer than her. Described in this way, the image is composed of four layers, with layers one and three featuring significant objects on the left-hand side (*Foreign Correspondent* Hitchcock and the woman) and suffering from a comparative lack of focus, and layers two and four holding more sharply focused objects on the right (*Stage Fright* Hitchcock and the bus).

The lack of focus on the left-hand side of the screen and the overall flattening of perspective are due, in part, to the post-production blowing up of the *Foreign Correspondent* footage which converts a medium shot of Hitchcock walking towards the camera into a medium close-up. This magnification results in a blurring of the image as well as an increase in its level of grain, and this, too, provides a contrast between the footage culled from each film.

Finally, the seam binding the two images together is kept visible in the composited frame. The join appears as a diffuse ray of light shining behind *Foreign Correspondent* Hitchcock's left shoulder, engulfing the front of the bus at the back of the frame. The original cameo performances were themselves edited together from multiple images, owing to the use of back projection to fill in the background street settings in each case (the separation between background and foreground is especially marked in *Foreign Correspondent*). In *Double Take*, the artificiality of the original compositions is compounded by creating a series of material distinctions between different visual elements across the screen, as well as between foreground and background, and by creating the impression of the image being composed of at least four layers, rather than one or two.

I am suggesting that there is an uneven texture to the image that strikes the eye of the viewer. Graininess is more or less apparent on different patches of the screen, different layers exhibit distinct levels of blur or sharpness from front of frame to back, and a non-diegetic shower of light cuts the screen down the middle. The shot's distinctive 'feel' is even more apparent when set in action within the film. Played in slow motion, the viewer is allowed to linger on the different textures of the image for longer than would have been possible had it run at normal speed. In addition, the shot is repeated four times across the film and this also facilitates a lingering look that can take in the image's contours. This motivic shot provides different kinds of stimulation for the eye and, to use a term that has become quite commonplace in film studies, might be described as particularly 'haptic': that is to say, there is a texture to the image that appeals to our sense of touch.

This book is centrally concerned with films that juxtapose materially different types of images and sounds, in a way that brings out their sensuous qualities in an especially vivid manner. Despite their actual status as machine-made recordings, the sounds and images acquire a 'living' texture that engages the viewer's senses in a particularly intensive way: this texture constitutes, in part, the sensuous quality of film, and I shall elaborate on this concept in Chapter 1. The films' use of an aesthetic of juxtaposition results in the distinctive texture of each image and sound being highlighted by its placement next to images/sounds of contrasting consistencies.

The ability of cinema to engage the senses has been noted in all kinds of writing about (and promotion of) film. In the last twenty years, there has been a steadily growing body of work within film studies that explores cinema's sensuous capacity, and that seeks to understand film viewing as a fully embodied, intense and immersive experience. The critical motivation for considering cinema in this way varies but, as I shall explain in Chapter 1, this kind of writing often sets itself against an approach that is concerned with the apparently less sensuously engaged activities of, for example, apprehending a story or forming a particular point of view on an individual character or dramatic situation.

The central claim of *The Sense of Film Narration*, as its title suggests, is that a film's sensuous qualities can be intimately connected to its storytelling processes. In what follows, my readings of films are designed to demonstrate that movies can make viewers particularly aware of their senses in order to help them make sense of the events, behaviours and attitudes pertaining to a particular fictional world. Rather than adopting a position that sees the sensuous experience of cinema as necessarily opposed to, disruptive of, or simply coincidental with a narrative experience, I argue that the appeal to the senses can contribute fundamentally to a film's dramatic rhetoric.

Another take on the *Double Take* cover image will help to illustrate the complementary relationship between the sensuous and the dramatic that I wish to pursue. So far, I have discussed the qualities that make the image seem particularly tactile and, therefore, appealing to the senses. The image is also 'appealing' narratively, however. It has been captured at the point where the *Stage Fright* Hitchcock turns around and looks at the figure he has just passed (the shot actually begins with the *Stage Fright* incarnation of the director entering the front of frame, screen right, his back to the camera). This is a moment of dramatic intrigue for character and viewer alike. The character registers surprise that he has seen his doppelganger walking past, his quizzical expression offering a bodily manifestation of the thought processes that may lie underneath – who is this man who looks so like me? For the viewer, the character's act of turning his head confirms what can only be intimated at the beginning of the shot: that we have, in fact, seen two versions of Hitchcock pass each other. How can this be and what is the significance of this encounter? Understood in this way, the image encourages the viewer to ask narrative-oriented questions at the same time as it connotes a thought process on the part of a character that also exhibits a desire to place an event in some explanatory order.

For the viewer, the *Foreign Correspondent* Hitchcock is equal to his *Stage Fright* alter ego as a source of dramatic interest (it is the uncanny nature of the two of them occupying the same space that is so intriguing). In terms of his bearing, however, this other Hitchcock is evidently less agitated towards dramatic cogitation than his double. Yet, he is still pointedly wrapped up in processing stories. On its first appearance, five minutes into the film, this 'master shot' of their encounter is prefaced by a closer shot of the *Foreign Correspondent* Hitchcock, just before his alter ego walks past him (the cut to the next shot brings his double into the frame). This closer shot begins just as Hitchcock raises a newspaper nearer towards his face, registering an increased attention to whatever he is reading. He does not notice his alter ego because his eyes remain trained on the page as he walks past. He, like his double and the viewer, is engrossed in following a story, albeit one pertaining to the world of public events, rather than the private sphere (as experienced by the other Hitchcock), or one appreciated as a fiction (as understood by the viewer).

Story-related activities permeate the *mise en scène* of this pivotal image from the film and, I suggest, are also prompted in the viewer. These activities occur at the same time as the unusual texture of the image evokes a tactility that engages with the viewer's sense of touch. I argue that the simultaneity of these responses is not merely coincidental.

In this particular case, the peculiar texture of the image can be related to narrative comprehension in at least two ways. On a local level, the different degrees of grain and blur apparent in the representation of each Hitchcock differentiates them despite their similarities. The *Foreign Correspondent* Hitchcock appears to be in a world of his own, oblivious to passers-by, his procession towards the camera steady and gaining the quality of a glide by the use of slow motion. The *Stage Fright* Hitchcock, in contrast, resists the pull towards an even 'ethereal' movement facilitated by slow motion, by consequence of the more varied and halting nature of his actions: he exerts a more physical presence by breaking into the frame (rather than simply already being there) and moving into it, and by stopping and turning to look at his alter ego. This Hitchcock appears as a more solidly human figure than the self-absorbed double that glides past him and this contrast is augmented by the visual sharpness associated with the *Stage Fright* Hitchcock when set alongside the comparatively grainy and more softly focused quality of the figure from *Foreign Correspondent*. In these ways, the image suggests that there may exist 'real' and 'spectral' versions of Hitchcock, and this connects with a key narrative strand of the film, followed intermittently across its duration, in which a 1962 version of Hitchcock, in voice-over, recounts a strange encounter he has with a figure claiming to be his future self. This strand provides the focus for my extended analysis of *Double Take* in Chapter 3, and the first appearance of the shot described here coincides with an early passage of voice-over in which the story is introduced ('I have pondered many times but somehow never understood the meaning of that fateful encounter one August afternoon in 1962 . . .').

On a more global level, the early appearance of a shot so obviously 'full' of both story *and* texture, along with its reoccurrence throughout the film and its overpopulation by an authorial presence (not one, but two, versions of the 'master' cinematic storyteller, Alfred Hitchcock), encourage the viewer to understand it as a 'rhetorical figure of narrational instruction'. This phrase is taken from George M. Wilson's book *Narration in Light: Studies in Cinematic Point of View*, and Wilson explains the concept in this way:

> In such a scene or shot or limited series of shots the primary function of the local narration is to establish a stressed configuration of audio-visual elements which adumbrates features of the way in which the global narration is to be read. It provides instruction in the forms of perceptual intelligibility that the film proposes and flags the segments where the realization of these forms principally occurs.[2]

Understood in this way, the shot instructs the viewer that the texture of the image will be especially intertwined in this film with the apprehension of an unfolding dramatic scenario and that this intertwining may be particularly intense in those segments concerning the encounter between the two Hitchcocks. *Double Take* invites the viewer to appreciate the relationship between the texture of the image and the development of its story, and my analysis of the film in Chapter 3 constitutes an acceptance of that invitation.

Each chapter of the book features close analyses of films that, I shall argue, also encourage the viewer to link sensory experience with narrative understanding. This connection is facilitated by a juxtaposition of sensuously contrasting materials which combine to express the film's fictional world. For example, in Chapter 3, as well as discussing *Double Take*, I consider a moment from the CGI animated movie *Toy Story 3* (Unkrich, 2010) in which the default pristine sheen of the image is interrupted by a much more lo-fi visual aesthetic, cued by the film switching to the representation of a home video recording. This juxtaposition is obvious and, while its narrative justification is more overt than some of the other instances I discuss, the unconcealed movement from one kind of visual format to another is indicative of the clear distinctions made between the material quality of different visual and aural elements in all the films I consider. Each film discussed involves an evident collision between different sensuous qualities, and this constitutes a particular aesthetic that is not shared by all movies (as the earlier description of many forms of mainstream cinema as 'seamless' indicates).

This raises the question of the more general applicability of my readings to a wider body of films, and I want to deal with that matter here by discussing a moment from *It's a Wonderful Life* (Capra, 1946), a film that is often held up as a key exemplar of Classical Hollywood, the type of cinema most commonly associated with principles of seamlessness. Even here, however, there is evidence that sensuously different visual registers are being combined in a way that helps to articulate the film's dramatic scenario.

The moment features a transition through which the responsibility of portraying the film's lead character is handed from one actor to a different one, a phenomenon that provides the focus for my analyses in Chapter 5. In *It's a Wonderful Life* this transition is straightforward, narratively speaking. We are being told the backstory of George Bailey, the film's protagonist, who, at the start of the film, is contemplating suicide. Seen initially as a child (played by Bobbie Anderson), the handing over of performing duties involves the story jumping forward from 1919 to 1928, at which point Bailey is seen in adult form, performed by James Stewart.

The transition is well ordered. The replacement of one performer by another is explained by off-screen voices, already established as those of the angel Clarence (Henry Travers) and his heavenly mentor who are involved in a briefing about George before Clarence is sent down to Earth to try to save him. We have just witnessed George as a boy spotting a potentially deadly mistake made by his employer at the chemist at which he works. A fade to black is followed by an opening out on to a scene set in a shop in which an adult character, played by James Stewart, is considering buying a suitcase. Stewart is viewed from just above waist up, initially in side profile. Just as he turns his face towards the camera and stretches out his arms to demonstrate the dimensions of the case he wants, the image is frozen. At this point, any doubts as to the relationship between this figure and the boy are allayed, as the angels have the following conversation:

CLARENCE: What d'ya stop it for?
MENTOR: I want you to take a good look at that face.
CLARENCE: Who is it?
MENTOR: George Bailey.
CLARENCE: Oh, you mean the kid that had his ear slapped back by the druggist?
MENTOR: That's the kid.

If the soundtrack 'smoothes over' the transition from one performer to another, however, clarifying the purpose of the formal disruption and the identity of the figure in view, there is still a disturbance in the visual register that provides the viewer with a sensory experience which is different from what has gone before. The decision to provide the first view of James Stewart as George Bailey through freeze-frame is a visually arresting one, and it gives the passing of time a material quality: this is what time looks like when it is frozen. Furthermore, the viewer is allowed, along with Clarence, 'a good look at that face', an opportunity to observe its contours without the distraction of movement: to take in the raised eyebrow and the creases it causes on his forehead, the drooping lower lip, and the shadows playing on the right side, his hands caught in a gesture that seems to be beckoning our attention towards *that* face.

This is the point at which the film speeds through the years to call the adult George Bailey into view thereby bringing closer the moment of his breakdown which Clarence has been ordered to remedy. As such, it is an important moment narratively, and its pivotal nature is registered by the film's characters (the heavenly mentor explains why he has chosen to freeze the story at this particular point) but is also felt by the viewer as a distinctly different sensory experience. The adult George Bailey could have been introduced without the use of the freeze-frame but its deployment allows the viewer a unique opportunity to savour the physical features and gestural capacity of the character as embodied by the film's star. The freezing of the moment offers an intense impression of the expressive capability of George Bailey, laying down a marker as to what will be lost to the world (and, in particular, his hometown of Bedford Falls) should he commit suicide.

In this way, *It's a Wonderful Life* appeals to the senses as part of its appeal to the viewer's engagement with story. It is possible, therefore, to find the sudden presentation of different sensory stimuli for dramatic effect even in films that are not predicated on the sustained juxtaposition of materially different visual and/or aural elements. It is equally conceivable to discuss the relationship between the sensuous and the dramatic in films that adopt an entirely consistent visual and aural aesthetic.

My decision to focus on films that are very clearly marked by multiple visual qualities and/or diverse consistencies of sound is governed by a concern to understand an important part of the sensuous appeal of cinema as resulting from an 'internal' interplay between a film's constituent parts. As I explain in Chapter 1, much sensuous scholarship on film posits a 'fusing' between the body of the film and the body of the spectator that disavows the notion of a movie constituting a world in its own right. This book explores the consequences of redrawing a boundary between the real-life placement of the viewer and the fictional world of the film, a critical position I also elaborate in Chapter 1. The concentration on the internal relationships constructed between materially disparate elements within a particular movie helps to make clear this distinction between viewer and fictional world.

I assert that the specific combination of its materials encourages a viewer to sense a film in a particular way and to find a distinct significance in this act of sensing. This general claim will be plausible only if the close readings of particular films that follow are deemed to be convincing. These analyses rely on a fine-grained attention to details of the texture of the soundtrack and the image, and one possible problem, in terms of the universality of the claims I make, is the partiality of the viewing context upon which the readings are made. The analysis of all the main case studies is based on the viewing of DVD versions of the films, studied on various screens (computer monitors and television sets) and played through systems of different quality. Any comments I make about details of the soundtrack are based on a combination of listening through headphones and hearing the films in a cinema equipped with a 5.1 surround-sound system.

It is certainly the case that the same film will look and sound different depending on the format in which the visual and aural information is stored, as well as the quality of the technological apparatus used to disseminate it. One response to this is simply to be clear about the viewing context that resulted in a particular analysis of the film, as demonstrated in the previous paragraph.

The notion of the films setting up internal relationships, including sensuous ones, between their elements is also helpful in determining how 'definitive' my readings may be. It is likely that any changes in image or sound quality from one version of a film to another will apply evenly to all aspects of what is viewed on-screen or heard on the soundtrack. This means that, as constituent parts of a fictional world, the relationship between the different elements will remain intact even if the sensory stimulus the viewer has to deal with from one version to another is qualitatively different. For example, the film stock used in *Amores Perros* (Inarritu, 2000), discussed in Chapter 2, underwent a distinctive bleach-bypass process, one effect of which is to increase the graininess of the image. Any alteration of grain levels in the transfer from celluloid to DVD and in the DVD's display on different screens would be proportionate across the film, meaning that the quality of the relationships between the different elements would be preserved.

There are limits to this line of argument: viewing *Double Take* on a black-and-white monitor would negate my commentary on the film's play between colour and monochrome, for example. The texture of image and soundtrack may be affected more unevenly than my generalisation allows when a film is transferred from one medium to another. The readings that are offered throughout this book, however, are made on the assumption that they derive from an accurate description of the film's visual and aural phenomena, as experienced through multiple viewings, and that these phenomena are able to be perceived by other interested viewers of the film (there would be no point in disseminating the analysis if I did not feel this to be the case). Of course, the claims I make about the films are partial (like any reading of a film) and open to challenge on their own terms. Additionally, any alternative versions of the films (in terms of the texture of sound and/or image) may provide the material for a different interpretation. If this book were to provoke such critical activity about the particular movies under review, I would take that as an indicator of its success as much as I would if the general approach practised throughout the study were considered in future sensuous scholarship on completely different films.

Given its predominant focus on the feature-length fiction film, the main body of the book is divided quite simply into three sections, each dedicated to a fundamental aspect of (nearly all) fictional movies: the image (Chapter 3); the soundtrack (Chapter 4); the performer (Chapter 5). Before this, I establish the critical approach that informs my discussion of the sensuous aspects of cinematic storytelling. In Chapter 1, this involves situating my concerns within two key areas of debate: the consideration of film as a sensuous medium, on the one hand; and the understanding of films as fictional worlds, on the other. There is a considerable body of literature in both areas, and my review concentrates on writing that helps me to synthesise the two approaches. By the end of the chapter, I am in a position to summarise the key principles underpinning the analysis I undertake in the rest of the book.

Chapter 2 features an extended comparison between the four crash scenes of *Amores Perros*. Each scene renders the same accident using materially distinct visual and aural components, and my analysis considers the dramatic significance of doing so. Without being tied to the more specific concerns that drive Chapters 3 to 5, the commentary in Chapter 2 functions as a general example of the type of reading that is possible when attending to the arrangement of sensuous detail within a fictional world.

Chapters 3 to 5 each deals with potentially very broad areas (image, sound, performance) but do so by focusing on specific phenomena in each case. Chapter 3 considers the storytelling role of 'flawed' images in environments which also (sometimes overwhelmingly) exhibit a visual aesthetic that draws towards the pristine. The collision between images of different technical quality is understood through recourse to discussions about the avant-garde found footage film which habitually places together images that are clearly 'mismatched' in terms of their formal characteristics. The key case studies are a collection of CGI-animated films, produced by the Hollywood studio Pixar, and *Double Take*. Despite being very different types of film, the Pixar movies and *Double Take* are linked by their status as digital productions and, therefore, the chapter considers the deployment of the flawed image specifically in relation to debates about digital aesthetics.

Chapter 4 focuses on an aural device that is especially associated with storytelling, namely the voice-over. I consider the significance of the voice's material qualities to its narrational role, recognising those qualities as 'natural' ones, emanating from the body of a particular character but also machine-made, resulting from a recording process. At different points I consider the voice-over's human and mechanical properties, privileging attention to a voice's timbre, seemingly incidental details of vocal delivery and/or the sound's technological signature. As in Chapter 3, I focus particularly on moments of 'imperfect' voice-over, whether that be in the hesitations of the speaker or the foregrounding of 'system noise' that would normally be erased. A key contention of my analysis is that voice-overs need to be understood as part of a sonic weave, containing multiple aural elements, rather than simply in relation to the image. The case studies for the chapter are all films that deploy the relatively uncommon practice of using more than one voice-over narrator, the comparison between different 'disembodied' voices offering another point of contrast that helps to define the unique material qualities of a particular voice.

Chapter 5 considers the material frisson that can occur when the responsibility of portraying a film character is passed from one performer to another. This practice is most usually kept hidden: for example, the film industry's routine use of body doubles in the production process is not meant to be noticed in the final film. There are occasions, however, when the viewer is made to notice the physical differences between performers, and it is at these points that those differences may become significant in constructing the character. I divide my analyses between examples of a 'motivated' switching between performers (the most common kind) and the rarer phenomenon of 'unmotivated' multiple casting. In both cases, I concentrate on the precise moments of transference from one body to another, again privileging instances that are marked by 'imperfection': that is to say, a relay between performers that is depicted as laboursome, awkward or collisive, in which the distinct qualities of each performing body are made apparent.

The topics considered in Chapters 3 to 5, therefore, are relatively specialist, and are encapsulated within an overall approach which focuses on films that favour an aesthetics of juxtaposition. The intention of channelling the investigations of this book fairly narrowly is to provide a set of case studies that are detailed and that avoid abstraction. The first two chapters, however, do provide a wider framework in which to understand the significance of the more niche enquiries that follow. Furthermore, the intention of the book as a whole is certainly not to suggest that an approach which connects sensuous and narrative aspects of the film viewing experience can take only this form. Rather, the topic areas represent particular areas of enquiry, among many other possibilities, while the close readings of the films are designed to open up discussion about the sensuous dimensions of storytelling in the particular movies under review, but also more widely.

Notes

1. The mainstream form of cinema most routinely associated with a seamless aesthetic is Hollywood, particularly in the 'Classical' period (1918–60 according to Bordwell, Staiger and Thompson, *The Classical Hollywood Cinema: Film Style & Mode of Production to 1960*). This notion has been ubiquitous in film studies: one example that demonstrates the pervasiveness of this understanding of Classical Hollywood is the fact that the discipline's most heavily used undergraduate textbook, Bordwell and Thompson's *Film Art*, has, across its many editions, asserted the seamlessness of this cinema's style. See, for example, the analysis of continuity editing in *The Maltese Falcon* (Huston, 1941), pp. 238–42 (ninth edition).
2. Wilson, *Narration in Light: Studies in Cinematic Point of View*, p. 49.

CHAPTER 1

Analysing Film Texturally

One of the most enduring elements of cinema's origins' story is the legend surrounding the screening of the Lumière brothers' *Arrival of the Train* at the first public film showing in Paris in 1895. Numerous commentators, over a long historical period, have perpetuated the myth that the sight of a train coming towards the camera caused spectators physically to panic for fear that it was about to burst out of the screen.

Martin Loiperdinger has demonstrated convincingly that there is no evidence that such a reaction was actually apparent (or that the film was even screened at this particular event). In debunking the myth, however, he provides a number of examples of the writing that has sustained it. In these accounts, two common themes emerge: first, that the film provided a sensational experience which inspired a spontaneous bodily reaction from its audience (for example, 'the spectators in the Grand Café involuntarily threw themselves back in their seats in fright');[1] and second that, despite its two-dimensional, monochrome properties, the cinematographic image was capable of conveying the 'real-life' texture of the objects it depicted ('an impression of depth and relief' according to a contemporary commentator).[2]

Figure 1.1 shows a poster by Albert Truchet from 1896, offering a

Figure 1.1 *1896 Albert Truchet poster for* Arrival of the Train

somewhat different account of the reaction *Arrival of the Train* might have inspired in its viewers. Loiperdinger cites it as counter-evidence to the hyperbolic accounts of the audience's supposed panic but I want to use it for a slightly different purpose, to explore cinema's invitation to the viewer to be simultaneously drawn in and kept at a distance. The image *does* counter, as Loiperdinger suggests, the notion that the film's audience was reduced to a state of 'perceptual shock'.[3] The female viewers betray no indication that they have been overwhelmed by the spectacle though they are clearly engaged with it. They look composed but also responsive to specific movements in the image, drawn to the train on the front left of the screen.

In the poster, the physical separation of viewer and film is indicated by the representation of the screen as a distinct presence. Its bottom right corner is cut off by the hat of one of the women, making clear that each entity occupies a separate position in the depicted space. Countering this, a seed of dissolution in the boundary between screen and spectator space appears at the bottom left corner, as the train tracks extend beyond the frame into the auditorium.

Loiperdinger takes issue with an exposition catalogue's retrospective suggestion that the extended tracks represent a 'cataclysmic' invasion of spectatorial space.[4] Instead, he argues that 'they graphically illustrate the movement of the train, nothing more, nothing less'.[5] While sympathetic to Loiperdinger's determination to counter the hyberbole of the catalogue entry, I think his own description is too reductive. The tracks do not just indicate a motion contained within the frame: their extension beyond it surely does convey something of the sense of the film 'reaching out' to its viewers in a tangible way. The testing of the screen's surface is also suggested by, at the front of the frame, the human figure whose outline is bolder than the crowd behind him, indicating he occupies a different plane to them. He is also leaning forward as if trying to press against the screen to escape it. The 'impression of depth and relief' observed by the commentator cited earlier is alluded to here as on-screen objects are characterised by a presence that presses itself towards the space occupied by the viewer.

The dissolution between the spaces of screen and spectator is expressed tentatively. The tracks peter out before fully reaching the edges of the poster's frame. The man screen-front remains 'inside' the image despite his pressing outwards. Even if the train really were to escape into the auditorium, the viewers depicted in the poster would be at a safe distance, sitting aside as they are from its path. The poster indicates something of film's capacity to '"ma[k]e sense" sensually, as pure stimulation',[6] a propensity that Jennifer M. Barker associates in particular with early cinema. It also represents a relationship between spectator and screen characterised by a certain distance, however, a quality not usually acknowledged in writing focusing on cinema's sensuous properties but one fundamental to my own understanding of film spectatorship.

In this chapter, I offer a definition of my own critical position which accepts, and finds interest in, cinema as a sensuous medium but does so from an understanding of the viewing experience as a 'distanced' one. I first demonstrate how an interest in the sensuous properties of cinema can be identified in the work of the 'classical' film theorists André Bazin, Siegfried Kracauer and Sergei Eisenstein. In particular, I make a distinction between work which is concerned with exploring how cinema can capture 'real-life' qualities of texture and tactility in its presentation of on-screen objects (and, occasionally, sound) and that which focuses on the sensuous properties of cinema itself as a technological apparatus. In this writing, the stress tends to be on one or the other whereas, throughout this book, I attempt to explore the sensuous aspects of both.

The second section attends to more recent writing on cinema and the senses. A significant body of work now exists in film studies that might be classified as 'sensuous scholarship'.[7] Two strands dominate: one taking a phenomenological approach, indebted to the writing of philosopher Maurice Merleau-Ponty; the other inspired by the thinking of Gilles Deleuze (some of the writing makes significant reference to both Merleau-Ponty and Deleuze). Whatever their philosophical underpinnings, both approaches tend to oppose 'classical' film theory's separation between spectator and screen and both are dedicated to a thick 'textural analysis' which is sensitive to tactile qualities of image and soundtrack that have been underexplored in previous writing on film.

On the whole, these works are reluctant to countenance the notion of films as worlds of their own: to do so would be to suggest a separation between viewer and film that might fundamentally contradict the way they theorise the spectator's experience. One consequence of this is that much contemporary sensuous film scholarship pays little heed to intricacies of story, characterisation and point of view, some of the elements that contribute to an understanding of the film as a world. The third part of the chapter looks to writing that *does* consider films as worlds of their own in order to establish a different point of orientation for the textural analysis that follows.

The chapter concludes with a summary of the principles underlying my analytical position: one that is sensitive to the sensuous capacity of cinema but considers how this might deepen, rather than distract from or supersede, the viewer's interest in a film as a distinctive fictional world.

Textural Analysis in 'Classical' Film Theory

Much contemporary writing on cinema and the senses adopts philosophical positions that are *relatively* new in film studies, the thinking of Merleau-Ponty and Deleuze gaining a foothold in the discipline in the 1990s. This does not mean, however, that earlier writers have not attended to cinema's sensuous potential. Martine Beugnet cites Antonin Artaud, Germaine Dulac, Jean Epstein, Luis Buñuel and Sergei Eisenstein as critics and/or practitioners writing in the 1920s who were all interested in cinema's 'intrinsic . . . capacity to trigger our senses'.[8]

A recent guide to film theory sees fit to introduce the field's entire history 'through the senses'.[9] This suggests that thinking about cinema in this way is a common contemporary critical preoccupation but it also demonstrates that there is something in earlier writing that makes the book's organisational rationale plausible. In the chapter most focused on contemporary sensuous scholarship in film, 'Cinema as skin and touch', the authors identify Siegfried Kracauer as a classical film theorist whose work can be understood in relation, rather than opposition, to more obviously phenomenological approaches.[10] Kracauer's writing is a fundamental reference point for at least one contemporary example of sensuous scholarship and this influence will be discussed presently. The first classical theorist I want to address, however, is André Bazin.

On the one hand, Bazin's notion of realism, as commonly understood, *is* inimical to contemporary phenomenological or Deleuzian accounts of the cinematic experience. Bazin argues, famously, that film is a recording of a pre-existing reality, 'mummified' for the scrutiny of the film spectator.[11] This posits a certainty about the world existing outside subjective experience (there is an objective reality that film can preserve) and establishes a separation between spectator and screen (the viewer looks through a window on to an imprint of events that have already taken place). Despite their differences, phenomenological and Deleuzian accounts both share an understanding of cinema as a process of becoming, in which identities are forged only through the encounter between the viewer and the film: there is no analysis of a level of reality that might pre-exist this encounter.

On a quite simple level, however, Bazin's realist thinking *is* concerned with the sensuous nature of the medium, and this makes his work as potentially relevant to my enquiry as more contemporary writing, even if the conceptualisation of the film–spectator relationship is different. Bazin prizes the movie camera's ability to capture 'the flesh and blood of reality',[12] which it preserves, albeit in 'mummified' form. He praises those forms of cinema that retain this flesh-and-blood quality most directly (in his view), such as Italian neo-realism. Bazin, then, appreciates cinema's propensity to relay the natural properties of texture belonging to the objects depicted, thereby appealing to the viewer's sense of touch. This is illustrated in Bazin's discussion of Roberto Rossellini's *Paisa* (1946). Bazin defines first the 'shot', 'an abstract view of a reality which is being analysed'[13] for a functional narrative purpose which Bazin explains through the following invented example: a close shot of a doorknob that registers the optical point of view of a condemned prisoner who has been nervously eyeing the door of his cell.[14] Against this, Bazin celebrates *Paisa*'s composition from 'image facts' which retain the 'concrete reality' of the things themselves:

> These are in a sense the centrifugal properties of the images – those which make the narrative possible. Each image being on its own just a fragment of reality existing before any meanings, the entire surface of the scene should manifest an equally concrete density. Once again we have here the opposite of the 'door-knob' type of scene, in which the color of the enamel, the dirt marks at the level of the hand, the shine of the metal, the worn-away look are just so many useless facts, concrete parasites of an abstraction fittingly dispensed with.[15]

The details, Bazin suggests here, that *should* be indispensable to narrative are sensuous ones: materials that offer different sensations when touched (enamel, the hand, metal) and that are bestowed a further differentiation of texture by the addition of another surface (dirt) or the erosion of its own ('worn-away'). These are also objects that have clearly been touched or have engaged in acts of touching (this is how the doorknob's surface has been worn away and how the hands have acquired dirt). Bazin also observes the material ways in which the objects appeal to a sense of sight: the colour of the enamel; the quality with which the metal shines.

It is telling that Bazin's example here is an invented one. It is entirely illustrative of Bazin's generally stated belief that film can capture such materiality particularly intensely but it is also the case that his writing on the specifics of films is not usually focused on such sensuous detail. For example, the essays collected in both volumes of *What Is Cinema?*, the most referenced collections of his work, pick out such detail only sporadically and in relation to a few select film-makers (Rossellini, Carl Theodor Dreyer and Robert Bresson).

Despite the limited extent, in practice, to which Bazin's writing can be said to focus on the sensuousness of film, his writing is influential in two ways on the approach this book takes. Firstly, unlike more contemporary writers on cinema and the senses, he emphasises the connection between the sensory and the narrative – in the passage cited above, the intimation is that the material details of on-screen objects (and human figures) provide a reality without which stories cannot take place; secondly, his understanding of film as a window on the – material – world suggests that the sensory is being framed for the scrutiny of the viewer rather than providing the occasion for an experience where the division between spectator and screen disappears entirely.

Along with Bazin, Kracauer is viewed as one of the seminal advocates of cinematic 'realism'. As my earlier reference to *Film Theory: an introduction through the senses* suggests, his work is more explicitly focused on the sensory experience offered by cinema and, as such, has been influential on writers that take up this subject as a central concern. Brigitte Peucker's *The Material Image: Art and the Real in Film*, for example, uses Kracauer as a touchstone in its enquiry. Peucker characterises the basis of Kracauer's interest in the sensuous in this way:

> Echoing the work of Bazin as well as his own earlier writings, Kracauer's *Theory of Film* claims that films are proportionately more cinematic the more they cling to the surface of things, their relation to reality seeming mystically to extend beyond the merely mimetic.[16]

Kracauer goes further than Bazin, however, in describing the corporeal response of the viewer on receiving a sensory input from a film:

> Repeatedly, Kracauer privileges what he calls the 'psychophysical' response of the spectator, the affective response to sensory stimuli, in other words, and the movement of film's images has a major role to play here. Movement evokes the 'flow of life', setting up a 'resonance effect' between spectator and image: moving images provoke visceral responses in the 'deep bodily layers' of the sense organs, producing 'organic tensions, nameless excitements'.[17]

It is not surprising that Peucker goes on to link Kracauer's 'resonance effect' with the phenomenology of Maurice Merleau-Ponty and, through this, to Vivian Sobchack. The idea that this resonance stems from the 'life' that flows through the image attributes to film a 'pulse' that belies its status as an inanimate object, suggesting it to be a kind of sensate being; the identification of this resonance occurring 'between' spectator and film imbricates both in a process of sensuously forged signification. Both these concepts, film as a living being and cinematic spectatorship as a process whereby viewer and film 'touch' each other, are central to recent phenomenological understandings of cinema.

Peucker's interest is the intersection of art and the real in film which leads her to a body of films that work dialectically in different ways (for example, in a number of chapters, she discusses films that combine references to, or images of, painting with the 'cinematic' image). This establishes common ground with my book in terms of the choice of case studies which also revolve around films that self-consciously combine, and focus attention on, the materiality of 'mixed media' materials (for example, film stock and video footage, monochrome and colour, sung voices and spoken voice-over). This means Kracauer can help Peucker only so far, as his interest is, fundamentally, solely in the real. As Peucker notes: 'In [Kracauer's] *Theory of Film*, the filmic medium is not the place for discursive reasoning; dialectical materialism and its expression through montage are rejected in favor of a phenomenological interest in the material world.'[18]

Bazin, too, demonstrated an ideological distaste for montage. This attitude comes through revealingly in a comment about the problems he sees with the use of process shots to composite images together:

> It is a fact that other devices such as process shots make it possible for two objects, say the star and a tiger, to be seen together, a proximity which if it were real might cause some problems. The illusion here is more complete [than montage], but it can be detected and in any case, the important thing is not whether the trick can be spotted but whether or not trickery is used, just as the beauty of a copy is no substitute for the authenticity of a Vermeer.[19]

Bazin's absolute rejection of even 'invisible' montage reinforces the notion that he is interested in how the 'wholeness' of things in the world are revealed in their cinematic incarnations: part of this wholeness, for both Bazin and Kracauer, is an object's sensuous properties, and it is at this level that their interest in the sensuous capacity of cinema resides.

This is certainly one quality of cinema that I address in my analysis. I consider how the sensuous attributes of objects (and people), as they are understood in the world, are represented in particular fictional scenarios in specific ways. This is only one aspect of my study, however. The other is to consider how the materiality of film, as a technological medium, is also involved in the display of these objects and their arrangement in particular film worlds. To pursue this, I have deliberately chosen films that contain a montage of sensuously different materials. To investigate a heritage of writing about the senses and cinema that is attuned to the different materialities of film itself, it is necessary to look to a different writer.

Sergei Eisenstein is routinely set against Bazin and Kracauer as the chief early proponent of a 'formalist' theory of film, opposed to Bazin and Kracauer's 'realism'. Rather than seeking to provide a window on to the world, formalist critics focus on film's capacity for self-conscious and overt manipulation where, to paraphrase Bazin, the image is evaluated according to 'what it adds to reality' rather than what 'it reveals of it'. Eisenstein's montage theory is the most renowned evidence of the formalist position in early film criticism, and part of it specifically addresses the sensory experience cinema should provide, through a self-conscious exploration and manipulation of its base materials and tools of production.

The question of how montage effects should make the viewer *feel*, in a physiological sense, is taken up most directly by Eisenstein in his essay 'The Filmic Fourth Dimension'. Using a musical analogy, Eisenstein explains how 'orthodox montage', arranged according to 'particular dominants', might be augmented by 'overtones' that provide a more intangible resonance within particular shots and across entire montage pieces. For Eisenstein, techniques which draw attention to, rather than conceal, film's technological basis, are particularly likely to produce such resonances:

> All sorts of aberrations, distortions, and other defects, which can be remedied by systems of lenses, can also be taken into account compositionally, providing a whole series of definite compositional effects (employing lens-openings from 28 to 310).
>
> In combinations which exploit *these collateral vibrations* – which is nothing less than *the filmed material itself* – we can achieve, completely analogous with music, *the visual overtonal complex of the shot*.[20]

Eisenstein summarises the effect of this newly identified montage element in the following way:

> For the musical overtone (a throb) it is not strictly fitting to say: 'I hear'.
> Nor for the visual overtone: 'I see'.
> For both, a new uniform formula must enter our vocabulary: 'I feel'.[21]

Here, Eisenstein valorises a potential in film that Bazin, in particular, suppresses: that technology helps to establish a resonance in the image (and, by extension, the soundtrack) that allows it to activate a physiological response from the viewer. In keeping with the dialectical impulse, Eisenstein argues that these resonances should be arranged on the principle of variation so that, for example, 'the montage of the beginning of the religious procession [in his *Old and New* (1929)] is according to "degrees of heat saturation" in the individual shots'.[22]

In 'The Filmic Fourth Dimension', Eisenstein establishes two principles directly relevant to my study, beyond the interest in cinema's capacity to stimulate the senses. The first is the acknowledgement that the technology of film finds material expression on-screen and on the soundtrack. In the quotation above, Eisenstein is discussing the manipulation of lens openings for particular visual effects but there is a host of other possibilities, many of which are pursued in the chapters that follow (for example, the choice of film stock, the highlighting of the 'surface' features of the digital image, the production techniques through which the human voice is given a particular kind of texture). Second, Eisenstein is interested in the relationships between different overtonal effects rather than in those effects in isolation. My study, too, concentrates on films which self-consciously explore the differences

between the sensuous qualities of their collected materials, whether they
be the contrasting material properties of archive television footage and DV
film images in *Double Take* or the interplay between voices in the 'Wise Up'
musical sequence of *Magnolia*, all of which carry material traces of different
degrees of technological manipulation.

This selective review of earlier, foundational writing on film demonstrates
that an interest in cinema's sensuous qualities was apparent even if, as in
Bazin's case, this was only an intermittent focus in the analysis of actual films
or, as in Eisenstein's, was expressed within an overarching theory of montage
that envisaged many other types of non-physiological effects. In my study, the
two approaches that remain separated here – one investigating the sensuous
qualities of the objects depicted, the other recognising the material effects of
film's technological mediation – are drawn together and understood in relation to a particular understanding of films as fictional worlds. As such, my
analysis of Bazin, Kracauer and Eisenstein establishes the areas of interest, in
terms of the materials of film I shall focus on, but it does not indicate the relationship I am positing between the spectator and what is seen and heard on-
screen. Before clarifying my understanding of films as worlds, I shall review
more contemporary sensuous scholarship on film. This displays a deepened
commitment to pursuing the sensory aspects of the cinematic experience but
also indicates fault lines in relation to my own approach, in terms of how the
relationship between spectator and screen is envisaged.

TEXTURAL ANALYSIS IN CONTEMPORARY FILM WRITING

At this point my review of relevant writing jumps from the 'classical' era in
which Bazin, Kracauer and Eisenstein are located, to the 1990s and beyond.
This abrupt transition no doubt involves omission of work between that does
attend to film's sensuous appeal but the shift also indicates a general lack of
attention to such bodily matters in the grand theories of film studies in the
1970s and 1980s. Vivian Sobchack's *The Address of the Eye: A Phenomenology
of Film Experience*, published in 1992, positioned itself explicitly against the
'objective' and 'scientific' stances taken by the psychoanalytical and neo-
Marxist film theory that prevailed at that time:

> I would argue that in the final analysis (indeed, perhaps as a result of the
> 'objective' process of analysis), both psychoanalytic and Marxist film theory
> in most of their current manifestations have obscured the dynamic, synoptic,
> and lived-body situation of both the spectator and the film.[23]

Describing psychoanalysis's concern with human existence as an 'interior'
one (dealing with the mind) and Marxism's as an 'exterior' one (dealing with

socio-political relationships),[24] Sobchack sees neither as being equipped to analyse 'the embodied experience of labor, alienation, engagement, and transformation I have every time I go to the movies'.[25] It is cinema as an experience that Sobchack wants to capture, and this experience is understood as a fundamentally sensuous one. In a later essay, Sobchack advances the notion of the cinesthetic subject, an entity that originates in the conjunction between the spectator's body and the stimulus of cinematic representation. The senses are fundamental to this encounter between spectator and screen: 'the cinema uses our dominant senses of vision and hearing to speak comprehensibly to our other senses'.[26]

Two themes emerge here that are distinctive in contemporary phenomenological work on cinema. First, the idea is expressed that all kinds of sensory feelings are involved in our embodied experience of the movies, even if films are literally composed only of sights and sounds and even though the viewer is typically sedentary during their consumption of them. Sobchack, for example, claims that 'our embodied experience of the movies, then, is an experience of seeing, hearing, touching, moving, tasting, smelling'.[27] Second, the spectator–screen relationship is characterised by a 'reversibility'. This is a more general concept, developed by Merleau-Ponty, and rests on the belief that perception is an embodied process that involves a reciprocal relationship between the perceiver and the perceived. Barker uses Merleau-Ponty's image of a person's one hand touching the other as a starting point for her own adoption of his philosophy to establish a theory of film spectatorship:

> When I touch one hand with the other, he explained, each hand plays the role of both the touching and the touched, but my experience of touching and being touched is not quite simultaneous. *Either* I feel one hand touching the other as an object, *or* I feel subjectively one hand being touched by the other, but I can't feel both at once . . . Instead, they each vacillate between the role of touching and touched . . . This structure of reversibility . . . involves a shifting of attention and intentionality from one aspect of the encounter to another.[28]

Sobchack reuses this imagery in her description of the film experience in which she claims she becomes 'the toucher but also the touched'.[29] In this way, the film is seen not as a pre-existing entity which the viewer observes from a distance but rather as a 'body', capable of an expression and perception, that engages with that of the viewer. It is in the contact zone between the two that the film experience occurs.

The notions of expression and perception are taken from Merleau-Ponty's observation that the 'lived body' is in a constant process of perceiving expression and expressing perception, a taking in of sensory experiences and an offering out of them. A key move of film phenomenologists has been to suggest that the film is as much of a lived body as the viewer. Barker builds on Sobchack's initial suggestion, that film lives 'an embodied existence in the world', by pinpointing the specific means at the disposal of the medium to do so. For example, she claims:

> The camera perceives and expresses through dolly tracks, tripod, wide-angle lens, and so forth; viewers do so by means of posture, muscle tension, visual concentration, facial expressions, and human gestures. As the film [Andrei Tarkovsky's *Mirror*] pulls us toward and away from the scene of therapist and stuttering boy through tracking and zooming, for example, the viewer may move with or against the film's movements by squinting at the screen to counteract the shift in focal point, or leaning forward to resist the pull away from the increasingly distant figures. The point, though, is that all these bodies – characters', actors', viewers', and film's – are entities whose attitudes and intentions are expressed by embodied behaviour.[30]

It is important to note that, as here, writers such as Sobchack and Barker are careful not to anthropomorphise film: they do not suggest that human beings and films are indistinguishable from one another. Nevertheless, Barker reinforces Sobchack's appropriation of Merleau-Ponty by insisting that the film experience is one of intimate mutual exchange between two embodied entities:

> We do not 'lose ourselves' in the film, so much as we exist – emerge, really – in the contact between our body and the film's body . . . we are embedded in a constantly mutual experience with the film, so that the cinematic experience is the experience of being both 'in' our bodies and 'in' the liminal space created by that contact.[31]

The notion of films as worlds in their own right, with particular boundaries that allow them to be experienced by the viewer from a certain distance, is thoroughly disavowed in this writing. Indeed, Sobchack explicitly identifies the notion of film as a distant object as one of the presuppositions of existing theory that needs to be challenged.[32]

One consequence of this rejection of distance in conceptualising the relationship between spectator and film is a decreased attention to elements of films that are commonly regarded when they are discussed as objects viewed from afar: identification, authorial point of view, narrative. In contemporary writing, a heightened interest in film as a sensuous experience is usually accompanied by a stated disinterest in film as a medium for storytelling.

This statement is made with more or less force in different writing and with varying levels of qualification. Nevertheless, it does recur as a repeated refrain and, it should be noted, is equally a feature of recent sensuous scholarship that is based on philosophical precepts other than existential phenomenology. For example, Steven Shaviro's *The Cinematic Body*, published a year after Sobchack's *Address of the Eye*, is inspired by the writing of Gilles Deleuze. Shaviro characterises 1970s and 1980s film theory as a 'phobic construct' in which 'images are kept at a distance, isolated like dangerous germs'.[33] His opening analysis of Kathryn Bigelow's *Blue Steel* (1989) highlights the film's 'visual excess' rather than discussing it 'only in terms of script and performance, of character, plot, and genre'.[34] He closes his introductory chapter by claiming:

> Even those all-too-common movies that – on the level of character and narrative – purvey the most reactionary stereotypes of gender and sexuality have their own potentialities for change and reversal, their 'lines of flight'. The cinematic apparatus has at least this virtue: that it tends to subvert the metaphysics that would privilege an intelligible, phallocratic order at the expense of the contingency and multiplicity of sensation, and to rupture the acquisitive mastery of the gaze.[35]

In this passage, Shaviro announces his intention to pursue the politics of cinema's sensational affect, identifying it as a level of experience that remains distinct from an engagement with character and narrative. This distinction is maintained throughout the book and leads to the following conclusion: 'Film theory should be less a theory of fantasy (psychoanalytic or otherwise) than a theory of the affects and transformations of bodies.'[36]

Yet more direct statements of a reorientation of focus away from narrative matters are made in other writing in the field. Early in *Cinema and Sensation*, Beugnet writes:

> Familiar with mainstream cinema's standardised formats, we have become used to thinking of and enjoying feature films first and foremost in terms of plot and characters, identification and narrative logic. A sensual apprehension of film works affords different, yet equally potent gratifications.[37]

In her chapter on 'Skin' in *The Tactile Eye*, Barker remarks:

> The chapter proceeds by way of several 'textural analyses' – not 'readings' of films so much as 'handlings' – in order to demonstrate the ways in which careful attention to the tactile surfaces and textures involved in the film experience might illuminate complexities and significance that might be overlooked by a focus on visual, aural, or narrative aspects. Even those films that seem dominated by narrative and cognitive concerns might possess secrets that we miss at first glance, secrets we may only discover when we begin to scratch the surface with a more tactile form of analysis.[38]

In these statements, each writer proposes a similar analytical standpoint, albeit expressed in different ways: Shaviro calls for a 'theory of the affects and transformations of bodies'; Beugnet for 'a sensual apprehension of film'; and Barker 'a more tactile form of analysis'. In each instance, this is differentiated from an interest in elements associated with storytelling in film, such as script, plot, narrative logic, performance, character, identification, genre and the notion of film as fantasy.

Yet, it is also revealing that, in other passages, each writer qualifies this distinction between sensual apprehension and narrative analysis. In his conclusion, Shaviro begins by restating his interest in the sensuous dimensions of the viewing experience, but with a caveat:

> I am affected by continuities and cuts, movements and stillnesses, gradations of color or of brightness. This does not mean that my experience of film is nonmimetic or abstract: these variations have to do with the actions and events being enacted, and not just with the plastic or formal qualities of the image.[39]

While Shaviro's connecting of sensational affect to the 'actions and events being enacted' occurs as an afterthought, Beugnet and Barker admit to their interest in narrative more extensively. Beugnet, for example, states:

> This book's focus, then, is on an aesthetic of sensation, where the material dimension of a cinematic work is initially given precedence over its expository and mimetic/realistic functions. These functions, however, are not discounted; they are, rather, addressed through the prism of the medium's material qualities.[40]

Similarly, Barker explains:

> This is not to say that an analysis that foregrounds the sensual aspects of the experience of these films is one that dismisses such concerns as narrative, theme, psychology, and history. Rather, this approach should simply remind us that those aspects of a film cannot be separated from – indeed, are conveyed and understood through – our sensual, muscular experience of the films.[41]

The focus for all three writers is, predominantly, on the feature-length fiction film. These qualifications suggest that, in that context, attention to the sensuous aspects of the film experience cannot entirely ignore the 'experience' these films have more commonly been thought to offer the viewer, namely that of being made witness to a story.

That said, these statements are presented as qualifications to a line of argument whose key focus is away from the film's storytelling qualities. This leaves room for work that reverses the polarities of the contemporary sensuous scholarship reviewed so far by insisting on the fiction film as a story world. This would involve addressing a film's material qualities through the prism of the invented world it proposes to the viewer. To establish such an approach, it is necessary first to understand how films might be characterised as worlds of their own before considering how these worlds invite the kind of tactile response from their viewers suggested by the writers reviewed so far.

FILMS AS WORLDS

To understand a film as a world of its own is to admit to a particular kind of distance between viewer and the material represented on-screen, a distance that contemporary sensuous scholarship on film would normally disavow. It is possible, however, to understand the viewing position as a 'distanced' one without that involving the kind of 'phobia' Shaviro aligns with 1970s and 1980s film theory. In this section, I want to: introduce the concept of film as world; elaborate on the viewing position such a characterisation of film might assign; and consider how the 'sensory' is still involved as an aspect of the film world and the viewer's engagement with it.

In his article, 'Where is the world? The horizon of events in movie fiction', Victor Perkins explores the 'worldhood' of films through close analyses of moments from movies such as *Citizen Kane* (Welles, 1941), *You Only Live Once* (Lang, 1937) and *The Night of the Hunter* (Laughton, 1955). Each analysis is used to demonstrate how 'understanding the events of a movie as taking place in a world is a prerequisite of the intelligibility not only of plot but also of tone, viewpoint, rhetoric, style and meaning'.[42] For Perkins, each film presents the viewer with material that insinuates a larger fictional world and that offers a particular vantage point from which to judge the events that take place within it.[43]

The world of the film, conceived in this way, 'is everything (in space and in time) surrounding and embedding our immediate perceptions'.[44] In this manner, Perkins characterises films as worlds that can be extremely expansive but are also, crucially, presented through acts of disclosure that establish certain boundaries. The sector in view at any particular moment makes apparent what is and what is not significant within a specific film world: the activity of the viewer is one that involves making judgements about what is meaningful *within* the invented world based on the evidence placed in front of her/him. This is a quite different conception of viewer activity to that proposed by much sensuous scholarship whereby moments in films are seen as 'triggers' that initiate a process of exploration of the self (in terms of the sensory response stimulated in the body).

By contrast, the engagement outlined by Perkins is one that remains focused on understanding the dimensions of the fictional world from which the viewer is kept at a productive distance. This is not to say that films have no relationship with the outside world. Perkins considers the dialectic of distance and proximity between the film world and 'our' world when reflecting on the ending of *Citizen Kane*. Famously, the film ends with the burning in a furnace of Kane's childhood sledge, named Rosebud. Perkins ponders the significance of this event being made visible to the viewer but not to any of the film's characters. It is worth quoting this passage at length as it lays the basis for the understanding of a viewer's engagement with film that underpins my analysis throughout the book:

> That we can be present as an audience to witness the absence of witnesses is an index of the separation between our world and the world of the fiction. It climaxes the anomaly that places *Citizen Kane* both in and beyond our world, our 1941 world. Of course this is our world. It shares our economy, our technologies, our architecture, and the legal systems and social forms that yield complex phenomena like slum landlords, divorce scandals and fame . . . But of course its world is not ours. Kane is famous throughout that world, and we have never heard of him nor of Jim Geddes, his political rival . . . These are some of the aspects that mark the world as fictional. They do not thereby negate its worldhood.
>
> The world of *Citizen Kane* is constituted as a world partly because, within it, there are facts known to all, to many, to few and to none.[45]

Here, then, is a conception of the fiction film as a world in its own right (albeit with connections to the real one) that the viewer partakes from outside. It is a world comprised – in part – of events and of characters who have different levels of knowledge about those events, and consumed by viewers whose access to knowledge about the film world is different again. By understanding the relationship between spectator and film world in this way, Perkins is clarifying a position adopted by a number of writers on film, often aligned with the thinking of film philosopher Stanley Cavell. In *The World Viewed*, Cavell describes the relationship between viewer and screen in this way:

> The world of a moving picture is screened. The screen is not a support, not like a canvas; there is nothing to support, that way. It holds a projection, as light as light. A screen is a barrier. What does the silver screen screen? It screens me from the world it holds – that is, makes me invisible. And it screens that world from me – that is, screens its existence from me.[46]

Cavell insists, like Perkins, on the separation between viewer and the world held (and screened) by the screen. In addition, he suggests that the viewing experience is an *invisible* one, rather than the corporeal one discussed in contemporary phenomenological accounts. Deborah Thomas also attests to the non-corporeal nature of our engagement with film worlds: 'Our sense of spatial exclusion from a film's narrative world – no matter how much visual and aural access to it we may have – does not appear to result from any over-awareness of our own bodies.'[47] Thomas elaborates by commenting on a filmic technique that underlines the exclusion of the viewer from the fictional world of the film:

> The technique of implying offscreen space in front of the screen through the use of onscreen mirrors which reflect parts of the offscreen narrative world, rather than reflecting us within the mirrors as we look, underscores our own invisibility rather than creating an illusion of bits of the narrative world exist-ing behind us, and this reinforces in a very blatant way the non-corporeal nature of our experience of viewing narrative films more generally.[48]

In Perkins's account, the viewer is separate from the film world: this is true of Cavell's and Thomas's film spectators, too, but they go further by conceptualising a viewer whose body is made to 'disappear'. Non-corporeal and distanced, the viewer conceived here would seem to be the antithesis of that posited by the kind of sensuous film scholarship I outlined in the previous section. On the other hand, writing that understands movies as worlds does bestow on them a greater 'body' than sensuous scholarship does, in the sense of attributing them a voluminous but defined shape: one that is both expansive (the film world contains much more than is presented to the viewer at any one moment) as well as bounded (Perkins: 'each world has its own norms').[49]

Is it possible, then, to combine an interest in film as a sensuous object, inspiring and interacting with the viewer's own sensory capacities, and film as a fictional world, comprised of events, facts, characters, attitudes and norms that are apprehended only by the viewer from a series of partial viewpoints, all of which are partaken from a distance? This question is raised explicitly by David Trotter. Trotter uses Laura U. Marks as his example of a writer who tends to see the sensuous – for Marks in the specific form of 'haptic visuality'[50] – as oppositional to the narrative:

> There is a problem, here. All feature films appeal in some measure (usually in very large measure) to narrative identification. Does that mean that they must abandon haptic visuality altogether? Or are there ways in which narra-tive cinema might incorporate haptic imagery, without ceasing to narrate?[51]

Through a reading of Lynne Ramsay's *Ratcatcher* (1999), Trotter goes on to demonstrate that the haptic and narrative can coexist. The bulk of this analysis is weighted towards the tracing of the haptic as a 'theme' in the film through the emphasis it lays on the protagonist James's relationship to mess (whose 'formlessness' Trotter links to the haptic). In the article's later stages there is also some attention to the haptic as an effect of the film's style, that is to say of its chosen mode of storytelling as well as the story being told. This change of focus is, in fact, first illustrated through commentary on Francois Truffaut's *Les Quartre Cents Coups* (1959) which Trotter uses as a point of comparison with *Ratcatcher* (both films about troubled children). Trotter's analysis of a particular moment from the film illustrates something of the approach I want to develop in this book:

> When his father (Albert Remy) turns him in for stealing a typewriter, Antoine ends up in a cage in the police-station. For the first time in the film, the camera identifies with his point of view. A slow pan reveals the prisoners in a second cage, a notice on the wall ('Deratisation'), a policeman at a table. More striking is the lattice of wire-mesh pressed so close to the lens that it blurs. To occupy Antoine's point of view, at this moment of maximum humiliation, is to begin to see the world differently. When the wagon arrives to take all the prisoners to holding-cells for the night, Antoine is last in . . . When we next see him from outside the wagon, tears stream down his cheeks. The shot dissolves to an indeterminate pock-marked surface, which gradually resolves itself, as the camera tracks along it, into a wall. This is haptic visuality, with a vengeance. 'Haptic visuality sees the world as though it were touching it', Marks observes: 'close, unknowable, appearing to exist on the surface of the image. Haptic images disturb the figure-ground relationship' (HV 1). In this case, the world haptic visuality fastens us to is all bad mess. The camera carries on past the end of the wall, to reveal a corridor, a gate, and a police-man silhouetted against the light. Optically rendered symbolism confirms the experience of confinement . . . The film's declassification of narrative – its lapse into the bad haptic – has already enacted his declassing long before the formalities of symbol and ceremony take place.[52]

This extract is instructive in terms of its relationship to the readings of films that follow in this book. Firstly, the focus of the analysis is on narrative detail. Whereas a sensuous theorist sees the film experience occurring in the body and in a 'liminal' space created by the contact between spectator and screen, Trotter suggests that the haptic visuality of this scene 'fastens us' to the film world. This indicates a particular intimacy between the film material and the viewer at this point but also retains the sense of the film as a discrete entity, drawing the (equally discrete) viewer in so he or she may appreciate the experience of a character within the fictional world.

Secondly, the haptic quality of the image is cast as an element of film style produced by particular techniques (for example, playing with different possibilities of focus) and interacting with other stylistic aspects (for example, camera movement), the combination helping to suggest a significance in the material presented to the viewer. Trotter's understanding of the moment, then, is predicated on a conception of how film communicates akin to Perkins's who states in 'Where is the world?': 'The image is displayed not only to relay information but to claim that it matters and to guide us towards the ways in which it matters.'[53] That said, Trotter's analysis is, self-admittedly, proposed as a starting point for a critical approach to films rather than as something more fully realised (the article offers thoughts *towards* a theory of haptic narrative). The readings of *Les Quatre Cents Coups* and *Ratcatcher* are quite narrowly focused on a specific aspect of storytelling, that is to say, the extent to which haptic imagery represents the subjectivity of the films' child protagonists. The analyses do not operate according to the more expansive notion of a film world expressed by Perkins in which the closing of the distance between the viewer's perspective and a character's is only one option among many, the scope of the 'many' established within the context of the individual world. Following Perkins, I understand the sensuous properties of film, at least in part, as an aspect of style intelligible through its taking place in a particular film world.

The inclusion of 'at least in part' is important to the preceding claim as the sensuous is not only expressed through the stylistic register of a film. As my analysis of *Amores Perros* will make immediately apparent, I consider a number of elements within the film world in terms of their sensuous qualities. Some of these may be understood as aspects of style, defined as the means through which the story is expressed, such as editing patterns, lighting effects and treatments of sound. I also give credit, however, to the notion of the objects and people (and animals) on-screen possessing a sensuous dimension, albeit one disclosed within a fictional environment shaped by stylistic choices which are delivered through film technology.

I also do not deny that a sensuous engagement between viewer and film can occur that is 'intelligible' in ways other than through recourse to an appreciation of the film world. Sobchack, keen to demonstrate how film can touch all the senses, offers the following two examples:

> Although, perhaps, smell and taste are less called on than touch to inform our comprehension of the images we see, I still remember the 'visual aroma' of my experience of *Black Narcissus* (Michael Powell and Emeric Pressberger, 1946), the film itself named after a perfume, or the pork-noodle taste of portions of *Tampopo* (Juzo Itami, 1986).[54]

Characterising these as experiences that occurred 'without a thought', Sobchack claims:

> In this regard we might wish to think again about processes of identification in the film experience, relating them not to our secondary engagement with and recognition of either 'subject positions' or characters but rather to our primary engagement (and the film's) with the sense and sensibility of materiality itself.[55]

I do not dispute that films can act upon the senses (and not just those of sight and hearing) inspiring a material reaction in and of the viewer's body. Here, Sobchack offers examples that are directly related to one of the five senses: the sight of food on-screen stimulates the viewer's taste buds; the evocation of a particular milieu is so vividly rendered that it activates the viewer's sense of smell. A whole range of other bodily responses, not so neatly connected to one sense or another, is also possible. Barker characterises the encounter between film and viewer as one involving, among other sensations, a process of caressing, piercing, grasping, clenching and breathing.[56]

To acknowledge this kind of bodily response, and to establish how my study approaches the sensuous quality of film from a different perspective, I shall end this review of relevant writing by discussing my own sensuous response to a moment from *Magnolia* (Anderson, 1999), the details of which I consider in Chapter 4. When I first saw the 'Wise Up' sequence from the film, in which the nine protagonists (this is a multi-character movie) sing, unexpectedly and non-naturalistically, a song by Aimee Mann, my body responded with a shiver which I experienced as involuntary.

This response could be worthy of study in itself and this study could take a number of different approaches. It could, for example, adopt the kind of sensuous theory practised by Sobchack. It could consider the response in relation to genre (as an example of the excessively affective qualities of melodrama, for instance) or in connection with pop music (often considered a particularly affective and bodily art form). It could contemplate the reaction as a learned response (so, in fact, not involuntary at all) which is deconstructed through a cognitive approach, or it could make use of the insights of contemporary neuroscience which has found evidence of a more intimate relationship than hitherto assumed between the activities of brain and body. Alternatively, it could review my response as part of a critical history of the senses (what might the fact that this response is possible at this particular time, in this particular viewing context, say about the culture more widely?). This is not an exhaustive list of critical possibilities but I cite them to establish what I do *not* pursue in this book.

Instead, the analytical chain in relation to my reading of this moment from *Magnolia* is as follows. It is offered as a response to an intuition I had about it on first viewing which partly manifested itself in a physical reaction. In the sequence, the 'untrained' voices of the characters are pitched against the melodious singing of the professional musician, Aimee Mann. I am fairly sure that the frisson between the different voices in the scene was responsible for my initial shiver and I know that this physical reaction was one of the things that made me 'feel close' to the moment as well as making me want to give it further thought.

In studying the moment, however, my attention has moved away from a further exploration of my bodily response to an interest in how the materials that I think triggered the response in the first place – that is to say, the singing voices of the characters pitched against that of Aimee Mann – take their place within a particular film world: what are the sensuous qualities of each voice? how do they work in combination? and what significance does this have in disclosing the different dimensions of the film world? Additionally, what attitude towards the material on display does the film encourage the viewer to adopt, including an attitude towards the scene's material qualities? These questions are distinctly different ones from those posed by Sobchack but do not mean that I am simply 'reducing' my focus to attention on a 'secondary engagement' with characters or 'subject positions': this presupposes a set of options for the viewer (direct identification with a character or interpellation into a particular ideologically bound imaginary viewing position) that is extremely limited. It also does not conceive of a *productive* distance (rather than alienating one) existing between viewer and film, a distance that I have identified as a crucial aspect of thinking about films as worlds.

To summarise, the following principles underlie all of the readings of moments from films that follow:

- A fiction film is a world. Its dimensions can be inferred by the viewer from the series of partial views of the world disclosed by the film's collection of images and sounds. The inferences a viewer (in this case, me) makes are not the *only* ones possible but their credibility can be tested against the material evidence offered by the elements of the world that *are* depicted on-screen and on the soundtrack.
- The aspects of a film that can be understood as taking place within a world include narrative (its events), characterisation, practices and beliefs (the norms against which behaviour and attitudes expressed within the world may be judged), style (the manner in which the dramatic material is delivered to the viewer), viewpoint (the selection of the material to be disclosed at any given moment and the impact that has on the viewer's relationship to, and understanding of, aspects of the film world) and tone (the attitude the film implies it is taking 'to the material and the stylistic register it employs').[57]
- The sensuous elements of a film world can assert a significant presence across all the different aspects listed above but this need not be the case: the credibility of a particular reading of a film, concentrating on the sensuous qualities of its world, will hinge on the extent to which its claims can be tested against the material evidence the film provides (so these are 'substantial' rather than 'subtextual' interpretations).

- The viewer apprehends the film world from a distance. Nevertheless, in relation to the senses, the film may 'reach out' to the viewer in two ways: the sensuous detail attributed to its depicted materials and the viewer's experience of those materials in the – historically and culturally specific – real world may closely correspond; gestures of the film may also provoke a response in the viewer that manifests itself corporeally (a bracing, a shiver, an intake of breath). Even in these moments of closeness, however, the actual absenting of the viewer from the film world allows him or her a position where this sensuousness can be both felt and observed. A gesture that stimulates a physical response in the viewer is one that takes its place in the context of its film world and gains significance from its connections with the film's other gestures; a sensuous detail in the film might resonate with a real-life experience of sensuousness on the part of the viewer but it also resonates with all the other sensuous details in the film world. By tracing these resonances, the viewer becomes involved in a way of reading that is both sense aware and respectful of the difference between our world and the film's 'world of its own'.

These principles established, it is now time to demonstrate the shape a sensuous reading of a film world might take. To do so, the next chapter contains a close analysis of four pivotal scenes from *Amores Perros*, all of which cover similar narrative terrain but which are differentiated by their sensuous qualities. By attending to these differences, I attempt to understand how the film expresses itself as a world.

Notes

1. Loiperdinger, 'Lumière's *Arrival of the Train*: cinema's founding myth', *The Moving Image*, pp. 90–1.
2. Ibid. p. 97.
3. Ibid. p. 93.
4. Ibid. p. 93.
5. Ibid. p. 94.
6. Barker, *The Tactile Eye: Touch and the Cinematic Experience*, p. 133.
7. See Stoller, *Sensuous Scholarship*.
8. Beugnet, *Cinema and Sensation: French Film and the Art of Transgression*, p. 22.
9. Elsaesser and Hagener, *Film Theory: an introduction through the senses*.
10. Ibid. p. 127.
11. See Bazin (translated by Hugh Gray), 'The ontology of the photographic image', in Bazin, *What Is Cinema?*: Volume I, pp. 9–16.
12. Bazin (translated by Hugh Gray), 'An aesthetic of reality', in Bazin, *What Is Cinema?*: Volume II, p. 25.
13. Ibid. p. 37.

14. Ibid. p. 28.
15. Ibid. p. 37.
16. Peucker, *The Material Image: Art and the Real in Film*, p. 3.
17. Ibid. p. 5.
18. Ibid. pp. 4–5.
19. Bazin (translated by Hugh Gray), 'The virtues and limitations of montage', in Bazin, *What Is Cinema?: Volume I*, p. 46.
20. Eisenstein (translated by Jay Leyda), 'The Filmic Fourth Dimension', in Eisenstein, *Film Form*, pp. 66–7.
21. Ibid. p. 71.
22. Ibid. p. 68.
23. Sobchack, *The Address of the Eye: A Phenomenology of Film Experience*, p. xvi.
24. Ibid. p. xiii.
25. Ibid. p. xv.
26. Sobchack, 'What my fingers knew: the cinesthetic subject, or vision in the flesh', in Sobchack, *Carnal Thoughts: Embodiment and Moving Image Culture*, p. 67.
27. Ibid. p. 76.
28. Barker, *The Tactile Eye*, p. 19.
29. Sobchack, *Carnal Thoughts*, p. 77.
30. Barker, *The Tactile Eye*, p. 10.
31. Ibid. p. 19.
32. Sobchack, *The Address of the Eye*, p. 20.
33. Shaviro, *The Cinematic Body*, p. 15.
34. Ibid. p. 2.
35. Ibid. pp. 64–5.
36. Ibid. p. 257.
37. Beugnet, *Cinema and Sensation: French Film and the Art of Transgression*, p. 5.
38. Barker, *The Tactile Eye*, p. 25.
39. Shaviro, *The Cinematic Body*, p. 255.
40. Beugnet, *Cinema and Sensation*, p. 14.
41. Barker, *The Tactile Eye*, p. 92.
42. Perkins, 'Where is the world? The horizon of events in movie fiction', in Gibbs and Pye (eds), *Style and Meaning: Studies in the detailed analysis of film*, p. 39.
43. Ibid. p.33.
44. Ibid. p. 22.
45. Ibid. pp. 19–20.
46. Cavell, *The World Viewed: Reflections on the Ontology of Film*, enlarged edition, p. 24.
47. Thomas, *Reading Hollywood: Spaces and Meanings in American Film*, p. 110.
48. Ibid. pp. 111–12.
49. Perkins, op. cit., p. 32.
50. Marks, *The Skin of the Film: Intercultural Cinema, Embodiment, and the Senses*, pp. 162–4.
51. Trotter, 'Lynne Ramsay's *Ratcatcher*: towards a theory of haptic narrative', *Paragraph* 31, p. 141.

52. Ibid. p. 154.
53. Perkins, 'Where is the world?', p. 20.
54. Sobchack, *Carnal Thoughts*, p. 65.
55. Ibid. p. 65.
56. Barker, *The Tactile Eye*, p. 21.
57. Pye, 'Movies and tone', in Pye and Gibbs, *Close Up* 2, p. 7.

CHAPTER 2

Sensation and Narrative Sense in Amores Perros

Amores Perros (Inarritu, 2000) works as a converging-fates film, as defined by David Bordwell, featuring unacquainted characters 'pursuing their own lives but intersecting occasionally by sheer accident'.[1] In this case, the convergence takes the form of a car crash involving Octavio (Gael Garcia Bernal) and Valeria (Goya Toledo), two of the main characters, which is witnessed by a third, el Chivo (Emilio Echevarria). The pivotal crash is represented four times during the film, reprised at various points in a narrative that investigates the lives of these three characters, pre- and post-collision. For the purposes of this analysis, the term 'crash scene' refers to the sequences that chart the characters' journeys towards the site of collision as well as the actual moment of impact and its immediate aftermath.

The accident is represented differently each time it is repeated and it is the significance of the differences that my analysis explores. Specifically, I am interested in the varying sensuous effects produced in the alternative versions of the scene and the implications these effects have for the viewer's understanding of the characters' places within the fictional world. As such, this section introduces an analytical approach that acknowledges the way films appeal to the senses, inciting the 'real world' bodies of their viewers. It also understands films as worlds of their own, however, consisting of fictional environments whose sensuous qualities draw attention to, and provide commentary on, aspects of story, setting, character and theme.

The repetition of the same narrative event enacted in these scenes is useful for my purposes as it offers multiple points of direct comparison between moments composed of materials that are closely related but imbued with different properties of texture and sensation. The commentary on these scenes is organised quite schematically in order to set out some of the general areas of enquiry that will inform my readings in the book as a whole. Like *Amores Perros* itself, my analysis passes over the crash scene four times: firstly, to establish the narrative context surrounding the rendition of each scene; secondly, to identify the visual means by which materials are bestowed varying sensuous properties; thirdly, to consider the different textures apparent on the soundtrack; and, finally, to relate the sensuous qualities of the crash scenes to those evident in other parts of the film. The repetition is designed to offer the sense that the same ground is being revisited to reveal new layers of detail in the textures of the film. All these textures, I argue, contribute to the production of moments where the experiencing of the sensuous qualities of the film and the understanding of the significance of relationships within the story world become part of the same process for the viewer.

THE CRASH SCENES AND THEIR NARRATIVE CONTEXTS

The film begins with three titles following each other silently, naming its production companies and its director, Alejandro Gonzalez Inarritu. There follows the title of the film itself, set in large lower case in the middle of a black screen, with 'amores' coloured red and 'perros' coloured white. There is no space between the two words. Traffic noise breaks the silence on the soundtrack just before the titles fade and the film cuts to its first live-action image: a shot of the white markings in the middle of the road viewed from the side window of a moving car. This turns out to be the first shot in a sequence lasting just over two minutes that represents the pivotal collision.

The first crash scene, then, is presented without a pre-established narrative context. It depicts two young men, later identified as Octavio and his friend Jorge (Humberto Busto), driving frantically to escape a truck occupied by a gun-wielding gang. From the dialogue between them, it is clear that Octavio has done something to incite their pursuers and that the story somehow involves the dog, Cofi, who lies bleeding in the back seat of their car. After a near collision with a bus and a brief moment when Octavio and Jorge think they have shaken off the truck, the scene concludes with the crash, a consequence of Octavio jumping a red light, which results in their car hitting the side of another vehicle whose occupant, later revealed to be Valeria, is viewed bloodied and trapped in the final shot of the sequence.

The first repetition of the crash scene occurs fifty-four minutes into the film, now following on in 'proper' narrative order from the events that lead to it. By this point, it has been established that Octavio has been entering Cofi into dogfights, culminating in a 'winner takes all' contest with a dog owned by local gangster Jarocho (Gustavo Sanchez Parra). Octavio had been banking on Cofi winning in order to raise the money to elope with Susana (Vanessa Bauche), the wife of his brother Ramiro (Marco Perez). On the eve of the fight, however, it appears that Susana has stolen off with Ramiro, using Octavio's money. The fight goes ahead, nonetheless, but, when Jarocho shoots Cofi to ensure victory for his dog, Octavio impetuously stabs him, and this is what leads to the car chase and crash as Jarocho's henchmen seek retribution.

The insertion of the chase and crash into a particular narrative context clearly affects the viewer's appreciation of these events as they are re-enacted. In the rendition of the chase itself, however, no new story information is offered to the viewer even though, as I shall discuss, the scene's 'feel' is entirely different from the first scene. This second version provides 'highlights' from the chase and cuts out abruptly just before the moment of impact between the two cars.

The third crash scene represents the perspective of Valeria and, in terms of its placement within the film, occurs just five minutes after the second rendition of the incident. By this point, it has been made clear that Valeria is a high-profile model who has been conducting an affair with Daniel (Alvaro Guerrero), a magazine editor. Between the second crash scene and the third, we see Valeria leaving the set of a television chat show and being led to an apartment which, she is surprised to discover, has been bought for her by Daniel who reveals that he has finally left his wife. Realising that they have no drink to toast this development in their relationship, Valeria pops out to the shops in her car with her pet dog, Richie, in tow. It is during this journey that Octavio's car crashes into hers, the scene concluding with the moment of impact.

The final version of the crash occurs forty minutes later, this time registered from the point of view of the film's third major player, the vagrant assassin el Chivo. At this point, el Chivo, surrounded by his coterie of dogs, is trailing a newly commissioned hit, following him to a restaurant and watching him from outside. The collision between Octavio and Valeria takes place on the road behind him, and he rushes to the scene of the accident, taking money from the semi-conscious Octavio's pocket, before helping him out of the car. With everyone else occupied with the human victims, el Chivo takes the opportunity to remove Cofi from the crash site, adding him to his pack.

The narrative placement of each rendition of the crash is important, and the significance of reviewing the scene from different points of view and with an accumulation of narrative knowledge will be considered as part of my analysis. The specific focus here, however, is on the sensuous aspects of the telling of these scenes and the way these qualities are dramatically significant.

THE SENSUOUS IMAGE

Each rendition of the crash offers a unique sensuous experience visually, and this can be accounted for by differences in the content of the *mise en scène* as well as variations within such fundamental filmic parameters as framing, camera movement, film speed and the tempo of cutting between shots. While these elements are likely to be considered in any close film analysis, the intention here is to concentrate on the tactile 'feel' of these features with a view to assessing their storytelling significance.

Crash scene 1: textured contrasts through framing

In the first crash scene, a distinct contrast is made between the framing of Octavio and Jorge, on the one hand, and the dog, Cofi, on the other. Despite the close confines of the car and the chaotic nature of the chase, Octavio and Jorge are predominantly shot in medium close-ups, allowing an intimate view of their frightened expressions and frantic gestures but also keeping the wider street environment in sight (Figures 2.1 and 2.2). By contrast, the shots of the dog are all in extreme close-up, drawing attention to the visceral details of its bloodied and sweating coat (Figure 2.3). There is a lingering on the surface of the dog's body, covered with fluid matter, that is forgone in the framing of the human characters at this point.

The special concentration on the texture of the dog's body is signalled in the moment that the camera is brought into the car for the first time. The sequence has opened with two exterior shots detailing an urban environment from a speeding car, one following the markings in the middle of the road, the other depicting a side view in which the cityscape becomes visible once the camera has sped past a line of trees. The third shot ties down these environmental images to a specific narrative situation. The camera is positioned pointing out through the back window of Octavio's car. The opening few seconds of the shot depict the traffic behind them and, by the evidence of cars trailing in the camera's wake, it is clear that Octavio is driving quickly. The camera then pulls back through the window, dipping speedily down the back seat, upholstered in rough, black-and-white striped corduroy and soaked with the blood of Cofi which is sprawled across the seat.

The closeness of the view of the bloodied upholstery reveals the grain of its texture with an intensity that has not been apparent up to this point. The 'presence' of the fabric, produced by its rough weave, its boldly conflicting colour scheme, the splattering of blood, and the closeness of the camera to it, contrasts with the abstract features of previous imagery (scenery whizzing past in a blur) and with its more neutrally representational aspects (buildings on the distant skyline, queues of traffic in the street). It introduces the viewer, visually, to the visceral and violent environment that the film will proceed to explore.

It is significant that the colour scheme in this moment matches that of the opening title, where 'amores' is typed in red and 'perros' in white, against a black backdrop. These titles are resolutely flat: the words fit symmetrically in the middle of the screen with a good deal of space around them; grammatical conventions are forgone in order not to disturb the evenness of the pattern ('amores' and 'perros' are uncapitalised and no space is offered between the two words). As the camera dips down towards the dog, the colour scheme and patterning are disarranged: flatness is replaced by rough-hewn texture, distance by extreme closeness, stillness by fast camera movement, and the separation between black, white and red is disturbed by the soaking of blood across the pattern of the fabric.

The track-down reaches the injured dog, the camera jittering as it essays its prone body. The framing is extremely intimate, allowing a registration of the detail of the blood and sweat on the dog's coat and its face. Jorge's hands move from Cofi's mouth to its body, offering the film's first close view of human flesh. The fact that these hands are slippery and glistening with the dog's blood is significant in terms of further indicating the violence inherent in the depicted world. It is also telling, however, that the extreme close-ups which reveal the messy materiality of the body do not continue in connection with the human figures for the rest of the scene. This shot revels in a tactile and textural intimacy to establish a possibility of visual framing that is subsequently suspended in relation to the film's human protagonists unless they are in physical contact with Cofi.

This distinction is revealed in the next series of shots which cut between medium close-ups of Octavio and Jorge as they wonder whether they have shaken off their assailants. There is then a return to the extreme close-ups associated with Cofi as we are offered a very close view of Jorge's hand on the dog's body over which he comments (in Spanish), 'shit, he's bleeding a lot'. The camera pans up to Jorge's face, caught in side profile, offering a much closer view than is allowed in the rest of the scene. As soon as the panning movement reaches his face, however, there is a cut to a more distanced medium close-up of Octavio as if to intimate that the film is not really ready to get too close to the human figures at this point. Octavio's suggestion that Jorge stem the flow of blood by pressing his finger on the wound motivates a return to the extreme close-up of Jorge's hands on the dog. This shot is given an even more intense tactile nature as we see Jorge lift his hands from Cofi causing the blood that had been underneath to ooze up.

Later in the scene, Octavio brakes sharply to avoid crashing into a bus, causing Cofi to fall off the back seat. Jorge lifts him back up and an extreme close-up shows him pressing his bloodied hands down on the dog's body to see if he is still breathing. Realising that the dog is bleeding even more copiously, Jorge takes off his shirt and uses this to try to stem the flow. The action of pressing the shirt against the dog's body is also shown in extreme close-up, offering a fourth material, after the car seat's upholstery, the dog's body itself and Jorge's hands, into which Cofi's blood is seen to seep (a very brief close shot of the T-shirt on Cofi's wound later in the scene registers an increased staining of blood).

The scene as a whole uses a variety of techniques to involve the viewer viscerally in the action. Camera movement is shaky and shot lengths are short, and these help to convey the physical sensations of a frantic chase. The framings of the human figures, however, are *relatively* lacking in intimacy compared to the access allowed to Cofi whose body ejects a flow of blood and sweat that is shown in grisly detail. Indeed, the moment of impact between Octavio's and Valeria's cars is shown by a series of exterior and interior shots in which no human figure is shown. The scene does end with a shot of a human character suffering but this is Valeria who has not been introduced to the viewer until this point and whose distressed and bloodied body is seen only from a distance through the misted glass of her car-door window.

Given that the distinction between relatively distanced framings for the human characters and texturally detailed close-ups for Cofi is made at the start of the film, at least two ways of understanding the contrast are possible: firstly, the relatively excessive visual attention on Cofi, given the lack of a framing narrative context, bestows a symbolic value on the dog which will be developed as the film progresses; secondly, the relatively distanced view of the human figures allows the film space to 'fill in the gaps' about these characters at a later point. Testing these hypotheses against the evidence of the subsequent renditions of the crash scene, it does become apparent that the film is interested in using the figure of the dog for thematic purposes (all three of the main characters are associated with dogs) and in the different possibilities of representing the detail of the human body.

Crash scene 2: disembodied sensations

Whereas the first version of the crash takes place in a narrative void, relatively speaking, the second rendition is narratively redundant. The viewer now knows the events that have led to the car chase, and the representation of it the second time contains no new information about its progress. It does offer the event as a novel type of sensational experience in comparison to its predecessor, however. The excessively visceral aspects of the scene are no longer carried by the images associated with Cofi. In fact, none of the extreme close-ups of the dog is repeated and the only sight of blood is on the hands and arms of Jorge viewed through medium shots as he picks Cofi off the floor and places him back on the car seat.

Blood is the key sensuous element of the first crash scene: it oozes, glistens, soaks into fabric and smears over human skin. That its absence in this version is deliberate is indicated by the image that precedes the re-enactment of the chase. A camera tracks behind Octavio as he runs out of the dogfight venue having stabbed Jarocho. It stops to view him driving off in his car with his pursuers running over to their truck on the other side of the road. The camera then lurches down to the ground to reveal the bloodied knife that Octavio has dropped during his escape. At exactly this moment, a non-diegetic machine-like dirge appears on the soundtrack (commented upon later) indicating a movement to a less realist audio-visual register. The second crash scene then begins.

The knife, therefore, carries a dramatic and figurative value at the same time: it has drawn the blood of Jarocho but, in the passage that follows, it also draws the blood away from the cinematic rendition of the car chase. Instead, the sequence offers an alternative set of sensations that represent what the moment *feels like* to Octavio, in particular, rather than defining him through his contribution to the bare facts of the events.

His experience of the chase is demonstrated to be a strangely dislocated one. The scene's dominant texture in this incarnation is one of ghostliness as sights and sounds are remixed in disembodied patterns. In purely visual terms, the opening two shots of road markings and the cityscape whizzing by, repeated exactly from the first sequence, set the mood precisely. In the first crash scene, the abstracting effect of motion blur in these two shots is superseded by the intensely visceral nature of the extreme close-up of Cofi. In the second version, however, the blurring effect is maintained, partly through distortions and displacements taking place on the soundtrack but also through the compression of the sequence in to a much shorter screen time (forty-five seconds as opposed to the first crash scene's running time of two-and-a-half minutes). The images may be ordered in the same sequence (though this is complicated by the work of the soundtrack) but they slip by with a speed that is fleeting in its own right and also experienced as such through comparison of what the viewer has seen of the event before. This sensation of excessive speed contributes to the feeling that Octavio is being propelled through events over which he has no control, thus linking a sensuous experience on the part of the viewer (in this case, the perception of speed) to an understanding of the level of power held by a character within the film's fictional world.

There is, of course, the possibility that the scene may be read simply as an instance of formal play that exists to engage the viewer in a fresh manner to compensate for the repetitions taking place in terms of story information. The understanding of the scene's sensational aspects as relevant to an appreciation of Octavio's character, however, is supported by surrounding evidence. Throughout the film, Octavio's desire to take control of situations is thwarted. Most prominently, his ambition to be with Ramiro's wife,

Susana, is frustrated even after his brother is killed. A funeral parlour holding Ramiro's open coffin is the venue for Octavio's and Susana's first meeting after Octavio's accident. He is still determined that Susana come away with him and tells her that he will be travelling on Sunday and that he will wait for her. Susana is clearly angry at being propositioned at this time, and the film's final image of Octavio depicts him waiting, fruitlessly, for Susana to join him at the bus station.

Octavio's timing, at this point, is all wrong, and his overall lack of control is indicated by the film's formal temporal strategies as well. In the second crash scene, this is represented by a severe compression of the events of the chase and a mistiming between sound and image, discussed later. In the film's latter stages, Octavio's vulnerability is suggested by his virtual disappearance from the screen. His story dominates screen time for almost the first hour of the film but he appears only twice more after that, in the scenes detailed above. The limited appearance of Octavio in the film's second half reflects the petering out of his ambitions, and his helplessness is made even more apparent by having these two scenes interspersed with the story of el Chivo whose control of events is conspicuously more assured.

Finally, the action that thwarts Octavio's original plans to elope with Susana is disclosed at two different moments in the film from two different perspectives. In this way, it attains the rare privilege of reiteration from another point of view that is also allowed only to the crash scene. Firstly, in its 'proper' story order, the film shows Susana collecting her baby from her mother, followed by Octavio's mother breaking the news to him that Ramiro and Susana have suddenly moved out to an undisclosed location. Octavio then runs up to Susana's room to discover that the secret stash of money he had been saving for their elopement has gone. The visual evidence of Susana and Ramiro moving out, however, does not occur for almost an hour of subsequent screen time when they are seen walking past el Chivo in the final section of the film which has gone back in time to present el Chivo's pre-crash story.

The temporal organisation of Octavio's story subjects it to a kind of structural buffeting: the viewer's introduction to his character is compromised by seeing him at a pivotal dramatic moment (the first crash scene) without a narrative context having been established; the film then reveals his story in top-heavy fashion, focusing on him centrally in the first fifty minutes but then 'losing interest' as other narrative lines are developed. The moment at which his plans of elopement are shown to be fruitless is returned to later in the film from a different perspective, as if to remind the viewer that Octavio's insight into events is fatally limited. The temporal compression and uncanny dislocations of the second crash scene, then, offer a sensorily distinct experience that is in keeping with a commentary on Octavio that is woven in to the wider time-scheme of the film.

The bloodlessness of this second rendition of the scene is also revealing in relation to Octavio. His knifing of Jarocho is out of character: up to this point, within the tough world of dogfighting, gang rivalries and gun crime, Octavio has been portrayed as a *relatively* naive and gentle figure. He enters the world of dogfighting only by chance after Cofi shows unexpected aggression in killing two of Jarocho's dogs on the street. His motivation for doing so has a naively romantic dimension as he strives to raise the money that he thinks – incorrectly – will allow him to elope with Susana.

This provides the context in which Octavio's stabbing of Jarocho comes as a surprise, and the shock of the moment is exacerbated by the depiction of the events leading immediately up to it. After Jarocho has shot Cofi, he teases Octavio for his naivety, saying 'don't be cry-babies, that's the business', and tells him to complain to his brother, as if Ramiro is really the person equipped to confront Jarocho on a more even footing. Octavio seems to have accepted his place as the camera follows him and Jorge carrying Cofi down the covered corridor and out to their car. As Jorge places Cofi in the back seat, however, Octavio evidently decides on a new course of action, telling Jorge to get the car started and wait. In the same shot, the camera tracks back to accommodate the reverse journey of Octavio as he returns to confront Jarocho. Jarocho is evidently unconcerned, greeting him with the feminising and infantilising title of 'princess'. He, his gang, and the viewer are not prepared for Octavio's sudden pulling of a knife and stabbing of Jarocho in the stomach (the viewer has no idea Octavio even carries a knife). The same shot continues as it once again follows Octavio down the covered walkway, this time pursued by Jarocho's gang, the shot ending with the dive down to the bloodied knife that augurs the second crash scene.

The blood on the knife, then, is a consequence of an aberrant action on the part of Octavio, and the rendition of the chase, thereafter, indicates the shock to Octavio's system that this action has caused. It also represents, in its immateriality and bloodlessness, the final throes of Octavio's pursuit of a romantic fantasy that has been predicated on a disavowal of his real, power-less position within his violent environment.

The sense of this rendition as bloodless is finalised at the moment of impact between Octavio's and Valeria's cars. Instead of representing the crash itself, there is an abrupt cut to black followed by the revealing of a television-studio monitor in the middle of the screen, featuring a black-and-white image of the chat-show host who had been interviewing Valeria before Octavio and Jorge left the apartment for the fight. This not only replaces the kinetic sensation of the crash with something entirely static and banal but also continues the sense that the second crash scene has been determinedly 'colourless', editing out the sight of blood that had given the first crash scene its most striking visceral qualities.

The second crash scene, in summary, arranges its visual materials in such a way that their sensuous effects reveal something of Octavio's subjectivity as well as offering a more distanced commentary on him. The bloodlessness of Octavio, established by contrast with Cofi in the first crash scene and carried on as a narrative motif thereafter, finds phantasmagorically sensuous expression here, through various techniques which evoke a 'blurring' that casts Octavio as a ghostly presence. The qualities of disembodiment projected in this scene are only partly produced through the image, however, and attention to the soundtrack later in my analysis will complete the description and interpretation of the scene's immaterial texture.

Crash scene 3: non-sensuous visual framing

The third crash scene shifts perspective, depicting Valeria's journey, which culminates with Octavio's car crashing in to hers. Its sensuous qualities, in terms of the image, are more self-effacing than in the first two renditions. After a pan up her bare legs (a key asset for her modelling career but grievously injured in the crash), the camera remains relatively steady and static throughout the scene, cutting between medium close-ups and close-ups of Valeria driving, in profile from inside the car and occasionally viewed from outside (Figures 2.4 and 2.5). There are also shots of her dog yapping in the back seat and two dramatically instructive long shots of traffic lights at the crossroads, first of all turning red causing Valeria to stop, and then turning green causing her to go, whereupon her car is hit by Octavio's. Apart from motion caused by the progress of the car itself, there are only two significant independent camera movements: one pivoting to look back on el Chivo whom the car passes as he walks with his dogs on the side of the road, the other to follow her car to the left as it is rammed against by Octavio's.

The (im)material qualities that are evoked by the visual strategies of the first two renditions of the crash are notably absent in this scene. The relative composure of the *mise en scène* here is fitting for two reasons. Firstly, it elongates the suspense for a viewer who knows that Valeria is going to be involved in the crash because of the inclusion of the shot of her bloodied and trapped body inside her car at the end of the first crash scene. Anticipation has been heightened by the replacement of the moment of impact in the second crash scene with the banal image of the television chat-show host. This lends a sense of incompletion to this second rendition and provides a bridge between Octavio's story and Valeria's through the intermediary of the television presenter. To re-experience the 'pay-off' of the moment of impact, it is implied, the viewer must first learn some of the details of the situation occupied by Valeria, its other key participant.

After the scene in the apartment Daniel has brought for her, the return to a driving scene cues the viewer to anticipate a re-enactment of the crash (why else would we be watching Valeria on the way to buy groceries?), and the imminence of the collision is made even more acute by the shots of the traffic lights which remind the viewer of the lights skipped by Octavio in the first two crash scenes. The deliberately unexciting manner in which these events are presented visually contrasts with the viewer's anticipation of an inevitable dramatic collision.

The composure of the *mise en scène* is also an appropriate way of representing Valeria's character whose livelihood relies on maintaining a carefully constructed appearance. The big billboard poster of her advertising perfume has already been depicted twice in the film by this point, and the preceding scenes have revealed how her job entails the public face of her private life being as carefully presented as her physical appearance. In her television interview, she 'reveals' her boyfriend to be a famous actor who then appears on set with her. This relationship exists for public consumption only, fitting in with her glamorous persona and diverting attention from the affair she is having with the married Daniel.

The apartment Daniel has set up for her is testament to her investment in appearances. It features on its living-room wall a series of blown-up photo-strips taken from one of her modelling sessions and looks out on to a huge poster of her hung from the building opposite. Valeria's attention to her physical appearance is underlined in the car scene itself when she takes the opportunity to reapply her lipstick as she waits for the traffic lights to turn green.

The lack of sensuous detail, visually, in this rendition of the crash, then, is fitting for the reasons cited above. When compared with other aspects of the film, it also sets up effective contrasts in three directions: between the experiences of Valeria and Octavio, two characters far removed on the social scale; between the life of Valeria pre- and post-crash which sees her moving from a state in which she is able to keep her body under perfect control to one where all such certainty is erased and her body begins to work against her; and between Valeria and el Chivo whose portrayal in the final crash scene is notably more sensuous.

Crash scene 4: the tactility of el Chivo

The moment of impact in the third crash scene is rendered in a suitably detached manner, viewed from some distance behind the set of lights Valeria crosses, and featuring a composed pan to the left to follow the trajectory of the colliding cars. The collision in the final crash scene is also handled matter-of-factly, taking place behind el Chivo, who looks towards the camera in mid shot on the right of the frame, while the cars crash into each other behind him on the left. The collision is experienced as an intrusion upon a lengthy passage (two-and-a-half minutes) that has followed el Chivo trailing his newly commissioned hit. Playing against the assassin's attempts to go about his work unobtrusively, this passage produces el Chivo as an extraordinary physical presence within his environment. In particular, through a number of cinematic means, he is bestowed with tactile qualities.

The passage is marked by a decisive temporal and spatial shift as the film moves from el Chivo in his makeshift home at night to him walking outside in daylight. The introduction of a particular non-diegetic musical theme at this point underlines the fact that the film has moved to a new phase of action. The first shot of this passage sees el Chivo emerging over the brow of a hilly road, pushing a trolley, with his pack of dogs milling about him. This is presented as a distanced, head-on shot (Figure 2.6), the use of a telephoto lens giving the image a heat-haze shimmer, a synaesthetic effect that gives heat a visual and tactile quality. The expression of heat visually occurs again later in the passage with a shot pointing from the base of a tree directly upwards into the sun creating a lens-flare effect that spreads across the tree's trunk and its tangled branches. The next shot shows el Chivo sitting at the base of the tree looking up, retrospectively associating the synaesthetic effect with the perception of his character.

Tactile associations with el Chivo are manufactured in two other ways. Firstly, while he is trailing his target, he engages in various activities that emphasise touch: he reaches into his pocket to retrieve a titbit for his dogs which then lap at his fingers (Figure 2.7); and he plays with a yo-yo, stretching out the string in both hands (Figure 2.8). Secondly, his face is replete with textured qualities that appeal to a sense of touch. He sports straggly, shoulder-length white/grey hair, a bushy beard that is white around his cheeks and dark grey around the mouth, and he has weather-beaten skin that is marked by deep wrinkles. For considerable stretches of this passage, el Chivo just sits by the tree observing the movements of his target, and this allows the viewer to contemplate the pronounced textures of his face, particularly in the shot of him looking up towards the sun which produces patches of intense light on one side of his face and dark shadows on the other (Figure 2.9).

The showcasing of his face as a 'landscape', which sunlight affects in different ways, continues when he gets on the move to follow his target. At one point, el Chivo is framed at the rear of a backtracking shot which has his target and companion at the front of it. The camera pulls focus from front to back so that el Chivo's features are viewed in sharp relief, the sun creating a halo effect around the top of his head. The following tracking shot is set up from behind the head of el Chivo, who now blocks most of the front of the frame, so that the viewer can see how the light plays on the top of his head from a different visual perspective. Very shortly afterwards, there is a sidetracking close-up of el Chivo, which offers an intimate view of his rugged features, and this is succeeded by a backtracking shot that cuts off just as his face fills the screen. This gives way to a shot from inside the restaurant window into which the target has just gone, and this features a blurred view of a pattern on the window front of frame and an equally indistinct depiction of the traffic at the crossroads at the back of the frame. El Chivo steps in from the right and the image now has a focus in the form of his weathered face. All these shots are interspersed with much more distanced views of the people el Chivo is trailing, with the effect that the particularities of their physical features are passed over, and el Chivo's face appears all the more extraordinarily textured by contrast.

If the first two crash scenes offer different views of Octavio's experience, the third and fourth renditions are grouped together through their contrasting presentations of the film's other two main characters. The scenes make a distinction between the smooth, manicured appearance of Valeria, on the one hand, and the rough-hewn, 'natural' features of el Chivo, on the other. The film finds a visual style to represent these different kinds of bodies appropriately: carefully composed and relatively distanced in relation to Valeria; and using a variety of techniques which evoke the tactile in the case of el Chivo.

The moment of impact in the final crash scene functions, as I have mentioned, as an intrusion upon this investigation of el Chivo as a physical presence. The subsequent depiction of the aftermath of the crash benefits from el Chivo's influence, however, as it is imbued with sensuous detail that had hitherto been withheld from the portrayal of the collision itself.

The only visual evidence of the aftermath disclosed before the final crash scene is the shot of Valeria trapped in her car at the end of the first rendition of the collision. The second crash scene omits the moment of impact entirely while the third views the collision in a single shot from some distance. The final crash scene, then, acts as a kind of delayed 'gratification' for the viewer who finally sees the physical impact of the crash on Octavio (and Jorge), learns much more about the suffering of Valeria, and is given more access generally to the visceral details of the scene.

The viewer is guided to the crash site through the movement of el Chivo. After the cars collide with each other behind his shoulder, el Chivo looks round and immediately walks towards the collision. A backtracking shot picks up his movement in medium close-up as he climbs over a crash barrier and heads towards the cars, the film then cutting briefly to a tracking shot following his movement from behind him. A wider sidetracking shot succeeds this, chronicling el Chivo's arrival at Octavio's car. At this point, el Chivo struggles with another man to pull off the car door, and this is represented through another tracking shot from behind his head.

The journey into the scene of the crash, then, continues the focus on el Chivo's physical presence, viewed from different visual perspectives, that had provided the keynote of the sequence up until this point. The crash first intrudes on the languid atmosphere of a scene in which the viewer watches el Chivo watching but then becomes another setting in which to appreciate his presence, this time animated by more urgent movement.

El Chivo's act of opening the car door reveals a scene in which Jorge and Octavio exhibit a material presence previously withheld. The delay in revealing blood in association with Octavio continues in the first shot once the car door has been ripped open. The shot is organised so that part of Jorge's face occupies the front left of the frame in close-up, with Octavio slumped forward on the dashboard behind him. While Jorge's face is absolutely caked with blood, Octavio's injuries remain undisclosed to the camera. El Chivo is positioned back centre, looking down (Figure 2.10).

It is only through el Chivo's gaze that Octavio's injuries are finally revealed. The shot matching his look down dollies towards Octavio's left leg clad in jeans that are splattered with blood. It is only as el Chivo helps to lift Octavio out of the car, with the assistance of another man, that the viewer sees blood *flowing* from Octavio (Figure 2.11). A shaky hand-held shot shows Octavio in medium close-up from the side. His face is bloodied and a gloop of blood also drips from his mouth. In a subsequent shot, framed in the same manner, Octavio regains consciousness fully and screams in agony, causing the blood around his mouth and his scrunched-up eyes to well. He also raises his arms, revealing the blood that splatters them.

After he has been pulled out of the car, the full extent of his injuries is revealed. He lies writhing on the road, blood covering his face and neck and his T-shirt absolutely soaked with it. The colour scheme here harks back to the black-white-red motif that was employed in the film's titles and refigured in the tracking shot over the back seat of the car near the start of the first crash scene. Octavio is wearing a 'Scream' T-shirt, which features a picture of a white mask set against a black background. The blood that soaks into this T-shirt is especially noticeable in its staining of the white mask, thereby reproducing the invasion of red on black and white that was evident on the upholstery of the back seat of the car in the first scene. Octavio's jeans are also ripped, revealing a bloodied left knee and blood soaked more voluminously around the tear. The protruding knee breaking out of torn fabric gives Octavio's body the illusion of a three-dimensionality that contrasts with the 'flattening' effects involved in the representation of his body in the second car crash scene.

El Chivo, then, is cast as the narrative agent whose actions reveal Octavio's bleeding to the viewer after nearly two hours of the film have passed. It is also through his act of turning that the viewer is led towards the sight of Valeria trapped and bloodied in her car, in a shot that exactly reprises that used at the end of the first crash scene. It is at this point, through the mediation of el Chivo, that the viewer realises what the opening crash scene has omitted in terms of Octavio's suffering body.

Of the three main characters, then, it is el Chivo who is associated most with the sensuous qualities that the various enactments of the crash scene both withhold and draw attention to. During el Chivo's journey to the site of collision, the image is imbued with a number of sensuous and synaesthetic properties, centred around the tactile qualities of el Chivo's face. At the accident scene itself, it is through el Chivo's agency that the material reality of Octavio's and Valeria's injuries is finally revealed. This suggests that el Chivo occupies a privileged position within the film's fictional world, and this is something I shall return to after I have considered the sensuous properties of the soundtrack in the crash scenes.

THE SENSUOUS SOUNDTRACK

Crash scene 1: sensuous sound v. narrative sound

Sound precedes the introduction of live-action images in *Amores Perros*. As the title of the film is displayed, traffic noise emerges on the soundtrack, the familiar sound of cars moving at speed travelling across the stereo spectrum. In the gap between the fading of the titles and the opening live-action shot of the white markings of a road, heavy breathing emerges through the central speakers while the traffic noise continues. Once the shot of the road markings appears, engine noise with a lighter tone is added to the mix, weighted towards the right-hand speakers, contributing a third texture to the soundtrack.

Without a framing narrative context, these sounds, like the blurring road markings, are offered as a sensational experience in their own right, one that offers a sense of aural depth to a flat image. The heavy breathing exhibits

particularly sensuous properties, marked as it is by the physical labour of the
sentient body that produces it.

These opening seconds systematically layer sounds upon one another
and explore qualities of movement, depth, tone and grain in the soundtrack,
all of which contribute to the experiencing of the aural as richly textured.
When, however, the frantic dialogue between Jorge and Octavio emerges,
at first disembodied over the final stage of the shot of the road markings,
sound becomes much more straightforwardly expository. General traffic
noise continues to provide an ambient backdrop to the scene while dialogue
becomes synchronised with its on-screen speakers and listeners. The sound
of Octavio's car changes in acoustic character depending on the placement
of the camera inside the car or outside it, thus affecting a sonic naturalism. In
addition, more specific sounds are introduced or emphasised in conjunction
with relevant images to pinpoint various moments of the chase. For example,
Octavio's slamming of the brakes to avoid crashing into a bus is depicted
through two close-ups that are unusual in their scale in the context of the
scene. A frontal close-up shows him scrunching up his face and bracing
himself, the soundtrack registering the sound of a car horn that 'explains' his
change in posture. There follows a very brief shot of his foot slamming on the
brakes which is accompanied by a crunch and the screech of locking wheels.
The combination of a close-up of his foot slamming on the brake and a close
shot of his scrunched-up face as he hits the horn is also used just before the
car actually crashes. This time, the lack of crunching and screeching sounds
indicates that the brakes have failed, and the sound of the horn is truncated
as the car collides with Valeria's. Sound accompanies image in these instances
as written captions explain a photograph, clarifying the actions that Octavio
takes to avoid, or fail to avoid, a collision.

In the main body of the sequence, then, sound confirms the details of
on-screen action in a manner which does not leave room for the exploration
of sound's sensuous properties that is intimated at the start of the scene. The
fact that the film begins with a set of sounds and images that are not given
a narrative context and which are overtly textured, however, introduces a
line of enquiry around the sensuous properties of audio-visual material that
is elaborated upon at other junctures. Indeed, the first sequence ends with
sound once again being taken out of its narrative context thereby gaining
another kind of resonance. The car horn re-emerges as a dominant aspect
of the soundtrack once the sounds of shattering glass and crunched metal
associated with the collision die down. Evidently stuck, the horn continues
to sound out over the shot of Valeria trapped and bloodied in her car. In
turn, the horn, Valeria's anguished cry and that of the man trying to open
her car door continue as the screen fades to black and the title 'octavio y

susana' appears in the middle of the screen. These noises then fade out, to be replaced by the sounds of dogs barking, while the title still remains on-screen.

In these seconds, the viewer becomes more aware of the soundtrack as a series of layers which can be 'thickened' or 'thinned out' in a variety of combinations. The language of layering, thickening and thinning points to the emphasis this puts on the textures of the aural. Here, after the relative 'fullness' of the soundtrack in the main body of the scene, the relative isolation of the sound of the horn works by contrast to suggest that this particular episode is coming to an end. The 'bleeding' of Valeria's cries in to the succeeding titles also performs a narrative function, suggesting some kind of overlap between her story and Octavio's and Susana's. The fade-out of this segment of sound altogether, however, along with the fading in of the dogs barking, suggest that the viewer will have to wait to see how Valeria's and Octavio's narratives are entwined. In these ways, the varying texture and dynamics of the sound-track take on storytelling significance, signalling the coming to an end of one section, a potential continuity between storylines, and the introduction of a new narrative strand.

In retrospect, it is also clear that the sound of the horn is used to justify the shot of Valeria in her car at this point, even though the final rendition of the scene demonstrates that Octavio's retrieval from his car takes place beforehand. With this knowledge, the viewer can reassess the significance of the monotone sound of a malfunctioning car part being used in favour of the visceral display of Octavio's body at this juncture. The horn acts as a kind of sonic censoring of visual material involving Octavio which is only eventually revealed through the mediation of the film's most sensuously engaged character, el Chivo.

In the first crash scene, therefore, sound adheres to principles of narrative realism in its main body, with intimations of something more exploratory in terms of texture bookending the scene. In the second crash scene, the soundtrack is freed from its clarifying role, setting up instead a set of dynamic contrasts between sounds and offering a series of unsettling dislocations between sound and image.

Crash scene 2: representing Octavio's subjectivity through the 'pitch' of sound

The sounds of the second crash scene begin with the swooping of the camera downwards to pick out the bloodied knife Octavio has used to stab Jarocho, and which is now lying on the pavement. This movement signals the emergence of a drone that resembles the churning of a washing machine played at slow speed. Its regurgitating repetitiveness provides a suitably off-key sound-track for images which are in themselves being regurgitated in a distorted form from the first crash scene. The slowed-down nature of the sound also provides a counterpoint to the speeded-up quality of the images which compresses the chase sequence into a quarter of its original running time.

Here, then, different types of temporal distortion determine the sensational aspects of soundtrack and image. Together, the two elements combine to provide the disorienting experience of acceleration, on the one hand, and deceleration, on the other. In narrative terms, the dislocation between visual and aural rhythms contributes to the sense that the viewer is being presented with Octavio's subjective point of view at a moment when he has lost control. This experience of dislocation is furthered by the contribution of other soundtrack elements to the scene.

Extracts from the dialogue of the first crash scene are repeated in the second but are usually presented out of sync with the images. In addition, the voices are speeded up at times, resulting in a higher pitch and more shrill tone. These intermittent vocal screeches grate against the regular rhythm and thicker tone of the machine-like drone that runs through most of the sequence. As well as agitating against another element of the soundtrack, the accelerated and fragmentary quality of the dialogue complements the image's properties of excessive speed and fragmentation: it is difficult to ascertain whether the images have actually been speeded up in this sequence but this is the overall effect of placing small snippets of previously viewed shots together with frantic snatches of displaced dialogue.

The dislocating of dialogue has another effect, in drawing attention to the physical features of Octavio, as his mouth is seen to move without accompanying speech. This is particularly apparent when a frontal medium close-up shows him in a state of extreme agitation vocally which, in the original scene, was accompanied with him shouting 'get down' to Jorge as he has seen that their pursuers have pulled out a gun. In the second crash scene, all that can be heard is the non-diegetic machine-like drone, and this focuses attention on the facial gestures themselves rather than on their production of a verbal instruction. The removal of dialogue from its source, therefore, intensifies the viewer's appreciation of Octavio as a physical being under extreme pressure, allowing an increased experience of his suffering in comparison to the first scene in which the view of Octavio was relatively detached.

Two other soundtrack elements appear in the second crash scene, and these further contribute to the sense of Octavio's loss of control. As Octavio slams on the brakes to avoid hitting the bus, the close-up of his foot is heard with an accompanying screech of tyres, providing a split second of aural-visual synchronicity which is, in the context of the sequence's overall commitment to dislocation, disorienting in itself. The moment is further deranged by the simultaneous emergence on the non-diegetic soundtrack of a snippet from the hard-edged hip hop track, 'Pesada', by the Mexican band Control Machete. Here, then, two short, sharp attacking bursts of noise, one diegetic, the other non-diegetic, combine to provide an aural shock that is exacerbated by the sudden cessation of the machine-like drone just for this moment. The disorienting intervention of 'Pesada' occurs once more later in the sequence when a shot of a side mirror reveals the pursuers aiming a gun at Octavio's car, the machine-like drone again cutting off, before returning for the final seconds of the scene.

The final disorienting effect produced predominantly through sound occurs at the end of the sequence where the expected visualisation of the collision is withheld and the screen cuts instead to black. This is accompanied by the abrupt cutting out of the mechanical drone and its replacement with a synthesised drum roll. The soundtrack moves from an eerie type of synthetic sound to a 'clean' one, suggesting a movement to a different milieu within the film's multifaceted fictional world. The sudden emergence of sanitised sound after the aural chaos of the preceding minute also intimates that a movement is being made to a more orderly environment, at least on its immediate surface. Indeed, the black screen quickly gives way to a shot of a studio monitor, revealing a return to the television chat show featuring Valeria that Octavio and Jorge had been watching before the dogfight. At the end of the first crash scene, the fade out of Valeria's cries suggested a postponement of the taking up of her story but the introduction of the drums here heralds the moment her narrative is finally brought to centre stage. The familiarity of the drum sound as a cueing device within the television show genre also immediately suggests that Valeria's movement within her world is carefully choreographed, in antithesis to Octavio's experience.

Crash scene 3: 'flimsy' sound and Valeria

Indeed, the soundtrack of the third crash scene, which chronicles Valeria's journey towards the collision, is conspicuously controlled and ordered in keeping with the even framings and measured camera movement of the sequence. The consistent thread of sound up to the moment of impact is the upbeat Latin song 'Corazon' by Titan, the sonic quality of which is subject to change depending on whether the camera offers an interior or exterior view of the car. The effort to establish an 'objective' auditory perspective to match the visual point of view contrasts markedly to the subjective distortions of sound heard in the second crash scene that has taken place just five minutes previously.

Indeed, this contrast is the motivating factor for the seemingly prosaic realism of the music's presentation here. The realist quality of the sound does not exist simply for its own purposes, and this is signalled by the song actually being carried over, unrealistically, from the previous scene in Valeria's new flat. The seamless continuation of the song, now heard at raised volume, as the film cuts in space and time away from the apartment to Valeria in her car, casts doubt on the diegetic nature of the music even though the shifts in sound quality as the film cuts between interior and exterior views of the car do seem to be registering it as music that plays from the car radio.

The textures of the music change depending on the visual perspective of the scene, seeming to suggest an orderly correlation between sight and sound: acoustic clarity and visual intimacy on the one hand, and sonic muffle and visual distance on the other. This orderliness is built on precarious foundations, however, as it relies on the viewer discounting the initial logical assumption that the music's diegetic source was somewhere in the apartment. The synchronisation of image and sound is simultaneously overly neat and logically suspect, suggesting that the distinction between the aural chaos of the second crash scene and the rigorous order of this one is *too* marked to ring completely true.

This corresponds to a more general dialectic between surface order and underlying vulnerability that has been established in relation to Valeria, even in the limited screen time that has been allowed to her before this scene. The temporal ellipsis in the first crash scene, through which Valeria is viewed trapped and bloodied, forewarns that the well-being of her character, registered in the initial scenes that focus upon her centrally, is only temporary and superficial. Before these scenes, Valeria features as a presence in the film's fictional world without being identified specifically, in keeping with her very first appearance. On two occasions, Daniel receives phone calls in his family home which he is either unable to take, in the first instance, or which he has to answer under false pretences, in the second. Only in retrospect, when Daniel surprises Valeria with the new apartment, does it become clear that Valeria had been on the other end of the phone. For the first section of the film, then, Valeria appears as an intermittent presence, suffering physically and emotionally, but without any backstory of her own.

Valeria's character finally begins to be fleshed out through her appearance on the television chat show viewed by Octavio and Jorge before they leave for the dogfight. The moment she is revealed as an embodied presence is visually disappointing, however, considering that her physical beauty and qualities of (hetero)sexual attraction are announced as her major assets by the show's host ('with us today, someone no man would want to miss: one of the most beautiful women in Iberian America'). Her entrance is viewed through a close-up of the small television through which Jorge watches the show. This magnifies the horizontal lines of the television image and reveals the pallid nature of its colour (Figure 2.12), in contrast to the non-televisual images that surround it. In the first crash scene, a misted car window provides a textured screen that self-consciously provides a barrier between the viewer and an 'unhindered' view of Valeria's body (Figure 2.13). Here, another visual barrier is provided, in the shape of a lined and pallid televisual image. The visual 'inferiority' of television, when presented in the context of a 35 mm film, is demonstrated in relation to size as well as texture towards the end of this scene, after Octavio and Jorge have left, as the camera remains focused on a wide shot of Octavio's room, revealing that the television occupies only a very small proportion of the overall space.

Here, then, statements about Valeria's beauty – her most important asset in terms of her modelling career – are undermined by the presentation of her through a screen that is undernourished in terms of its sensuous properties, and undersized in relation to physical scale. The sonic shifts in the moment chronicling Valeria's journey just before the crash can be understood as similarly undermining. The seamless continuation of the song from the apartment to the car, together with the simultaneous raising of volume, suggest that the music is being continued to carry the happy mood enjoyed by Valeria at this point, now that her lover has finally left his wife. The song itself, now heard at full volume, certainly connotes joy, a Hammond-style organ solo rollicking over bubbling Latin beats. The lyrics consist of the single repeated refrain 'Corazon – mi Corazon' and are heard without any shift of aural perspective on their first two airings. The minimalism of lyrical content focuses attention on the manner in which the words are sung, rather than their 'meaning', showcasing a silky and smooth female vocal. The intermittent yapping of Valeria's dog, looking out the window in the back seat, adds to the sense of overall aural busyness.

The mood is interrupted, however, by the series of exterior views of the car which begin as Valeria pulls up to the lights at the crossroads where the crash will take place. The music ceases to be presented on its own terms and is put, instead, at the mercy of the visual dynamics of the scene. Just as her appearance on the television chat show is presented in a manner that deliberately underplays her 'natural' beauty, the seconds immediately preceding the crash undercut the fulsomeness of the aural environment as it has been momentarily established.

The only time Valeria is not presented in a state of suffering is in the scenes that occur, in terms of the story's chronology, just before the crash. In the fabric of their presentation, however, these moments are deliberately underwhelming, suggesting the fragile nature of Valeria's happiness even at this stage. During the apartment scene, Valeria rushes over to embrace her lover and the floorboards give way under her foot, exposing a hole that will later cause the accident that leads to her leg, already badly injured in the crash, having to be amputated. The image of the collapsing floor is reproduced metaphorically through the audio-visual staging of Valeria's activities in these scenes, the assured and optimistic nature of which remain unsupported by their flimsy formal presentation.

Crash scene 4: the sensuous and expository sound world of el Chivo

Of the three main characters represented in the crash scenes, only el Chivo inhabits a sound world whose coordinates remain stable. The soundtrack of el Chivo's journey to the crash scene is dominated by a sustained piece of – unambiguously – non-diegetic music. This music remains consistently low key and sparse, often consisting solely of a relaxed drum beat and moody bass line which are accompanied, on occasion, by a prominent simple shimmering guitar line and other instrumental and electronic samplings and swellings that remain low in the mix. It is flexible enough to react to narrative events, engineering a dramatic pause as the man who has commissioned el Chivo to take out his business partner notices el Chivo is following them. On the whole, however, its reflective tone sustains a mood appropriate for a sequence that is primarily concerned with exploring the details of el Chivo's physical features rather than advancing the story.

Diegetic sounds are also presented in a manner that secures el Chivo's position within his environment. For example, the moment of impact is presaged by the sound of Octavio's car, heard – before it is seen – from the right speaker, matching the car's direction of movement. This is an untroubling use of sound for two reasons: it matches sound accurately to the visual relationships set out within the scene itself; but it also repeats a sonic pattern established in the third crash scene in which Octavio's car was also seen, and heard, arriving from the right-hand side of the screen. The viewer's orientation in terms of audio-visual relationships is thus subject to a double guarantee, one emerging from the orchestration of elements within the moment, the other relying on the memory of a similar moment earlier in the film.

In this instance, a sound which has already been established in an earlier crash scene is reworked around el Chivo in a manner that makes sense spatially. The 'realist' quality of the diegetic soundtrack here would be unremarkable in itself but gains significance by comparison to the way sound is organised in the previous versions of the crash. Its straightforward quality, focalised through the point of view of el Chivo, reinforces the impression that he is more attuned to his environment, sensorially speaking, than Octavio or Valeria.

Figure 2.1   *Alejandro Gonzalez Inarritu,* Amores Perros *(2000)*

Figure 2.2   *Alejandro Gonzalez Inarritu,* Amores Perros *(2000)*

Figure 2.3   *Alejandro Gonzalez Inarritu,* Amores Perros *(2000)*

Figure 2.4   *Alejandro Gonzalez Inarritu,* Amores Perros *(2000)*

Figure 2.5 *Alejandro Gonzalez Inarritu,* Amores Perros *(2000)*

Figure 2.6 *Alejandro Gonzalez Inarritu,* Amores Perros *(2000)*

Figure 2.7 *Alejandro Gonzalez Inarritu,* Amores Perros *(2000)*

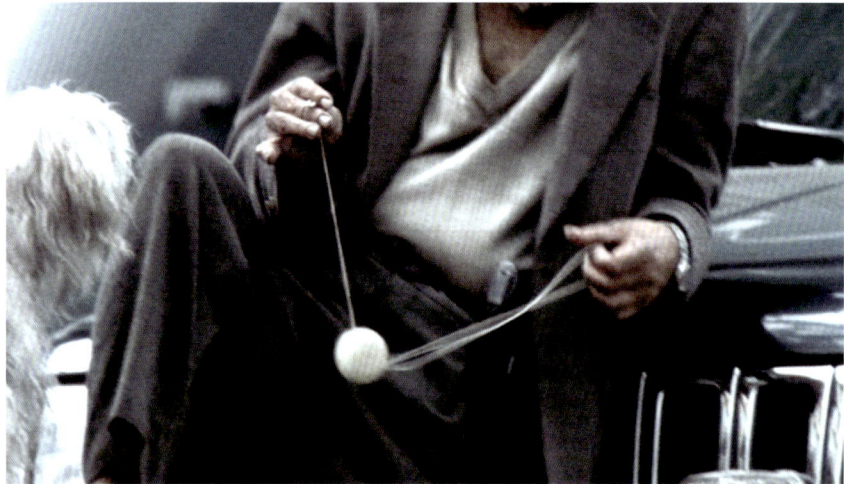

Figure 2.8 *Alejandro Gonzalez Inarritu,* Amores Perros *(2000)*

Figure 2.9 *Alejandro Gonzalez Inarritu,* Amores Perros *(2000)*

Figure 2.10 *Alejandro Gonzalez Inarritu,* Amores Perros *(2000)*

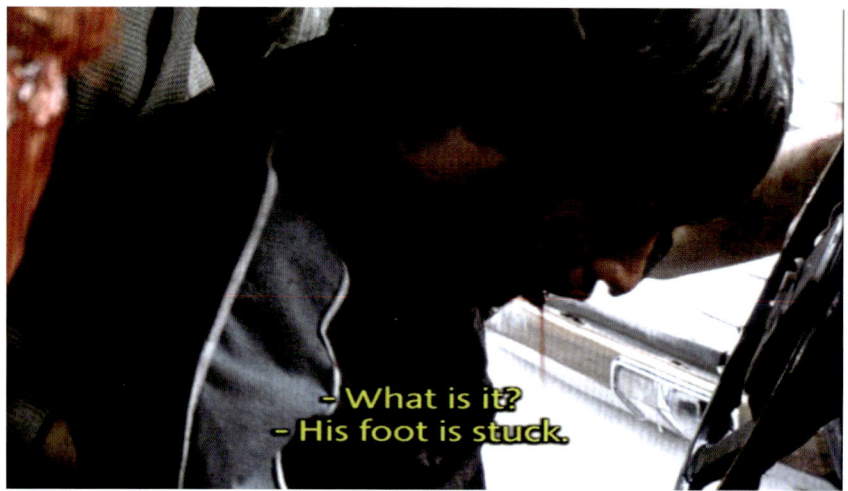

Figure 2.11   *Alejandro Gonzalez Inarritu,* Amores Perros *(2000)*

Figure 2.12   *Alejandro Gonzalez Inarritu,* Amores Perros *(2000)*

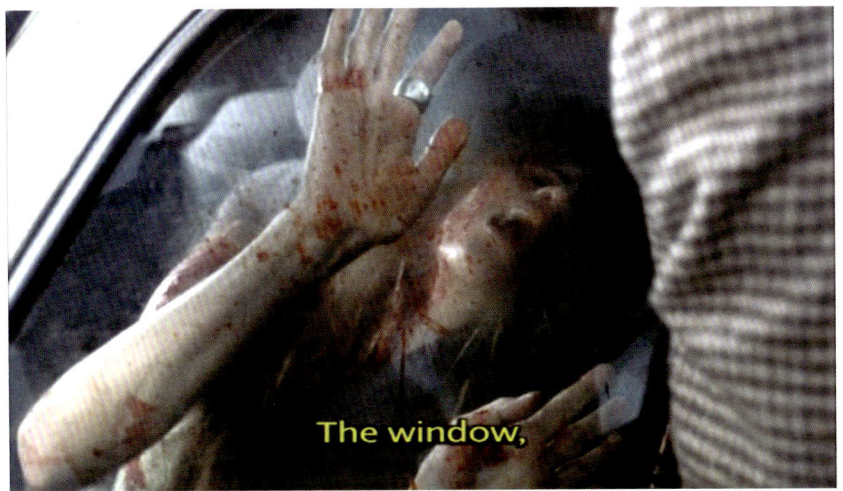

Figure 2.13   *Alejandro Gonzalez Inarritu,* Amores Perros *(2000)*

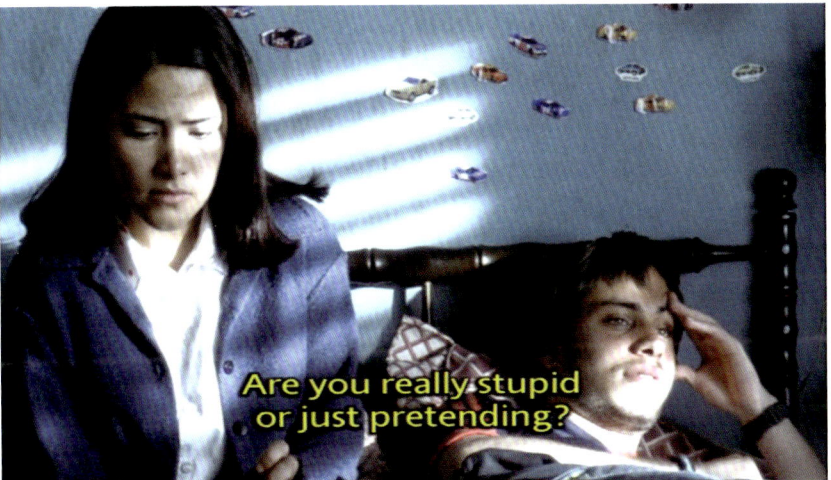

Figure 2.14   *Alejandro Gonzalez Inarritu,* Amores Perros *(2000)*

Figure 2.15   *Alejandro Gonzalez Inarritu,* Amores Perros *(2000)*

Figure 2.16   *Alejandro Gonzalez Inarritu,* Amores Perros *(2000)*

Figure 2.17 *Alejandro Gonzalez Inarritu*, Amores Perros *(2000)*

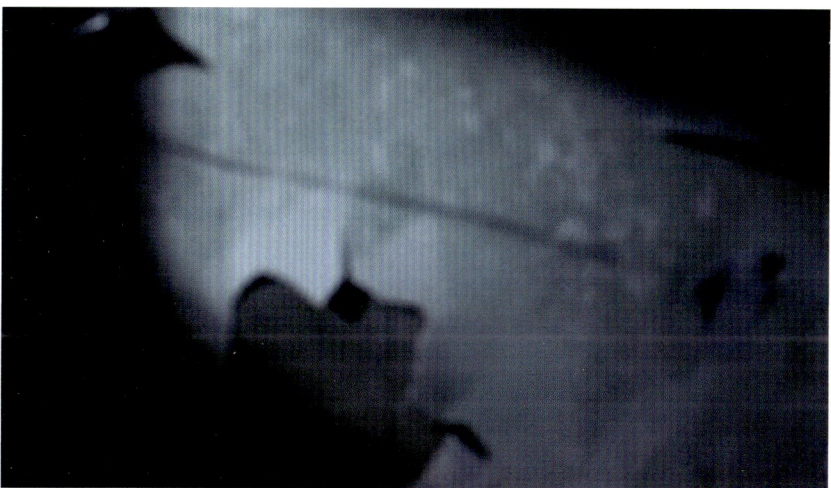

Figure 2.18 *Alejandro Gonzalez Inarritu*, Amores Perros *(2000)*

Figure 2.19 *Alejandro Gonzalez Inarritu,* Amores Perros *(2000)*

Figure 3.1 *John Lasseter, Ash Brannon and Lee Unkrich,* Toy Story 2 *(1999)*

Figure 3.2   *John Lasseter, Ash Brannon and Lee Unkrich,* Toy Story 2 *(1999)*

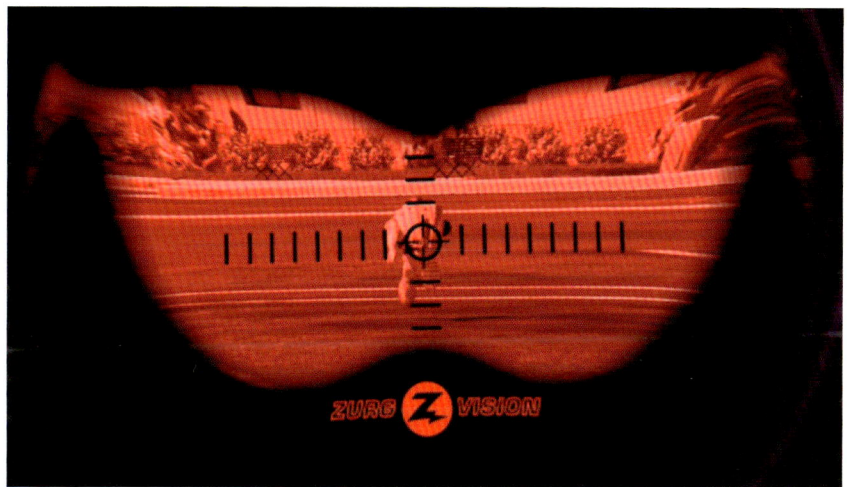

Figure 3.3   *John Lasseter, Ash Brannon and Lee Unkrich,* Toy Story 2 *(1999)*

Figure 3.4 *Lee Unkrich,* Toy Story 3 *(2010)*

Figure 3.5 *Lee Unkrich,* Toy Story 3 *(2010)*

Figure 3.6 *Lee Unkrich,* Toy Story 3 *(2010)*

Figure 3.7 *Lee Unkrich,* Toy Story 3 *(2010)*

Figure 3.8 *Johan Grimonprez,* Double Take *(2009)*

Figure 3.9 *Johan Grimonprez,* Double Take *(2009)*

Figure 3.10   *Johan Grimonprez,* Double Take *(2009)*

Figure 3.11   *Johan Grimonprez,* Double Take *(2009)*

Figure 3.12   *Johan Grimonprez,* Double Take *(2009)*

Figure 3.13 *Johan Grimonprez,* Double Take *(2009)*

Figure 3.14 *Johan Grimonprez,* Double Take *(2009)*

Figure 3.15 *Johan Grimonprez,* Double Take *(2009)*

Figure 3.16   *Johan Grimonprez,* Double Take *(2009)*

Figure 3.17   *Johan Grimonprez,* Double Take *(2009)*

In this final crash scene, sounds which have been reconfigured in previous renditions are put in their 'proper' place. In the first rendition of the scene, the sound of Octavio's stuck car horn bridges a shot of his wrecked vehicle and a shot of Valeria trapped in her car. In the final rendition, it becomes clear that the sound of the horn is stilled some time before this moment involving Valeria. Rather than appearing as a mysterious adjunct to the first scene, or withheld completely in the second and third renditions, Valeria's suffering, and its accompanying sounds, are now seen and heard to their full extent, perceived through the mediating point-of-view shots of el Chivo.

Through el Chivo's mediation, the sensational aspects of the crash scene are presented in a context that also renders faithfully the chronology of events and documents dramatic details much more fully than the previous scenes. El Chivo is given the fictional authority to harmonise the sensuous detailing and narrative explanation of the crash scene, in contrast to the more partial renditions of the scene offered up until this point.

In so doing, el Chivo is associated with an authority and breadth of perspective that are denied Octavio and Valeria. Of these characters, his is the one to demonstrate the greatest ability to move between different aspects of the film's world and to undergo personal change. For the purposes of this analysis, it is particularly significant that this superior mobility is registered, in part, by his association with particularly tactile activities. To conclude this chapter, I shall discuss how el Chivo's authority is also registered through his tactile relationship with photographs. My comments are intended to indicate how the characterisation of el Chivo in the crash scenes is continued in other aspects of the film. The particular concentration on photographs also allows me to engage with other writing on *Amores Perros* that tackles the same theme, thereby helping me to define what is distinctive about my critical approach.

CONCLUSION

El Chivo's story arc charts his decision to re-establish contact with his now grown-up daughter, Maru (Lourdes Echevarria), who was just two when he walked out on his family to pursue revolutionary goals. The death of his estranged wife exerts an emotional pull on el Chivo that makes him decide to give up his life as a vagrant assassin and to make his presence known to his daughter who has been led to believe that he is dead. Unable to confront Maru directly, el Chivo breaks into her house, steals a photograph of her graduation ceremony (in which she is embraced by her mother and her mother's new husband) and eventually returns to replace the photo which he has doctored by sticking a passport photograph of himself over the head of the new husband. Before he leaves his daughter's house, he deposits on her bed the money he has earned from his assassination assignments and records an emotional message on Maru's answerphone. El Chivo's handling of the photo, then, indicates both the distance el Chivo moves emotionally across the narrative (he can imagine himself again as Maru's father) as well as the limits of what he finds himself able to do (a photograph substitutes for an actual reunion).

El Chivo is shown to have a particularly tactile relationship to photographs which is contrasted to Octavio's and Valeria's engagement with photographs at different points. This tactility is registered literally, through el Chivo's handling of photos, and stylistically through an arrangement of *mise en scène* and choice of image quality that emphasises the texture of on-screen materials and of the film image itself.

Photographs are associated with el Chivo early on, in the scene which shows him in his makeshift home for the first time. A brief establishing shot of el Chivo sitting by a desk at the back of a dishevelled bedroom immediately reveals there is a framed photo above his bed. The preceding scene had shown Octavio in his bedroom for the first time and there is a contrast in the way the texture of the *mise en scène* of each room, and its inhabitants, are revealed. Octavio is involved in an exchange with Susana in which he notices her ear is bleeding. This is depicted through an over-the-shoulder shot/reverse shot pattern which resolves into a frontal two shot as Susana joins Octavio on his bed. The focus remains on the interaction between the two characters, carried through dialogue, with the result that there is minimal sense of the room being mapped as an integral deep space (Figure 2.14).

The depth of el Chivo's cluttered room, by contrast, is exaggerated by the low angle of the shot, the on-screen presence of both side walls tapering into the 'distance', and the use of deep focus (Figure 2.15). A sense of space is also generated by the placement of objects at the very front right of the frame and the positioning of el Chivo (the human interest of the scene) at the very back, and by the use of different pools of light to 'model' the space. The objects within the frame are also especially rough hewn which gives them a particular type of texture: the bedsheets and pillows are crumpled and piled up on the bed rather than laid flat; the paint on the walls is peeling; and the living bodies in the frame are marked by their straggliness, whether that be the dogs that lie on the bed and floor or el Chivo himself whose silver beard and long hair are picked out by the natural light coming in from a window at the back of the frame and a lamp on the table in front of him. The framed photograph, then, takes its place within a *mise en scène* that evokes the tactile generally and that contrasts to the functional framing of the scene in Octavio's bedroom.

The textured qualities of the photograph itself are brought into focus in the next shot which shows el Chivo in close-up from below, the camera tilted up so that the photo is captured at the top right of the screen, with el Chivo occupying the left side of the frame (Figure 2.16). This brings the photograph closer to the viewer but its features are less distinct than they might be, owing to the shallower focus being employed in the shot. The photograph's features are relatively soft in their own right, picturing a young girl in faded mono-chrome. Furthermore, the smoke from el Chivo's cigarette furls up directly in front of the photo, further softening our view of it and imbuing it with additional texture.

The photograph, like el Chivo, is depicted as a particularly textured object, and these textures associate it with the past (its faded monochrome quality) and the present (the smoke, generated at this moment, furling up in front of it, adding an immediate visual layer to its representation but also contributing to the depiction of a smoky and dirty environment that has given the frame its weathered look). Without knowing at this point who the photograph depicts, a connection is made with el Chivo (both are weathered objects with pecu-liarly tactile features) and this is contrasted to the depiction of Octavio in the previous scene. Octavio is also framed with 'pictures' behind him but these take the form of stickers of cars appended to his bedstead, as different as you could imagine, in their glossy flatness and generic quality, from the lived-in and intimate properties of the photograph of the girl.

At this point, el Chivo has yet to learn of his ex-wife's death so he has not received the impetus to reintroduce himself into Maru's life. As such, it is fitting that a relationship is suggested between the photograph and el Chivo without el Chivo being cast as an active partner in this relationship. The alternative focus he has at this point is registered by the different type of pho-tograph he actually handles in the same shot and subsequently in the scene: a photo of the man who is to be his next assassination target. In contrast to the picture of Maru, this is presented transparently rather than through a number of layers that provide it with a special texture and relate past to present. In fact, as el Chivo pulls the photograph from a drawer, it is the back of the photo, with its written facts about the hit (his name, age and address), that is revealed first. The hit is then shown in a cleanly composed colour still, stand-ing in profile, his facial features clearly illuminated. This is a photograph that provides information rather than evoking a tactile memory.

After putting the photograph down, el Chivo reaches back into the drawer and pulls out a gun. It is at this point that the viewer gets a first inkling of his profession. As a self-styled vagrant, el Chivo makes an unlikely assassin, and the incongruousness of his current situation is insinuated through textural contrast and tactile detail even before he pulls out the gun. He is shown holding the photograph on either side between his thumbs and index fingers, rubbing the surface of the photo briefly before setting it aside. His fingernails are overgrown and black with dirt (Figure 2.17). The handling of the photo here serves to contrast its glossy nature, and the world of high finance that that represents (the target is a chief industrialist, and el Chivo will be paid handsomely for the job), with the rough-hewn features of el Chivo: these hands seem far more at home later on, working on the DIY adaptation of Maru's graduation photo.

The photography motif is developed throughout the film, retaining a sensuous dimension. In a key moment late on, el Chivo puts on his old pair of glasses, a sign that he is ready to make some kind of reconnection with Maru and leave his current life behind. He is lying on his bed at this point and, just before he puts on the glasses, we see the peeling wall above him from his optical perspective, slightly out of focus, because that is how he views the world without glasses (Figure 2.18). After he has put on his glasses, there is a shot also from his optical point of view, but now clearly focused (Figure 2.19), moving up from the wall on to the photograph of Maru (which appears upside down because of the angle from which el Chivo views it). Taken on its own, the symbolism of this moment might appear heavy handed, depicting as it does el Chivo's movement towards some kind of emotional clarity through the regaining of a literal clear-sightedness (though Maru is still available to him only obliquely and this is registered by him viewing her photograph upside down). The moment gains resonance, however, through its association with other instances of el Chivo interacting sensuously with photographs and its contribution to the more general portrait of el Chivo as a tactile and sensuous figure, this quality distinguishing him from the other characters and giving him a special authority within the film's world.

The relationship between still photography and the moving film image is the central focus of Karen Beckman's essay on *Amores Perros*. Like me, she identifies el Chivo's special relationship with photography and pays particular attention to the moment he puts on his glasses and looks up at Maru's picture. She does so, however, to pursue an argument about the film's self-reflexive groping towards a new nationally specific form, a struggle she sees being staged through 'cinema's collision with various forms of the still image'.[2]

Paul Julian Smith also comments on this scene in his monograph on the film, citing it as a typical example of the film's reliance on image rather than verbal language to articulate plot developments.[3] In our accounts of this moment, the differences of emphasis between myself, Beckman and Smith are instructive in identifying the distinctive analysis yielded by an approach that combines an appreciation of a film's sensuous qualities with an understanding of it as a world. Beckman stresses the formal self-consciousness of the moment, so that the argument pulls away from an engagement with el Chivo, and his position within a fictional world, towards a metatextual level in which the aesthetic arrangement of the scene becomes a commentary on film aesthetics in itself. Conversely, Smith's reading is absolutely grounded in plot: form serves character development.

Like Beckman, my analysis has identified the formal self-consciousness of *Amores Perros*: when the same narrative event (in this case, the crash) is replayed multiple times, the different form each reiteration takes is likely to garner extra attention (as the bare story information is already known). The variety of stylistic registers the film uses to re-enact the crash scene, together with an overall sense of 'intensity' in the film's formal make-up,[4] contribute to a style of narration that is uncommonly upfront. This means that, even when the form of the film becomes more conventionally self-effacing, as in the iteration of the crash focusing on Valeria, this quality becomes, in itself, the subject of attention in its contrast to more overtly stylised and sensuous representations of the same event.

Unlike Beckman, however, I relate the formally self-conscious properties of *mise en scène*, editing and soundtrack to the disclosing of the facets of the film's world, its events, characters, norms of behaviour, style, viewpoint and tone. My brief analysis of the moment el Chivo looks at the photograph of Maru above his bed, for example, contextualises it within the film's unfolding story and discusses it in relation to el Chivo's development as a character, a development that is, in turn, contextualised within a world in which el Chivo becomes the locus of a set of representational strategies and behaviours that comes to stand for the values against which the other protagonists are (negatively) judged. Under this reading, the 'tone' of the film is judged as one that implies a sincere mode of address to its viewer in terms of its invitation to engage with, and take a view on, the lives of the characters inhabiting its world. This does not mean that Beckman's identification of another level of meaning, to do with the film's reflection on the possibilities of its own medium, is wrong. It does indicate a way of reading the film, however, that will pick up inferences and make connections which are missed by a more metatextual approach.

The understanding of character within the wider context of a film world also differentiates my reading from Smith's in that it provides a larger set of coordinates against which a particular moment may be judged (so it is not just a case of how form relates to character but also how these aspects relate to viewpoint, tone, behavioural norms and so on). Finally, my reading of *Amores Perros* is distinct from those of both Smith and Beckman in its consistent attention to the sensuous details of the film. In line with a phenomenological approach, I have tried to convey how *Amores Perros* 'feels' as an experience. One benefit in taking sensory aspects as the focus of the analysis is that they *are* ubiquitous. They are equally a feature of image and soundtrack and are as much a part of a film's stylistic register as they are the representational content. This means that connections can be made between any areas of the film world. For example, the moment of el Chivo looking at Maru's photo is as related to his representation in the fourth crash scene as it is to the more obviously relevant moment in which our first view of him in his home is accompanied by the sight of Maru's photo. That said, it is still possible and, indeed, necessary to give the reading of a film purpose, to identify particularly resonant relationships between a film world's sensuous materials, and this is what I have tried to demonstrate. The following chapters explore specific combinations of particular sensuous materials within fictional film worlds in relation to areas fundamental to their material expression: their images; their sounds; and their performances.

Notes

1. Bordwell, *The Way Hollywood Tells It: Story and Style in Modern Movies*, p. 97.
2. Beckman, 'Crash aesthetics: *Amores Perros* and the dream of cinematic mobility', in Beckman and Ma (eds), *Still Moving: Between Cinema and Photography*, p. 143.
3. Smith, *Amores Perros*, p. 74.
4. Smith titles one of his chapters, 'A two-hour shout?', taking his cue from a description offered by director Alejandro Gonzalez Inarritu who also uses 'visceral' as the term to sum up the film. See Smith, p. 59.

CHAPTER 3

Storytelling through the Imperfect Image

This chapter considers the way sensuous properties of the image are made significant to the storytelling processes of particular films. It begins by establishing a tradition of self-reflexive sensuous investigation of visual material in experimental audio-visual art. This tradition has been marked both by work that explores the material qualities of a particular media format as well as by pieces that combine different visual formats to draw out the specific sensuous characteristics of one format through juxtaposition with another. These works do not usually invite narrative engagement, and the critical discourse around them has often cast them as deliberately anti-narrative in the sense that narrative is normally understood.

After establishing this tradition and its accompanying critical discourse, I train the questions it raises about the materiality of visual media on to films that do clearly tell stories. My investigation focuses on two different types of cinema: a mainstream form of production exemplified by Pixar, the computer animation studio owned by Walt Disney; and *Double Take* (Grimonprez, 2009), an artist's film, discussed in the introduction, which is much more obviously part of the avant-garde tradition considered in the first part of the chapter. It is, nevertheless, strongly committed to constructing an intriguing narrative. Despite the different scales of their production, therefore, both of my case studies are bound by an interest in articulating the material qualities of their visual phenomena within a storytelling context. They are also linked by their status as digital productions, albeit of different kinds, and the chapter will consider the specific type of materiality associated with the image in the digital age.

VISUAL MATERIALITY AND THE AVANT-GARDE

Sarah Child's 16 mm *Between the Frames* (1977) opens by disclosing a variety of human activities. In a 15-second shot, the camera pans across a crowd of people milling about before it alights on a man wearing sunglasses; a swinging mirror discloses a woman holding a movie camera who is responsible, presumably, for filming the scene.

This opening shot might raise a number of questions to do with narrative: where is this scene taking place? who are these people? why is the man being singled out for special attention by the camera? why is the woman filming this scene? what is her relationship with the man? Upon reaching the man in sunglasses, however, the image freezes. Thereafter, for the film's 10-minute duration, the same shot is repeated, as it is subjected to various formal 'distortions': for instance, it is shown printed on negative film stock, run backwards, and is presented with strobing effects.

Sarah Child describes her ambitions for making the film in this way:

> The intention was thus to repeat and slow down by rhythmic printing etc. the relationship between the vertical planes of the filming situation, i.e. the film plane in the camera, the suggestion of the retinal 'plane', the foreground plane and mirror reflection, the background plane and subject and also the duplicated film planes (negative, framing factors) in the optical printing machine.[1]

Child's film stands as part of a tradition of avant-garde structural materialist film-making in which a filming situation is set up to investigate the material properties of a particular medium and/or to induce a severe self-consciousness about the viewing experience in the spectator. The film's title echoes avant-garde film-maker Peter Kubelka's assertion, in an influential lecture, that it is 'between the frames where cinema speaks'.[2] By calling attention to the single frame, rather than to the shot or a larger combination, Kubelka signalled an interest in the qualities of film at a micro level, which was pursued in his own practice but also in key work of the 1960s and 1970s by film-makers such as Paul Sharits, Peter Gidal and Malcolm LaGrice. Michele Pierson, discussing Kubelka and Sharits in particular, suggests:

> Both [Kubelka's *Arnulf Rainer*] and Sharits' flicker films can very much be seen as documentaries about the material properties and processes of cinema: the concrete materiality of celluloid; the illusionist effects of projection on the discrete reality of the individual film frame.[3]

As a key champion of structural/materialist film, Peter Gidal advocates the construction of a particular relationship between the material qualities of the medium and the represented content and formal structure of individual films:

> The dialectic of the film is established in that space of tension between materialist flatness, grain, light, movement, and the supposed reality that is presented. Consequently a continual attempt to destroy the illusion is necessary . . . Through usage of specific filmic devices such as repetition within duration one is forced to attempt to decipher both the film's material and the film's construct, and to decipher the precise transformations that each co/incide/nce of cinematic techniques produces. The attempt is primary to any

specific shape, otherwise the discovery of shape (fetishising shape or system) may become the theme, in fact, the narrative of the film.[4]

In both Pierson's and Gidal's characterisations, the exposure of the illusionistic capacity of cinema, in which what is represented is taken as reality, involves redirecting the viewer to the 'real reality' of film whether that is conceived as the materiality of the film frame or qualities of flatness, grain, light and movement. Through this redirection, the viewer is dissuaded from becoming seduced by the represented content of a particular moment, the temptation to assign narrative significance or the desire to identify an over-riding formal structure.

The engagement encouraged by these films is both tactile and anti-narrative: one type of immersion is seen to be incompatible with another. *Between the Frames* is axiomatic of this mode of address. The same shot is returned to and shown to exhibit different material qualities depending on how it is being reprocessed. Child's referencing to the multiple planes of the filming situation characterises the image as a complexly multilayered one and the recognition of the use of an optical printing machine (which is used to re-photograph the strips of film) offers the further sense that this is an image that has been excessively treated.

The tactile handling of the film serves to eliminate any narrative drive. The initial freeze-frame of the man may, on first viewing, be seen as an act of characterisation (pausing the image to establish the man's significance) but this turns out to be misleading: the freeze-frame in fact becomes one of a number of techniques that are used to discover different visual qualities in the individual film frames rather than conspiring to suture the frames together according to dramatic principles of story and character development.

MATERIAL JUXTAPOSITION IN THE FOUND-FOOTAGE FILM

In this chapter, I discuss films that also draw attention to their material qualities. They do so particularly keenly through their juxtaposition of different types of visual media, the contrasting properties of which serve to throw each other's material qualities into sharp relief. In this way, the films under discussion are connected to the avant-garde found-footage film in which existing footage, often from different sources, is taken out of its original context and recycled. Pierson sees the found-footage film as related to structural materialist cinema in its exposure and investigation of medium-specific sensuous qualities. Her main case studies are *pièce touchée* (1989) and *Alone. Life Wastes Andy Hardy* (1998) by Martin Arnold and *Outer Space* (1999) and *Dream Work* (2001) by Peter Tscherkassky. As the passage below indicates, however, she connects these film-makers with an avant-garde tradition that encompasses not only structural materialist film-making of the 1960s and 1970s but also earlier found-footage films and even Buñuel and Dali's landmark avant-garde classic *Un Chien Andalou* (1929):

> Buñuel and Dali rejected the overt symbolism that they associated with the new art cinema in favor of techniques for heightening or intensifying sensory experience, with the expectation or, at least, hope that they would more immediately and strongly arouse unconscious recollection and desire.
>
> The search for such techniques is also evident in Joseph Cornell's turn to the sensuous abundance of 'cinema in the raw' in his enormously influential found-footage film, *Rose Hobart* (1936). Shots taken from the original George Melford film, *East of Borneo* (1931), have been rearranged and mixed with shots of natural phenomena taken from other film sources from Cornell's extensive collection (a stone being dropped in a pool of water, a bunch of bananas hanging from a banana tree, palm trees, a lunar eclipse) to produce a film in which few clues are offered for deciphering the looks of determination, deliberation, contemplation, and anguish on the heroine's face. Stripped of narrative and its constraining causality, the Melford footage undergoes a kind of re-enchantment, which brings the strangeness of the baroque sets and the photogenic beauty of the film's star into sharper focus. The ambition to create films that strongly appeal to the senses runs through Arnold's and Tscherkassky's filmmaking too.[5]

Found-footage films can rework just one kind of visual material but, in *Rose Hobart*, Pierson chooses an example where the 're-enchantment' of the *East of Borneo* footage is, in part, made possible by it being juxtaposed with related visual material (the shots of nature) that is, nevertheless, derived discernibly from a different source.

Paul Arthur distinguishes between two different types of combination of material in the found-footage film which he designates as 'denotative and expressive collage'.[6] As the quotation below implies, denotative collage is associated with the establishing of a narrative and an argument whereas expressive collage is concerned with the exploration of the image's material qualities:

> For our immediate purposes, divergent conceptions of the function of collage can be reduced to matters of realism, to an ongoing commitment by partisans of documentary to features such as standard photographic images, a semblance of narrative continuity, and shared protocols for the presentation of argument and evidence [denotative collage]. The avant-garde, on the other hand, has almost by definition refused adherence to realist codes, adopting a constructivist approach to unsettling and creatively unmasking the materiality of the image [expressive collage].[7]

In Pierson's account, *Rose Hobart* falls into the category of 'expressive collage', bringing together different kinds of visual stimulus to bring forward sensuous qualities that are less apparent when presented in a straightforward narrative context. Arthur introduces these categories, however, to question the value of maintaining an absolute distinction between them. In his closing analysis of Emile de Antonio's Vietnam documentary, *In the Year of the Pig* (1968), Arthur highlights the extent to which the film's argument is carried through passages that 'seem calculated to inflame our affective sensibilities'.[8] The final shot of the documentary reuses an image of a statue of an American Civil War soldier, introduced at the very start of the film. Arthur discusses the moment in this way:

> The final shot of the film is a split-screen image, one half in darkness and the other featuring the initial shot of the Civil War solider, this time printed on negative film stock. The affective impact of this sequence is stirring, mournful, angry, and its resources of meaning have little to do with strictly analogical uses of found footage . . . it should sound a cautionary note to documentary scholars to pay more attention to the expressive, figurative dimension of found footage.[9]

Arthur implies that the moment is affective as much due to its 'expressive' as its 'denotative' qualities. The signs of the expressive in the image here are tactile ones, its 'skin' becoming apparent through the rough cut made into it (via a 'messy' split-screen effect), the contrast in texture between different types of darkness (the difference between the flat black of one half of the screen and the luminous silvery grey of the image of the statue) and the 'turning inside-out', in terms of visual tone, of the initial film image of the Civil War soldier (through a process called solarisation). Denotative meaning is clearly still important (it is not coincidental, of course, that the figure on screen is an American soldier) but this can only be felt as part of a visual experience, the sensuous qualities of which are key to the expression of a particular political argument.

Arthur's efforts to find significance in the sensuous combination of different types of image, in the documentary context, are echoed in my own exploration of the significance of sensuous visual combinations in the fiction film. In the two case studies that follow, I discuss different instances of films that mix various types of visual media (or at least seem to), paying attention to the different tactile qualities these media formats are shown to possess – qualities that are thrown into sharper relief by their juxtaposition with other visual formats. I do not, however, see the exposure of the material qualities of the image as an end in itself nor necessarily antagonistic to narrative development (as I argue is the case in *Between the Frames*). Rather, the attention to sensuous detail serves my interest in exploring the processes through which the films tell their stories.

MEDIUM SPECIFICITY IN SENSUOUS SCHOLARSHIP

Within the sensuous scholarship represented in Chapter 1, there has been some discussion of the specific types of sensory experience offered by different visual media formats. Laura U. Marks's *The Skin of the Film* offers one such example. Marks first establishes a base definition of haptic visuality, which is distinguished from a more common optical visuality, and may be produced through any visual medium:

> Haptic visuality is distinguished from optical visuality, which sees things from enough distance to perceive them as distinct forms in deep space: in other words, how we usually conceive of vision. Optical visuality depends on a separation between the viewing subject and the object. Haptic looking tends to move over the surface of its object rather than to plunge into illusionistic depth, not to distinguish form so much as to discern texture . . . while optical perception privileges the representational power of the image, haptic perception privileges the material presence of the image.[10]

Once this basic definition has been established, Marks then attributes some medium-specific differences between the haptic effects of cinema and video. For cinema, Marks notes that the following techniques, deployed on the physical surface of the medium, can be used to make a film 'look tactile': optical printing; solarisation; and scratching the emulsion. Film stock is also capable of registering a distinctive grain, particularly apparent on 8 mm film and higher-gauge film shot at high speed or in low light. Conversely, films of high resolution (such as 35 mm) can also exhibit a tactile quality owing to a sense that they 'contain more visual texture than the eye can apprehend'.[11]

According to Marks, video is a less controllable kind of image than film because it occurs in a 'relay between source and screen' rather than originating 'from a material object (of celluloid/acetate)'. In this lack of control resides the possibility of variations in image quality that, in themselves, give the video a haptic look. In addition, Marks points to the much lower pixel density and contrast ratio of VHS video in comparison to 16 or 35 mm film which yields a much less detailed image than the one registered by human vision. This lack of detail gives the image a relative depthlessness that works as a distinctive texture in itself. Finally, Marks sees the electronic manipulability of video, evidenced by a technique like pixellation (the intentional lowering of image resolution to give it an electronic 'grain'), as another potential source of haptic visuality.[12]

Vivian Sobchack also makes distinctions between different visual media formats, this time classified as the photographic, the cinematic and the electronic. Unlike Marks, she does not concentrate on specific techniques or physical properties in relation to each category but rather considers how each technology of perception and representation mediates the embodied viewers' relationship with the world around them. For Sobchack, the cinematic represents a 'centred and subjective spatiotemporal engagement with the materiality of the world',[13] whereas the electronic is experienced as a 'simultaneous, dispersed, and insubstantial transmission across a network or web that is constituted spatially more as a materially flimsy latticework of nodal points than as the stable ground of embodied experience'.[14]

Sobchack identifies an integral materiality to the cinematic experience that contrasts to the radical immateriality of an electronic one. This feeds into a debate about the perceived immateriality of digital media, in particular, and I shall represent this discussion more fully presently. It also registers a difference in opinion between Marks and Sobchack, however, about the way electronic materiality should be characterised. Marks stresses that she values video as a '*warm* medium'[15] and, indeed, it is this quality that she sees as crucial to her chosen films' success in engaging their audiences. By contrast, Sobchack views all electronic media (from television, through video to the Internet) as constituting an 'absolute electronic world of immaterialised . . . experience'.[16]

In both cases, the assertions being made about the sensory qualities of each medium are quite absolute. My analysis in the rest of the chapter does pay attention to some of the techniques and material properties associated with film and video, as they are identified by Marks. It also engages with the broad thinking about the sensuous aspects of different mediated experiences that characterises the writing of Sobchack. These issues, however, are all pursued in relation to their articulation within particular fictional worlds. Rather than accepting that different media formats exhibit an inherent set of characteristics or provide a uniform sensory experience, I understand the sensuous profiling of different media formats as something that is made apparent through the particular combination of different visual materials within a film's world.

MEDIUM SPECIFICITY POST-MEDIUM

All of the examples that follow are products of the digital age. As I explain below, the Pixar films I discuss have taken on a special status as the most commercially and critically successful manifestations of 'purely' digital filmmaking, in the sense that they do not involve any kind of filming in real life.

Double Take operates in a different sphere, in terms of its much more modest scale of production and level of distribution. It is still a digital production, however, in its use of digital cameras to capture original footage and its digital manipulation of the various kinds of found footage it makes use of.

Many critics have associated the development of digital technology with a 'post-medium' condition in which the boundaries between different media have become obsolete and notions of medium specificity redundant.[17] For example, the 'non-digital' media formats represented in the Pixar films (such as newsreel, VHS video, old photographs) are simulated digitally. I follow Rosalind Krauss, however, in regarding the term 'medium' as something that describes a supporting structure which is associated with 'expressive possibilities and conventions',[18] rather than a term that describes a physical apparatus. For example, I read the inserted VHS video footage at the beginning of *Toy Story 3* not as a straightforward material manifestation of an analogue technology within a digital environment but, rather, as a moment which refers to a mode of expression that has become associated with that particular format. For the purposes of this study, I concentrate on the sensuous aspects of this mode of expression. Crucially, I move from describing the conventional material properties of the video medium, as they are simulated in the film, to consider how those qualities are toyed with for a particular storytelling purpose.

The rest of the chapter continues with a more detailed elaboration of the debate about the materiality – or perceived immateriality – of the digital image. It progresses through a series of readings of moments from Pixar films, each of which simulates a different type of visual media format through digital means. This simulation might involve attributing a roughness, an excessive gloss or a 'naturalness' to a computer-animated image whose 'default' material qualities are often described in terms of their plasticity. Whatever the nature of the transformation, the interest in the analysis is the significance in relation to storytelling of the contrast between the textures of each kind of image: that is to say, the 'plastic norm' that characterises the image quality of each film as a whole and the momentary deviations in which the image temporarily adopts a different type of sheen.

The chapter concludes with an extended analysis of one of the narrative strands of *Double Take*, a film that uses digital technology in a different way from the Pixar films and, on the face of it, has more connection with the avant-garde found-footage films discussed so far in the chapter. Though I concentrate on the treatment of original images, I handle them as a kind of invented found footage, considering the recycling they are subjected to through the course of the film. The result is a mosaic of images that hold related represented content while exhibiting different types of materiality.

Rather than understanding the friction between these different materials as a purely formal matter or as an exercise in didactic montage (as the accounts of the found-footage films cited earlier tend to do), I consider how the sensuous contrasting of the different visual materials works in a dramatic context.

THE (IM)MATERIALITY OF THE DIGITAL IMAGE

Pierson, in her discussion of *Rose Hobart*, and Marks, in the films and videos she analyses in *The Skin of the Film*, are both dealing with the materiality of analogue audio-visual formats. Their commentary attests to the fact that the analogue image has a discernible texture to explore, and this has been seen to be a characteristic that marks the analogue: the images are perceived to carry a particular kind of 'grain'. Their own surfaces make themselves present to the viewer, and these are surfaces that may even be subject to wear and tear, thereby enhancing the sense of the image's fabric-like and tactile qualities.

The digital image is not usually represented as a material one, subject to potential damage or responsive to human handling, in the same way as the analogue image. Instead, competing discourses about the digital image have developed which either emphasise its immateriality (as the product of an abstract computation rather than as a tangible photochemical or non-digital electronic process) or, when the surface properties of the image are acknowledged, identify an unearthly flawlessness and lack of grain as key characteristics.

The characterisation of the digital image as somehow immaterial has taken two forms. The first represents a discourse of anxiety in which the image's generation from computer code is seen to disassociate it from the material world (echoing Sobchack's account of electronic media more generally). This was a common theme in criticism that accompanied the increasing use of digital effects (CGI) in cinema during the 1990s. Lev Manovich, writing in 1999, encapsulates the anxiety in this way:

> Even for director Andrey Tarkovsky, film-painter par excellence, cinema's identity lay in its ability to record reality. Once, during a public discussion in Moscow sometime in the 1970s he was asked the question as to whether he was interested in making abstract films. He replied that there can be no such thing. Cinema's most basic gesture is to open the shutter and to start the film rolling, recording whatever happens to be in front of the lens. For Tarkovsky, an abstract cinema is thus impossible ... But what happens to cinema's indexical identity if it is now possible to generate photorealistic scenes entirely in a computer using 3D computer animation; to modify individual frames or whole scenes with the help of a digital paint program; to cut, bend,

> stretch and stitch digitised film images into something which has perfect pho-
> tographic credibility, although it was never actually filmed?[19]

The immateriality of the digital image in this case lies in the absence of any solid real-life referent for the screen content, without which it is seen to be entirely at the mercy of the digital processes that brought it into being: the infinite manipulability of the image betrays its fatal lack of real-world robustness.

Whereas this anxiety laments the loss of the real in the digital image (the real being the quality that would give it a recognisable materiality), the second type of immateriality associated with the digital image is seen to be derived from the opposite concern: that digital images are capable of rendering visions of reality that are so credible that the sense of a material medium relaying screen content disappears. According to Julia Moszkowicz, this type of immateriality has routinely been attributed to CGI animation in a manner that runs contrary to both conventional understandings of animation as an obviously mediated form as well as to the routine awareness film studies has shown of cinema's 'mediating interface'.[20] Writing in 2002, she states:

> There is a sense in which the astounding digital productions of today are cel-
> ebrated for attributes that do not simply confront but fundamentally under-
> mine conventional understandings of the medium. Products such as *Shrek* are
> cherished as near perfect manifestations of literal form, capable of offering
> the status of objecthood to representations in the virtual realm . . . all such
> hyperbole is possible only if the focus of discussion tends towards notions of
> *simulation* over *representation* – of finished image over artistic process. It would
> appear that for many, the latest computer animations are not operating within
> the parameters of a visual idiom at all: they are simply acquiring enhanced
> naturalistic forms as the technology is progressively developed.[21]

When the digital image is viewed as *all* mediation, arrived at through a series of abstract computations, there follows a tendency to see the image's represented content as immaterial. Conversely, disregarding the mediated nature of the digital image entirely involves making the 'interface' invisible. This means that another type of immateriality arises, this time to do with the 'skinlessness' of the digital image itself, rather than the represented content.

There is an alternative strand of writing about the digital image that *does* acknowledge its 'skin'. On the whole, however, this skin is characterised as something that seems 'untouched', displaying none of the grain, body or other tactile qualities that are attributed to analogue images. For example, Andrew Darnley, writing about *Toy Story* (Lasseter, 1995), asserts:

> The new techniques of image and textual simulation at work in *Toy Story*
> produce *not* a simulation that is wholly indistinguishable from its model(s),

rather, a relatively unprecedented kind of image (and text) . . . akin to cinematography, yet different somehow, because it is just too *pristine*.[22]

Peter Lunenfeld argues that digital media generally are associated with a quality of 'crispness' that is contrasted to 'the more natural, less polarised, more curved' characteristics of the analogue.[23] Pat Power represents a distinction between traditional animation techniques (for example, hand drawn, stop frame, clay modelling) and CGI, the former demonstrating an 'indexical expressiveness'[24] through which the 'hands-on' process of animation is physically marked on the finished product, the latter 'indexically dehumanised through absence of such qualities'.[25]

Like Darnley, Jennifer M. Barker and William Schaffer both discuss Pixar's *Toy Story* as a landmark text, the first feature-length film to be entirely generated by – and thus have the overall feel of – CGI. Importantly, their discussions of the material qualities of *Toy Story* do not have the negative connotations implied by Darnley (and other writers). Indeed, Schaffer's article is conceived as a riposte to Darnley's criticisms. Both writers do still attribute an inhuman smoothness to the film's images, however. Barker claims:

> Its texture is completely manufactured and processed, and even if we didn't know that this film was the first feature in history to consist entirely of computer-generated imagery, we would *feel* it. This film's skin has no grain to it, no roughness, no messiness: it is as smooth as a plastic Magic Eight ball.[26]

Schaffer takes the reference to plastic further, claiming that the digital and the plastic are intimately connected:

> Plastic and digitality alike thus give rise to the utopic/dystopic vision of a world replaced entirely by its own resemblance, since both are capable of emulating any form, without partaking in any apparent resemblance or capture of traces at an ontological level. These two forms of synthesis resemble each other by at once resembling, and not resembling, anything at all. Plastic is to substance as digitality is to image.[27]

Here, then, Schaffer reiterates the view of the digital image being immaterial, free from any ontological traces of the objects it represents and possessed of a mutability that allows it to morph into any form it chooses. Schaffer continues by stating:

> The invisible metamorphic effect of CGI, as specifically imagined and realised in a Pixar production, is performed not so much *in* the image (as expressive fluctuation of form or dimensional inconsistency), than *as* the image (as a sort of miracle of plastic consistency).[28]

Both Barker and Schaffer reinforce the view that a plastic consistency characterises the texture of CGI, at least as demonstrated through the house style of Pixar. Plastic textures are, indeed, dominant in Pixar films. While these textures might connote an 'inhuman' production process, this does not mean that the look of the films will necessarily discourage a human response from the viewer (as might be implied by writing that identifies a soulless-ness in CGI animation). Both Barker and Schaffer discuss the ways in which *Toy Story* solicits empathetic identification from its viewer, predominantly through the association of the plastic feel of the film with real-life experiences viewers might have had of handling and playing with plastic toys. Barker's and Schaffer's accounts, therefore, are concerned with understanding the feel of the films in relation to a particular storytelling context and, as such, provide useful models for my own readings of moments from the Pixar films.

Both writers, however, overstate the extent to which *Toy Story* and other Pixar movies achieve an absolute plastic consistency. There are many moments in Pixar films where the plastic sheen of the CGI image is delib-erately roughened up, and it is the play between those moments marked as 'non-plastic' and the default pristine image quality of the rest of the film that I explore.

The presence of variations in image quality in Pixar films is discussed by Sobchack [in relation to the use of VHS video in *Wall-E* (Stanton, 2008)][29] and Colleen Montgomery [also in relation to *Wall-E* as well as the use of black-and-white video in *Toy Story 2* (Lasseter, Brannon and Unkrich, 1999)].[30] Both writers argue that a certain technophobia is evidenced through these instances and, with it, a nostalgia for obsolete media forms. These issues certainly form part of my reading of moments when the plastic sheen of Pixar is disturbed but I shall also comment on the more local storytelling contexts in which the moments take place and their significance in articulating these.

MIXED MEDIA IN THE FILMS OF PIXAR

Sobchack's and Montgomery's focus, on the general significance of the media format being represented rather than a concentration on specific material qualities of the image per se, is not surprising given the context in which the non-plastic moments most commonly occur. That is to say, there is nearly always a clear narrative justification for the image quality changing, with these moments predicated on the display of a particular type of audio-visual media technology within the film's fictional world. Unlike the artist films mentioned at the start of this chapter, or *Double Take*, the analysis of which closes the chapter, there are no moments where the introduction of a different media format occurs without a narrative pretext.

That said, a closer focus on the materiality of such moments is justified, given the fact that every Pixar feature to date has featured scenes that ruffle their plastic consistency. Even those films set in 'non-media' worlds contrive to include instances where a different image format is introduced. *Brave* (Andrews, Chapman and Purcell, 2012) is set in a fairy-tale past but still conjures moments where overtly mediated, lo-fi images find a place on screen via the holographic visions that come out of a witch's cauldron. *A Bug's Life* (Lasseter and Stanton, 1998) is the Pixar production most committed to representing a world of nature free from human interference and, thus, the least likely to include examples of man-made audio-visual technologies (at any rate, this is a type of anthropomorphism in which the film chooses not to indulge). Even this film, however, features as a key narrative element a visual device that allows the opportunity for images to be seen in alternative ways to the plastic norm. Early on, the ant protagonist Flik (voiced by David Foley) invents a telescope to impress Atta (Julia Louis-Dreyfus), the princess of his colony, and this device turns out to be a key aid in the ants' fight against their grasshopper enemies. The lens of the telescope is made out of a drop of water, the material qualities of which are used to provide an alternative texture to the film's skin at certain points.

In terms of representing more contemporary mediated forms, the following types of existing (audio)-visual media are given a significant presence: photographs [in *Up* (Docter and Peterson, 2009), *Finding Nemo* (Stanton and Unkrich, 2003), *Ratatouille* (Bird and Pinkava, 2007) and *Toy Story 3*)]; Movietone-style newsreel [in *Up* and *The Incredibles* (Bird, 2004)]; television [in *Monsters Inc.* (Docter, Silverman and Unkrich, 2001), *Ratatouille*, *The Incredibles*, *Toy Story*, *Toy Story 2*, *Cars* (Lasseter and Ranft, 2006) and *Cars 2* (Lasseter and Lewis, 2011)]; video (the kinescope recording of 'Woody's Round Up' in *Toy Story 2* and the live-action VHS recording of *Hello Dolly* in *Wall-E*); computer games (in *Toy Story 2*, *Wall-E* and *Cars 2*); CCTV (in *Monsters Inc.*, *The Incredibles* and *Toy Story 3*); and big 'event' screens (in both *Cars* films). There is also a number of instances where futuristic audio-visual forms are represented, such as the communication screen on the collars of Charles Muntz's dogs in *Up*; the various types of James Bond-style audio-visual gadgetry featured in *The Incredibles* and *Cars 2*; the ubiquitous translucent, interactive screens in *Wall-E*; and the bank of screens in the back of the lorry that is used to transport Lightning McQueen from race to race in *Cars*.

Finally, there are instances where the viewer witnesses events from the point of view of technological apparatuses that capture images rather than transmit them. These include the view through a still-camera viewfinder in *Monsters Inc.*, a video-camera viewfinder in *Toy Story 3*, and spy camera lenses and secretly 'weaponised' sports broadcast cameras in *Cars 2*. There is also a number of 'robotic' point-of-view shots where the action is rendered through the artificial forms of vision possessed by the robots of *Wall-E*, the robot antagonist in *The Incredibles* and Emperor Zurg in *Toy Story 2*.

The qualities of image used in the characterisation of Emperor Zurg will be the subject of my first case study of this phenomenon. I am interested in the way different forms of digital excess mark these images and the effect this has on the way the viewer is encouraged to understand a particular character. This example will be contrasted with the use of low-resolution home-video footage in *Toy Story 3*, the inclusion of which encourages the viewer to adopt a particular attitude to the visual qualities of the film's world as a whole.

DIGITAL EXCESS IN *TOY STORY 2*

The *Toy Story* films revolve around the conceit that toys are actually living entities that pretend to be inanimate when people are around. The recurring toy characters, led by the pull-string cowboy Woody (Tom Hanks), all belong to a boy called Andy (John Morris). In *Toy Story*, Buzz Lightyear (Tim Allen) is introduced as a delusional toy, believing himself to be really a space ranger, equipped with the ability to fly and charged with protecting his planet from the attentions of the evil Emperor Zurg (Andrew Stanton). By the end of the film, Buzz has learned he cannot really fly but finally accepts his status and value as a toy. *Toy Story 2*, however, opens by seeming to reinforce Buzz's initial claims that he is 'real'. This occurs through an *in medias res* introduction in which Buzz is seen flying through space towards Emperor Zurg's base planet.

Toy Story 2 begins, then, by giving a futuristic sheen to the image that is not present in the first movie. The CGI is used to pastiche the visual conventions of a big-budget science fiction film thereby leading to a double articulation of the film's digital status: CGI animation is used to emulate the pristine visual spectacle of a live-action film that would also use CGI to achieve its look. The opening scene of *Toy Story 2* presents itself as digital twice over.

Emperor Zurg's first on-screen appearance needs to be understood within this visual scheme. After a shot of Buzz running through a corridor in Zurg's hideout, there is a cut to a close-up shot of a monitor on which a yellow dot moves across a red background. This is accompanied by the beginning of a theatrically evil laugh which continues as the camera rapidly zooms away from the close view of the monitor (Figure 3.1) to reveal it is part of a control panel, labelled 'Zurg Vision' (Figure 3.2), which is being viewed by Emperor Zurg himself. By the end of the shot, the camera has moved to a position behind Zurg's left shoulder, and the emperor has proclaimed, in Darth Vader-like tones, the stock baddy line: 'come to me my prey!'.

The initial view of the monitor is so close up that its texture is exposed, consisting of chunky horizontal lines. The image quality is determinedly low resolution, and the quick revelation that this is what constitutes 'Zurg Vision' establishes limitations in the expressivity of the image in relation to the articulation of Zurg's point of view. This is aligned with the limitations in Zurg's vocal expressivity, associated as he is with the most basic baddy dialogue (an evil laugh and a clichéd line, both delivered with the utmost hamminess).

This action scene ends abruptly when Buzz appears to be blown to bits by Zurg, at which point, a cut to a television screen in which the action of the scene continues reveals to the viewer the fact that they have been watching a computer game that turns out to have been played by the dinosaur toy Rex (Wallace Shawn) with the real (that is, the toy) Buzz standing next to him. Retrospectively, this adds a third layer of digitalness to the opening scene, as the viewer now appreciates it as a digitally animated sequence, which makes visual reference to live-action digital sci-fi but within the context of the lower resolution digital imagery characteristic of computer games around the early/mid 1990s (the controller and console most resemble that of the Super Nintendo, a 16-bit computer game system that had been superseded by more powerful 32-bit machines by the time of *Toy Story 2*'s production).

The point of transition between the high-resolution digital image and the lower resolution one represented on the television screen is a tracking shot into a medium close-up of Zurg. Within the overall visual scheme, then, Zurg is represented twice in a low-resolution form that is not used to characterise Buzz. Indeed, the film immediately offers Buzz the opportunity to reassert his true self within the film's dominant visual regime of the plastic norm as he makes natural, everyday gestures to try to counter Rex's despondency at having lost the game again (Rex's attempts to master this game are a running theme throughout the film). The revelation of the real Buzz, moving naturally within a screen environment that mimics the photoreal but with a markedly pristine gloss, contrasts to the *overly* pristine nature of the first scene, as well as his initial unexpectedly straightforward (and clichéd) superheroic behaviour (which William Schaffer notes is 'desperately out of type').[31] In other words, the reintroduction of the real Buzz, established in the first *Toy Story* film, into *Toy Story 2* takes place within the visual regime and according to the storytelling principles identified as the Pixar norm by Schaffer:

> The *feel* of Pixar is inseparable from a subtly differentiated attitude to the potential 'realism' of digitally rendered imagery . . . [John] Lasseter [CEO of Pixar and co-director of *Toy Story 2*] repeatedly asserts that new technologies should be exploited to support engagement with characters in the context of imaginary worlds, and not, as in many other CGI creations, to foreground the technology itself.[32]

The film provides a false start for the viewer by encasing Buzz in a visual field that is marked too heavily by the digital (in relation to the norm established in the first film) and which results in him acting inconsistently in the context of the behaviour he has previously exhibited within *Toy Story*'s imaginary world. The return of the real Buzz signals a return to the Pixar plastic norm, one that combines state-of-the-art digital visual qualities with determinedly 'human' forms of characterisation. Emperor Zurg, by contrast, is frozen within the constraints of the inauthentic digital visual schemes set up at the start of the film.

This opening informs the moment later in the film where the viewer sees the world through Zurg's eyes. The main storyline of *Toy Story 2* sees Buzz leading his fellow toys on a mission to rescue Woody who has been taken by the owner of Al's Toy Barn who wants to sell him as part of a collection of toys associated with the old television show *Woody's Round Up*. During a retreat from the toy store, Buzz accidentally releases a version of Zurg from his box. Zurg immediately slips into character, showing no sign (unlike the toys owned by Andy) that he knows he is just a toy. He sees Buzz running away from him and immediately trains his gaze on him, before marching after him while intoning 'Destroy Buzz Lightyear' repeatedly.

The moment at which Zurg sets his sights on Buzz is registered through a point-of-view shot (Figure 3.3). This begins with a tracking movement that slides across the back of Zurg's head and then moves in through a hole that has 'Look Here' written above it. The movement through the hole reveals a mask-shaped viewfinder with a target in the centre and the 'Zurg Vision' logo underneath it. The perspective of what is shown through the viewfinder is distorted through the speed of movement of the camera through Zurg's viewfinder and the creation of an effect whereby one lens (belonging to the virtual camera which is one of the means through which the film is narrated) is seen to provide a distorted view of a scene captured by another lens (the one that is part of the Zurg Vision system).

In this way, there is a distinction made between Zurg's visual perspective and the authorial eye of the film. The impossibly smooth virtual movement of the camera through the hole in the back of Zurg's head into the viewfinder is contrasted with the very limited visual capacity of Zurg Vision itself which masks off much of the view in front of it (Zurg Vision is shaped as a Zorro-like mask in the middle of a screen that is otherwise blacked out, apart from the 'Zurg Vision' logo itself). It is also an impoverished image in terms of its colour palette, reducing the world it surveys to a uniform infrared, which is entirely unnecessary given that Zurg is chasing Buzz in broad daylight.

In the two scenes featuring different forms of Zurg Vision, the promise that this robotic mode of seeing might possess superior features is undermined by the way in which the limitations of its material qualities are exposed. The deviations in these instances from the plastic norm serve to characterise Zurg as a figure lacking the expressive capabilities of Buzz and other toys in the film and incapable of moving to another level of characterisation: Zurg remains convinced of his status as a real intergalactic dictator to the very end and is never given the opportunity to escape his position as a stock sci-fi baddy. The low-resolution imagery associated with Zurg casts him as a character who is too digital within an imaginary world that otherwise uses digital technology to pursue human forms of characterisation.

REVEALING THE HUMAN TOUCH OF CGI VIA VHS: *TOY STORY 3*

This example from *Toy Story 2* makes use of an invented viewing technology: Zurg Vision will have similarities to the viewfinder systems of a number of toys but it is not directly copied from a real toy. By contrast, *Toy Story 3* features a moment where the image quality changes because of the film's adoption of the point of view of an on-screen viewing device that is directly related to a real-life technology. It opens in a similar fashion to its predecessor featuring an epic action scene in which the key players seem to have transcended their status as toys. The scene does not work as a deliberately misleading one, however, partly because viewers aware of *Toy Story 2* will be primed for this type of opening but also because the scene features nearly all of Andy's toys and is, therefore, more obviously understood from the start as a movie-pastiche representation of a story Andy is making up with his toys. This refers back to the opening of the first *Toy Story* film which shows Andy handling his toys and narrating a story about them. The opening of the third film in the series, therefore, self-consciously combines elements of the first scenes of the previous ones.

What is more surprising, on first viewing, is the revelation that this is actually a story that Andy invented some time in the past in relation to the dominant time frame of the film. At first, the viewer's assumption that this is simply a movie-style version of a story Andy is making up is confirmed. Just as the story's villain, Mr. Potatohead (Don Rickles), appears about to destroy Buzz, Woody and the cowgirl Jessie (Joan Cusack) (Figure 3.4), there is an abrupt cut to the real toy Mr. Potatohead, sitting motionless in a box (Figure 3.5). This is followed by a cut to a shot of Andy handling similarly motionless versions of Woody, Jesse and Buzz (Figure 3.6). Andy continues to narrate the story which, before this point, had been presented omnisciently, using blockbuster conventions.

This expected 'twist' gives way to a more surprising one, however, when the widescreen image, presented as the plastic norm, is replaced by a VHS home-video-style image, with the sides of the screen blacked out (as this is a 4:3 image) and the basic viewfinder grid visible (framelines in the corners of the screen, a 'REC' symbol in the left-hand top corner and a battery-level indicator in the right). The camera is evidently being operated by Andy's mother (Laurie Metcalf) who encourages her son to keep on playing and gets confused as to whether the camera is still recording. Randy Newman's theme song, 'You've Got a Friend in Me', strikes up non-diegetically and there follows a montage of VHS video taken of Andy playing with his toys at around the age he appeared in the first two films. After this montage, there is a blackout, after which the film moves to the time it adopts for the rest of its duration, a point at which Andy is about to leave for college and no longer plays with his toys.

Whereas the opening of *Toy Story 2* begins by showing different parts of the same story through two visual regimes (as live-action CGI movie pastiche and as 16-bit computer game), three visual schemes are used in the rendition of the story that opens *Toy Story 3* (the movie pastiche, the plastic norm of Andy playing with his toys and the VHS home-video footage). This allows the viewer the opportunity to assess the significance of presenting the same story material through visual means that are materially different from one another. In this case, the differences enable a more general understanding of the film's narrative themes and representational strategies rather than feeding in to the construction of one particular character, as I have argued is the case through my reading of *Toy Story 2*.

The differences between the movie-pastiche section of the opening and the shots of Andy handling the toys and narrating that immediately follow (before the move to VHS footage) are not, strictly speaking, to do with the texture of the image. Both visual schemes exhibit the pristine image quality associated with the plastic norm, and the differences are more to do with the tone in which each segment is narrated. Visually, in the movie-pastiche section, the style is much more bombastic, in keeping with its self-conscious presentation as a blockbusting opening to the movie, following the precedent set by *Toy Story 2*. The difference can be illustrated through a comparison between the shots of Buzz, Jesse and Woody 'handcuffed' (with plastic monkeys) to the desert ground, just preceding the movement away from movie pastiche, and the parallel shots of the three of them after it is revealed this is a story being told by Andy. In the earlier shots, each character gets his or her own close-up, the camera moving down towards them as they brace themselves for the moment when Mr. Potatohead presses the button that will destroy them (these close-ups are interspersed with shots of Mr. Potatohead laughing maniacally and reaching for a big red button). These close shots allow for a registration of melodramatic performance (the characters all grit their teeth and flinch) that is augmented by lighting (the modelling of the characters is extremely 'rounded', the shadows cast underneath them adding to a sense of volume in their representation) (Figures 3.4 and 3.7). Finally, the soundtrack, featuring Mr. Potatohead's hectoring laugh and a bombastic music cue, augments the feeling that, visually and aurally, the style is approaching sensory overload, at least within the context of the plastic norm, much like the aesthetic present in the opening of *Toy Story 2*.

The movement to the characters in their true toy form indicates a stepping away from this sensory excess without signalling a complete deflation of the aesthetic as was the case in the movement from sci-fi spectacle to computer game in *Toy Story 2*. When we see Buzz, Jesse and Woody in this segment (after the shot of Mr. Potatohead in the cardboard box), they are featured lying next to each other on Andy's bedroom floor in one static overhead shot taken from a more distanced position than was the case at the end of the movie-pastiche section. This, together with the fact that their facial expressions are now fixed (as they are not allowed to reveal they can really move and talk while Andy is around), make the characters seem flatter than in their previous incarnation. This is not offered as a criticism, however, but rather as a necessary deflation in visual style that returns the characters, and their relationship with Andy, to the state with which the viewer has become familiar over the course of the first two films.

The most significant aspect of this moment, in relation to sensory experience, is the fact that the viewer sees Andy handling the toys. Indeed, all we see of Andy in this section is his hands: in the initial overhead shot, his left hand grabs and shakes Woody and his right hand snatches up Buzz, whereupon a closer shot shows the intricate manipulations and prodding Andy undertakes to act out a scenario in which Buzz shoots a laser at Woody's sheriff badge so that it can deflect off it on to the airborne spaceship (actually the cardboard box) of Mr. Potatohead and bring him to the ground (the successful execution of which is also achieved by Andy's hand knocking the box in the following shot).

To provide an example of the discourse which values the human qualities of 'hand-crafted' animation over the perceived coldness of CGI, Pat Power quotes a director from the animation studio, Aardman, which is predominantly known for producing stop-motion clay animation:

> Aardman's supervising director Richard Goleszowski insists that audiences can tell the difference between CGI, drawn and stop frame, and that in contrast with the automated, synthetic, even plastic-looking nature of much 3D animation, if 'you know it's a hunk of plasticine and occasionally you can still see the fingerprints – some of the process is revealed and that actually helps you tune in to the character'[33]

In this scene, the process of getting one's fingerprints on to a character to animate them is made into an event in the film's fictional world. For Andy, the toys come to life only under his touch and, even though the films are based on the premise that the toys actually do have lives of their own, it is a golden rule that Andy does not find this out.

The tactile activity in this scene can be understood in self-reflexive terms. Like the toys in the fictional world of *Toy Story*, the characters created by computer in Pixar productions do not actually need to be touched by a human being to be animated. It is important to the distinctive aesthetic of the films, however, that a discourse is evoked in which human contact is deemed necessary to bring the characters to life. This discourse can be articulated extratextually through statements by the film-makers or critics about the hands-on aspects of the production process and the perceived human 'warmth' of the final products. The discourse can also be insinuated within the films in moments like these, however. As previously stated, the level of discontinuity between the opening action scene of *Toy Story 3* and the events that follow is much lower than that between the opening of *Toy Story 2* and the rest of the film. By following the hyperspectacular style of the opening moments of the film with scenes of intimate handling of the same characters, in a continuation of the same narrative scenario, the film reflects back on its opening moments to suggest that they are just as much a product of tactile handcrafting as the scenes in which the viewer literally gets to see inanimate figures being brought to life by human touch.

The theme of touch is continued in the switch to the VHS-style video footage. The transition is made through a cut to just outside Andy's bedroom seen through the viewfinder of the video camera. Andy's mum's hand appears in front of the camera to open the door whereupon Andy is revealed still making up the same story. Andy's mum then steps into the room urging him to continue playing.

The video develops into a montage showing Andy playing with his toys at various stages of his childhood. The footage has a worn quality as if this is a videotape that has been played over and over again (in the DVD commentary, director Lee Unkrich refers to the image quality as deliberately 'cruddy'). Throughout the montage, however, as already mentioned, the viewfinder markings, including the 'REC' symbol and battery indicator, remain intact, suggesting that this might actually be the view from the camera at the point of recording rather than something that has been edited and is being played back.

The retention of the viewfinder indicators on the skin of the image is important to an understanding of the extent to which the camera can be seen as an extension of Andy's mother. The camera *almost* becomes her eyes in this montage, a notion introduced by seeing the camera caught in the course of her normal movements, her hand appearing before it in the same way as she would see it with her own eyes, and the camera moving into the room according to her walking pace.

While the camera is humanised in this way, it still retains a distinct technological presence. When Andy's mother points the camera towards her own face, asking 'does the red light mean that it's still going?', the separateness of the technological apparatus from the human operator is clearly being indicated. The viewfinder markings also serve as a reminder of the camera's non-human status as does the low quality of the image (in terms of its basic resolution and the visual noise that is apparent on it). The two extra layers to the image here, however, the viewfinder markings and the lo-fi noise that differentiate the montage from the plastic norm, work to construct a sense of human warmth at the same time as they indicate the presence of a mediating technological interface.

The constant reminder that the viewfinder offers of these scenes as recordings in progress attests to the ability of the home video camera to capture intimate moments spontaneously. Furthermore, the illogical presence of a battery indicator that never wavers, even though these scenes have clearly been recorded at different times, suggests an inexhaustible capacity of the camera to capture such moments. The simultaneous presence of visual signifiers of playback in the montage pays testament to the ability of the camera to memorialise events and to keep them alive long after they have occurred. The other content of the image is, of course, significant in indicating the poignant relationship between Andy and his toys. The 'extra' markings on the image, however, implicate the technological aspects of the video camera in the very human activities of bearing witness to events and remembering them.

In this way, the home video camera is granted great power in the signification of human emotion. The degraded quality of the image connotes something worth going back to rather than something that carries the negative connotations of the 'too digital', low-resolution images associated with Emperor Zurg in *Toy Story 2*. The linking of the intimate, marked, home-video footage with the scenes that precede it, via the connection of each visual regime to Andy's invented story, is also significant. By relating the VHS material narratively to the plastic norm image that precedes it which, in turn, is linked to the initial movie-pastiche material, a chain of association is made between all three types of image. The preceding visual schemes benefit from their association with the home-video footage and this carries through to the film's visual aesthetic as a whole. The digital image becomes trusted as something that has been constructed, figuratively, in a hands-on manner and functions as a suitable medium through which to explore the human themes of memory and the ageing process that drive the film: the central dilemma for the toys is that they face retirement now that Andy no longer plays with them; the key issue for Andy is what to do with toys which he remembers playing with fondly but which no longer seem relevant to his present. The home-video footage is presented as something that both captures the ageing process (Andy seen at a particular point in his life that is now past) and is itself marked by age (through the noise that has accumulated on it). The placing of footage coded as analogue in a chain of sympathetic associations with imagery cast as digital lends the digital footage an 'agedness' it does not naturally possess.

These opening moments present the film image – whatever its origins – as something that needs to demonstrate a human handling to be emotionally effective. The question of how the toys should be 'handled' is also a theme that runs throughout the film: the toys initially fear they are going to be thrown away or put in the attic never to be touched by human hands again; they then suffer the wrong kind of handling when they are given a new lease of life at Sunnyside Daycare nursery only to be tricked into occupying the room for toddlers whose playing is too rough for them; when it appears that the toys are about to be incinerated, they respond by engaging in the tactile act of holding each other's hands; and, finally, Andy draws a line under his time with his toys by getting them out of their box once more and handling each of them in turn as he passes them over to their new owner, the little girl, Bonnie (Emily Hahn). In this way, the film's self-reflexive exploration of the capacity of different kinds of image-making processes to retain a sense of the human touch is imbricated in the developing narrative themes of the film.

In her analysis of the use of a VHS recording of a scene from *Hello Dolly* in *Wall-E*, Sobchack states:

> Sitting centrally as it does in this computer-graphically rendered mise-en-scène, the videotape functions not only narratively as a remainder/reminder of a once vibrant, long-gone humanity capable of song, dance and romance, but also formally as a remainder/reminder of a once live-action but long-gone photochemical cinema capable of an indexicality that exists even when its subject is a fantasy. What strikes me most about the videotape, however, is that it is a videotape. It stands, then, not only as a substitute for the loss of cinema and the loss of humanity, but also for a peculiarly absent (if presently ubiquitous) DVD – or, given this is Pixar via Disney, Blu-ray. Indeed, in this scene, the videotape effectively serves, both narratively and formally, to overwhelm signs of 'new media', and of WALL-E's own digital mode of animation.[34]

Here, Sobchack characterises the relationship between analogue video and digital animation as an estranged one: the video footage overwhelms the signs of the digital. In my readings of moments of 'mixed media' I have attempted to explore the constructive interactions between types of image that are coded as different from one another. These interactions are sometimes estranged ones (the visual aesthetic associated with Zurg Vision separates Emperor Zurg from the 'good' toys which are associated with the plastic norm of the film). They are just as often complementary ones, however, or at least interactions where continuities between media formats are suggested.

I have also tried to go beyond stating the fact of the films' referencing of different types of audio-visual media. To this extent, I am doing something different from Sobchack who states that her chief interest in the videotape of *Hello Dolly*, as presented in *Wall-E*, is that it is a videotape. In this particular article, it is not Sobchack's intention to pursue an interest in the visual qualities video (or other formats coded as distinct from the plastic norm) bring to the Pixar films, or to consider the narrative significance of such qualities. This has, however, been the central focus of my investigation and I conclude this chapter with a narrative reading of the 'surface' qualities of the digital image in *Double Take*, a film that, at first glance, appears far less structured around clear storytelling principles than the Pixar examples.

DOUBLE TAKE: FICTIONALISING HITCHCOCK

One quality of *Double Take* which distinguishes it from the Pixar films and which, potentially, makes its visual textures harder to read in dramatic terms, is the absence of a central scheme that the viewer can identify as the norm of the film's visual narration. *Double Take* features a combination of original digital video, archive news footage detailing the development of the Cold War between the United States and the Soviet Union in the 1960s, coffee advertisements and different types of material related to Alfred Hitchcock (for example, clips from his films, promotional footage, skits from his television show *Alfred Hitchcock Presents*). Sometimes the same images, including the original footage, are reworked and presented in different visual forms in a way that *could* be equated to the purely formal experimentation enacted in *Between the Frames* and the found-footage films considered earlier. Indeed, Steven Jacobs discusses *Double Take* at the end of a chapter on artist films that appropriate Hitchcock footage in which he suggests a persistent tendency of this body of work is to assert the primacy of images by disconnecting them from a narrative context.[35]

It is my contention, however, that the play with the different surface features of images in *Double Take* is keyed in to the film's unfolding of a dramatic scenario. I intend to demonstrate this by discussing how the combination of differently textured images works to develop Hitchcock as a fictional character within the film's world. I shall focus on images that accompany a voice-over purporting to be by Hitchcock himself (though, at the very start of the film, we see the real actor who has been hired to impersonate Hitchcock's voice). In these images, Hitchcock is seen only obliquely, and this means that an unusual weight is placed on other visual characteristics – including the materiality of the image – to support the narrative that is being relayed through the voice-over.

The voice-over details an uncanny meeting between the Hitchcock of 1962 and an older alter ego who has somehow travelled back in time from 1980. The narration is attributed to the younger Hitchcock, and the story unfolds in several sections spread across the film. It takes place in August 1962 during the production of *The Birds*. Hitchcock is filming his own cameo when he is called away to the production office to meet a mysterious visitor. He enters the office to find that it has somehow changed, now resembling a well-appointed tearoom. A cigar-smoking older version of himself awaits him in the room, telling him that this is a meeting the two of them have scripted. The uncanniness of the situation convinces the younger Hitchcock that the meeting constitutes a matter of life or death and, indeed, the tense encounter concludes with the passing away of his older alter ego. In the final passage of voice-over, Hitchcock refers to another encounter in which a younger version of himself visits him on a movie set, on 29 April 1980. As a news montage in the film clarifies, this was the day the real-life Hitchcock died so the implication is that this meeting, too, ends in death.

The meeting between the alter egos is represented through a complex montage of found footage and original material, shot on digital camera. The original footage features a number of recurring visual motifs and possesses a variety of textures. These range from a severe graininess, which inhibits the full disclosure of the objects it portrays, to one that exhibits a crystalline sheen. Much of the original footage is repurposed as the film proceeds. The fictional characterisation of the Hitchcocks, therefore, is communicated, in part, through the various surface qualities of the images that are used to represent him even when (as is usually the case) these images do not feature a recognisable human figure. A key motif in the representation of the director in the voice-over sections is a bowler hat, and my analysis will centre upon the texture of shots featuring the hat. The main body of my commentary will consider the variations in image quality of the hat shots themselves but attention will also be paid to the relationship between these shots and the tactile properties of other footage.

THE HAT AND THE OLDER HITCHCOCK

Recurring motifs in the voice-over sections include murky, prowling tracking shots through corridors, often featuring the bowler hat upon which my analysis will centre; a glossy black-and-white shot of a crow posed in front of a chandelier; shots, in colour and monochrome, of cups of tea and coffee being served; and close-up glimpses of the older Hitchcock (portrayed by a lookalike) smoking a cigar. These stylised shots contrast with the film's more naturalistic original footage which offers a documentary portrait of the Hitchcock impersonator, Ron Burrage. The differences and occasional continuity between the texture of the hat shots and the Burrage footage provide a link between the film's fictional narrative and its documentary aspect. This is also a facet of the film's aesthetics, in terms of the arrangement of its textures, that my analysis considers.

The hat accompanies five passages of voice-over and one sequence that contributes to the documentary portrait of Burrage. It appears first with the voice-over that introduces the narrative about the uncanny encounter. The hat is depicted upturned towards the front of frame, lying in the middle of a hallway that leads on to a corridor extending into the depth of the image (Figure 3.8). The camera is at floor level, demonstrates a slight shake, and the image is monochrome. Owing to the lack of artificial lighting (the light comes from three lamps on the ceiling of the corridor but the hallway at the front of the frame is dimly lit), certain elements of the image display a graininess which provides it with some of its tactile quality. Attention is further drawn to the surface qualities of the image by two means. Firstly, the shot is taken from inside the viewfinder of the camera so that the frame markings on the finder are visible just as was the case in the example from *Toy Story 3*. This provides an extra layer, at the very front of the image, that would normally be effaced. Secondly, the shot is marked by intermittent digital glitching as if there had been electrical interference during the process of filming or as if what we are seeing is an image on digital tape during playback, at a point where the tape has become damaged.

The presence of the viewfinder and of the glitch is dramatically significant. Exactly the same shot is used soon after to herald a return to the voice-over and, thus, the encounter of the two Hitchcocks. Once more, it is accompanied by digital glitching, this time preceded by an effect that mimics the switching of channels on an analogue television (the storyline is being reintroduced straight after an old television commercial for Folgers Coffee). The impression of a messy transition from one mode (analogue) to another (digital) is emphasised by the addition of a scrambled sound effect. In one way, then, the glitching indicates a switching from one strand of the film to another and fits in with other, channel-changing visual effects that are used throughout the film.

The glitching also helps to establish the sense that Hitchcock is retelling the story of his encounter with his double from a position of temporal distance, with all the unreliability of memory that that may entail. The digital interference present in these shots may suggest material that has become damaged by overuse or age. This association is made explicit by the Hitchcock voice-over following the first appearance of the bowler hat. Hitchcock says: 'I have chewed the details over and over so repeatedly that the memory of it has become inaccurate like a film scratched and faded by the years.' If the video footage in *Toy Story 3* brings a sense of the human touch to the film's visual scheme as a whole, here the glitching, in combination with the voice-over, introduces a note of human fallibility.

On the other hand, just like *Toy Story 3*, the visible presence of the view-finder in the shots lends an immediacy to the footage that counters the sense of it as a recording of events long past. Here, the cohabitation of two different layers on the surface of the image (the viewfinder and the glitches) compete to suggest different temporal assignations for the footage: the question of whether the glitch in the first shot can be understood as a power surge during filming or damaged tape in playback thus becomes more central to the drama than it might have first appeared. Indeed, the question of *when* this story is playing out becomes one of the central points of debate between the two Hitchcocks.

The different layers occupying the surface of the image also exert an influence on the representation of the bowler hat. On its first appearance, the hat exhibits a lifelessness that contrasts to the activity at the image's surface (the glitches). All the elements around it, the carpet on which it lies and the corridor behind it, are depicted with a contrasting graininess that bestows texture on their surfaces: the fabric of the hat and the lighting around it are simply too dark to take on this grain, and the hat thereby adopts a two-dimensional, cardboard-cut-out quality. It takes on more animated properties as the film proceeds, eventually coming to represent the characters of the younger and of the older Hitchcocks. It gains character through the development of its tactile qualities, and this is partly contrived through the different types of image quality through which the hat is represented.

Twenty seconds after its first appearance the hat reappears (Figure 3.9). This time it is seen tumbling down a flight of stairs, shot from below, filmed through the viewfinder as in the first shot. The image is still monochrome and full of grain but, within this environment, the hat establishes a weightier, more three-dimensional presence. Sound is important here, as a disproportionately loud thud has been added to accompany the hat each time it hits a step. A slow-motion effect registers this newfound weightiness in the visual realm, with the hat seeming to progress more slowly than it should considering its actual lightness. This effect also produces a grainy motion blur to the rim of the hat as it tumbles down, thereby highlighting the relative thinness of material of one part of the hat (the rim) in comparison with another (the headpiece itself): the edges of the hat are flimsy enough to be subject to blur in a way that its centre is not.

The same shot is used with variation seconds later. The action is the same but the image has been subjected to a post-production zoom so that the focus is more tightly on the hat. The process also reveals much more grain in the image, meaning that the differentiation between the blur of the rim and the centrepiece of the hat is less pronounced, lost in the overall grain. The reduction of the accompanying thud to an almost subliminal level also reduces the sense of an object 'coming to life' that had been intimated in the preceding view of it. In this form, the shot offers a visual representation of an idea that is stated in the voice-over just before its appearance. Pondering on his encounter, Hitchcock says 'the episode seems too strange to be real'. As if in response, the hat acquires a ghostly immateriality, appearing as something that does not seem real. The gradual development of the hat into a more solid representation of character(s) occurs hesitantly in an overall context of other-worldliness.

The characterisation of the hat begins in earnest in the following passage of voice-over. It appears at the very end of this segment, at the close of a shot that prowls through a corridor, with leaves blowing through it in slight slow motion (Figure 3.10). This is a much sharper monochrome image than any of the corridor/stair shots in the previous section, and there is no longer a visible viewfinder to function as a reminder that this is film footage. The relative clarity of the image is accompanied by a lightness of movement within the frame as if objects can traverse it more easily now that it is rid of its grain. The hat floats in like the leaves, this time with no disconcerting sonic thud. Its appearance coincides with the voice-over's promises that there is a number of surprises to come. The hat actually tumbles into the frame after the camera has turned to the right, as if it has perceived the hat's presence. The camera continues to traverse towards it as it comes to a rest, the right way up. There is a fade just as the camera reaches its side.

From its initial upturned appearance as a cardboard-cut-out, anonymous shape, the hat has been transformed into an entity with weight (this time its lightness is accentuated by association with the leaves), a capacity for movement, and an increased material presence (it no longer competes with the viewfinder markings or the glitching). This coincides with the hat responding more actively to the dramatic situation being described in the voice-over. It enters the frame, and comes neatly to rest, as if it represents the surprise Hitchcock is about to encounter: that is, his older self. The relative clarity of the image of the hat, therefore, is part of its more particular characterisation as a synecdoche for the older Hitchcock. The quality of the image relaying the hat changes in tandem with the development of its storytelling role.

The contrast between the hat's initial lifeless appearance and its subsequent animation is emphasised in the next voice-over segment. The sequence ends with a shot of the hat in very vivid colour as it rolls along a patch of lush green grass. This is portrayed through the smooth tracking movement of a camera trained on the ground, the hat entering the frame from the bottom of the screen and exceeding the pace of the camera so, by the end of the few seconds the shot lasts, it is in danger of disappearing out of shot (Figure 3.11). The camera allows a view of both the hat rolling along and its shadow (indeed, at one point, the hat bounces up off-screen, meaning that the only sign of it within the frame is its shadow). This reinforces the sense of the hat as a three-dimensional object making an impression as it moves through space, the sudden introduction of colour giving it a newfound vividness. The energising force of these representational strategies is augmented by the sense that the hat is outpacing the camera as it moves towards the top of the frame: from its initial position of inertia, fixed within the tramlines of the viewfinder, it is now engaged in a game of hat and mouse, the camera struggling to keep it in its field of vision.

This image of the hat offers a wordless coda before the film moves on to a different scenario. Like previous shots, it represents visually a sentiment that has been stated in the voice-over. Hitchcock has just expressed his surprise at entering his production office to find that it now resembles a tearoom. The sudden movement to an exterior setting signalled by the shot of the hat rolling on grass allows the viewer to experience the shock of alighting on an unexpected location, just as Hitchcock has. The material qualities of the image reinforce the surprise: nothing to this point prepares the viewer for the appearance of lush colour.

At this moment, the viewer's attention is caught between following the movement of the hat itself and its shadowy alter ego and this, too, engages the viewer in perceptual activity that is related to the narrative. It is in this passage that Hitchcock acknowledges a fear that he is entering a trap 'instigated by another mind, another director'. The characterisation of the hat as object and shadow continues to develop it as a representation of the mysterious Hitchcock doppelganger, an elusive presence sensed but not yet glimpsed by the *The Birds*-era director, leading his prey inexorably towards their meeting. The richer sensuous impression of the image, indicated by its bold, fulsome colour scheme, indicates a movement into a world where encounters between human figures and their alter egos become a reality. The viewer is led to expect a time when the hat does not slip out of the frame and the meeting between the two Hitchcocks takes place.

Indeed, the hat's next appearance immediately precedes the moment where the younger Hitchcock sets eyes on his older self. The camera is at ground level, as it was in the first shot of the hat, but closer to it and closing in (Figure 3.12). The viewfinder grid and glitching have gone, and the framing and camerawork are now justified by on-screen human movement, the camera moving in tandem with a pair of feet. A difference is also signalled by a use of colour in this shot but it is muted, rather than vivid as in the shot of the hat traversing the grass. The palette is in keeping with that used to portray Ron Burrage. The connection between the Burrage segments and the fictional voice-over sections is explored further later in the film, as I shall discuss.

The surface qualities of the image are not flaunted as they have been in previous shots of the hat. The scenario in which Hitchcock approaches his double is made to look as real at this point as the naturalistic portrait of Burrage, a non-fictional figure. This indicates that the 'impossible' meeting between two Hitchcocks is about to become reality, and this is emphasised by the figure on-screen picking up the hat and lifting it off-screen (the camera continues to follow his feet). It is as if the hat has fulfilled its premonitory purpose and can now be cleared off-screen. Indeed, there follows the first intimation of the older Hitchcock as a flesh-and-blood character, evidenced by his shadow and a hand holding a cigar.

All these events take place within the first fifteen minutes of the film. In this time, the hat undergoes a process of representation that plays on the surface qualities of the image to suggest a movement of the object towards the corporeal: the hat leads the younger Hitchcock (and the viewer) to his older self, at which point a flesh-and-blood character takes over. This would suggest that the hat has fulfilled its narrative function, a quarter of an hour into the film, and there is, indeed, a lengthy passage in which the hat does not feature (lasting nearly forty minutes of a seventy-five-minute film). The hat does return three more times, however, in ways that reiterate the material qualities, which have already been showcased, but also extend them.

THE HAT AND RON BURRAGE

The hat's next appearance occurs at the end of a sequence that concentrates on Burrage's career as a Hitchcock impersonator. This is the only occasion in the film that the hat is not associated with a passage of voice-over. Instead, its presence suggests a connection between the documentary portrait of Burrage and the fictional encounter between the Hitchcocks. For the purposes of this analysis, the central question is the following: how do surface qualities of the image, including the hat, shade our understanding of the relationship between the two narrative strands?

The hat is presented within a *mise en scène* familiar from its earlier appearance where it had blown into a corridor strewn with leaves (Figure 3.10). The shot is not an exact reprise in its action but the most obvious difference is a 'surface' one. This image is in colour rather than in monochrome (Figure 3.13). It uses the same muted colour palette in representing the corridor as in the earlier shots of the hat being picked up off the floor (Figure 3.12). There, I suggested, the use of muted colour links the fictional scenario with the portrayal of Burrage, through its deployment of a similar palette, lending the impending encounter between the directors a sense of reality. The reverse process occurs in the colour shot of the hat here, resulting in the Burrage portrait acquiring some of the supernatural atmosphere of the fictional encounter. This is achieved by the disturbance of the naturalistic sheen of the image via various ghostly visual effects. The first of these is the slight slow-motion effect reprised from the initial monochrome shot of the hat and leaves in the corridor. This produces a motion blur around the edges of the hat as it rolls in the corridor (the relative thinness of the rim allowing the blurring effect) akin to the one produced when it was seen bouncing down the stairs (Figure 3.9).

The characterisation of the hat as thin, in this respect, is counteracted in the shot by the forceful movement of the camera away from the hat's edges and towards the inside of the bowler. The cut occurs just a few frames before the image is darkened entirely by the camera moving 'into' the hat, this movement acting as a (nearly completed) fade to black. As a film that relies on the juxtaposition of different elements and that emphasises surface qualities of the image, *Double Take* deploys the fade to black extremely sparingly: as an editing technique, it breaks the flow of the montage and as a visual form it is devoid of the variations of grain and light with which the film otherwise makes great play. This makes the occasions on which the fade *is* deployed especially significant.

The first is at the end of the zoomed-in shot of the hat bouncing down the stairs. After the fade, a sprightly fanfare accompanies an archive intertitle from a Universal International News newsreel, describing Hitchcock's address to the National Press Club (to announce the release of *The Birds*). The division of the two shots by a decisive fade brackets off – for now – the spectral nature of the original footage from the 'real-life' activities of Hitchcock in the archival footage. This corresponds to the initial presentation of the voiceover as a fantastic narrative that only subsequently acquires more 'earthly' dimensions.

The second and more pronounced fade occurs at the end of the monochrome shot of the hat and leaves in the corridor (Figure 3.10). The camera is homing in on the hat but the fade to black is concluded just before it actually reaches it. It functions to separate the atmosphere of the voice-over story from the world of real events, like the first fade, superseded similarly by a fanfare and newsreel inter-title. It also serves a premonitory function, gesturing towards an engagement between the camera, the fade and the hat, that is only completed in the colour version of the hat and leaves shot.

In the colour version, the exploration of the hat as a material form has developed to the extent that the camera now makes use of its fabric to enact a fade-to-black process more commonly completed 'off-screen' (that is, in post-production). The use of muted colour in the shot conjoins it with the naturalism of the strand of the film which profiles Burrage but everything else points to the implication of this aspect of the film with the concerns and atmosphere of those passages focusing on Hitchcock's encounter with himself. It is as if the tracking shot into the hat represents Burrage's fall into this other-worldly narrative, and this sense is confirmed by his next appearance: for the first and only time in the film, he is accompanied by Hitchcock's voice-over, at the point where he spitefully says to his older self, 'I hate your face, which is a parody of mine'. The fade-through-hat moment, therefore, has the storytelling function of transporting Burrage explicitly into the world represented by the voice-over. In so doing, the film subjects Burrage, by association, to questions about the parasitic nature of his career choice which are not explicitly asked of him by his interviewer or addressed by him in his spoken comments. The investigation of the materiality of the hat, in its filmed form (in this case its capacity to block out on-screen light entirely), serves to link two key strands of the film together, 'reaching over' to Burrage and pulling him into the invented scenario's orbit.

THE HAT AND THE YOUNGER HITCHCOCK

The final images of the hat are reintegrated into the voice-over narrative. After its appearance in the Burrage section, it is next seen in a familiar pose (Figure 3.14), upturned on the floor of the corridor, that is featured throughout the voice-over. The last time it was seen in this position, it was picked up by a man, and this action is repeated as if the film is reminding the viewer of the progression of events surrounding the hat in the fictional scenario. The continuity of action between these shots consolidates the inclusion of the hat as a 'real' part of the drama rather than as a symbol or synecdoche, and this sense is developed across the segment as the man actually sports the hat, the first time it has been worn. The sequence features a proliferation of human figures with three men, all suited and wearing hats, forming a procession down the corridor.

The hat is involved in continuous action in this passage, now attached to the head of a human figure (as you might expect it to function in real life) rather than operating autonomously, as if it had (or represented) a life of its own. To an extent, the surface qualities of the image reflect the hat's involve-ment in action rendered through relatively realist codes (in the continuity of time and space suggested in this sequence of shots). The palette is the muted colour associated with Burrage, a slight grain in the image registering the absence of artificial means to boost light levels but not exaggerated to the extent that the grain becomes the focal point of attention.

Other qualities of the image, however, draw attention to the surface of the frame and particular elements within it. The slight slow-motion effect, used so often in these scenes, is retained so that a blur remains apparent as the feet move down the corridor. This lends a ghostly wispiness to the figure (it does not possess a complete earthly solidity). This immateriality is also indicated in relation to the other figures in the scene who are always viewed out of focus, most strikingly in a quasi-point-of-view shot from the perspective of the man who has picked up the hat (Figure 3.15).

These shots, then, register a combination of the 'real' (hats placed on heads where they should be, continuous action, naturalistic colour and lighting) and the other-worldly (the figures do not move with a human weight and the lines of their bodies are too soft; the symmetrical movement and rhyming pattern of the figures, all walking the same line down the corridor, are uncanny). This creates an uncertainty over the status of what is being presented to the viewer at this time, an equivocation that extends to what the hat's role in the drama ultimately is.

I have argued that the hat functions as a premonitory figure of the older Hitchcock in the opening sections of the film. In its return, towards the end of the film, the hat is actually placed on someone's head and this figure is most plausibly understood as an embodiment of the younger Hitchcock, the story's narrator. The accompaniment of the voice-over with a quasi-point-of-view shot from this man's perspective strengthens the association. If this is the case, the younger Hitchcock is adopting the clothes of his older self even though he expresses a consistent fear of his alter ego and a desire to keep his distance from him.

The uncertainty of identity is a theme that pervades *Double Take*, and it is one that is articulated particularly intensely as the fictional encounter comes to a close. This intensity is signalled by the proliferation of Hitchcock clones at this point, both visually (parading in a line down the corridor) and through the voice-over, as the older Hitchcock raises the possibility 'maybe there's three or four of us'. This line coincides with the cut to the shot of three figures walking down the corridor, with the figure that might be taken as the younger Hitchcock closest to the camera, a glimpse of his face now apparent for the first time, hat on head. At the same time as he takes on his seemingly most solid visual form, doubts are raised, through the voice-over, as to whether this really is who we have been led to believe it is. The sudden appearance of multiple figures in this sequence, walking along the same paths, exacerbates the sense of them as part of a production line, interchangeable with one another. In this scenario, the figure at the front of the frame could just as well be the older Hitch with whom the hat is first associated.

The final appearance of the hat occurs towards the end of this passage of voice-over. The hat lies upturned in the corridor, this time in a shard of sunlight coming from an open door, the hat casting a distinctive shadow (Figure 3.16). The camera is angled above the hat so that its inside is visible, the leather lining worn in patches but not in others, and a shadow covering part of it while the light from the door shines on the rest. Here the textures of the hat, the qualities that render it as a three-dimensional real object are presented without overt mediation or stylisation: the shot uses a naturalistic colour palette; there are no surreal additions to the *mise en scène* (such as leaves blowing inside); and the variation of texture is granted by the hat's own features (the worn leather) and the natural play of light on it.

The camera then begins to track backwards, however, with the effect that these details of texture are lost. The motion of the camera in all the shots in the corridor (whether featuring the hat or not) has never been backwards until this point, marking this movement as a particularly significant one. It represents a final retreat from the hat as a motif in the story and, in so doing, manufactures a moment in which the extremes of the representation of the hat are summarised: at the start of the shot the hat is viewed as an object that may exist in a real world of three-dimensionality and earthy textures; at the end of the shot, the hat is reduced to the one-dimensional form characteristic of its first appearance (Figure 3.17).

This final shot occurs after the older Hitchcock tells his younger self that 'my whole life has been a setting to film of this moment. Now events have caught up with the film and overrun it. It will end badly for someone, just as it did last time.' The younger Hitchcock then reports his own reply: 'I know what you're thinking. It's the murderer who will tell the story.' The shot of the hat coincides with the following lines: 'As I spoke the words, fear surged inside my chest, sharp as a knife. It dawned on me that this might be my own death scene playing itself out.' This exchange iterates, through speech, the same question that was raised during the first appearance of the hat, through the digital glitches playing on the surface of the image. The older Hitchcock refers to the event ending badly, 'just as it did last time', raising the possibility that this is a repeat of something that has happened (multiple times?) in the past. The younger Hitchcock worries that he has experienced an uncanny shift forward in time, his older alter ego representing himself at the point of his death. The glitching brings to the foreground the materiality of the digital image but this moment exists neither as a purely formal gesture nor to interrupt the viewer's immersion in the film's fictional world. Rather, it plays a key role in supporting the 'glitch in time' scenario of the story, allowing two temporally disconnected versions of the same person to meet. The digital glitch can be seen as a mark of the past (a tape wearing out through use) and an indicator of the present (a power surge at the moment of recording); the temporal location of the story is poised ambiguously in the present, the future and as something that is replaying the past. The procession of Hitchcock figures in the corridor provides a visualisation of past, present and future Hitches caught in a never-ending loop. Similarly, the movement of the camera away from the hat in its last appearance captures, through tactile detail, the involvement of the hat within this looping structure: moving towards a three-dimensional and textured 'real-time' presence as the narrative unfolds, only to recede back to its starting point as (this iteration of) the story comes to its denouement.

CONCLUSION

The close analysis of the bowler hat shots in the film reveals how the tactile qualities of similar material [the same prop, filmed via the same technological means (a digital camera)] can be presented to the viewer in a variety of connected but often contrasting ways. Furthermore, my reading of these moments is designed to draw attention to the storytelling role this investigation of sensuous qualities can have. The hat shots are presented as a kind of invented found footage: this is indicated from the start by the presence of the viewfinder which signals its status as footage, and the digital glitching which suggests the kind of damage that might have been done to footage that has been found. As in the found-footage films discussed earlier in the chapter, the images are subjected to a material interrogation, as the same shots – or very similar ones – are reused and sometimes retreated through techniques like a post-production zoom.

Despite their very different scales of production, *Double Take* and the Pixar films all make use of digital technology to manufacture 'disturbances' on the surface of the image. Despite the critical discourse around the digital's plasticity, digital technology can be used to make images 'dirtier', and this is a practice that is now commonplace (as demonstrated by the hugely successful mobile phone application Instagram which allows users to choose filters to change the look of their photos before sharing them). In the main case studies of this chapter, however, the repurposing of the material is not an end in itself. I have attempted to understand the tactile investigation of the image as a form of storytelling, albeit one that makes sense only in combination with other narrational devices.

Notes

1. http://lux.org.uk/collection/works/between-frames (accessed 23.04.2012).
2. Kubelka, 'The theory of metrical film' in Sitney, *The Avant-Garde Film: A Reader of Theory and Criticism*, p. 141.
3. Pierson, 'Special effects in Martin Arnold's and Peter Tscherkassky's cinema of mind', *Discourse*, p. 32.
4. Gidal, 'Theory and definition of structural/materialist film', in Gidal, *Structural Film Anthology*, pp. 1–2.
5. Pierson, 'Special effects in Martin Arnold's and Peter Tscherkassky's cinema of mind', *Discourse*, p. 39.
6. Arthur, 'The Status of found footage', *Spectator*, p. 64.
7. Ibid. p. 64.
8. Ibid. p. 67.
9. Ibid. p. 68.
10. Marks, *The Skin of the Film: Intercultural Cinema, Embodiment, and the Senses*, pp. 162–3.
11. Ibid. pp. 173–5.
12. Ibid. pp. 175–6.
13. Sobchack, 'The scene of the screen', in *Carnal Thoughts: Embodiment and Moving Image Culture*, p. 154.
14. Ibid. p. 154.
15. Marks, *The Skin of the Film: Intercultural Cinema, Embodiment, and the Senses*, p. 176.
16. Sobchack, *Carnal Thoughts*, p. 153.
17. For a critical analysis of debates about the post-medium condition, as they specifically relate to cinema, see Kim, 'The post-medium condition and the explosion of cinema', *Screen*, pp. 114–23.
18. Krauss, *A Voyage on the North Sea*, p. 26.
19. Manovich, 'What is digital cinema?', http://www.manovich.net/TEXT/digital-cinema.html (accessed 23.04.2012)
20. Moszkowicz, 'To infinity and beyond: assessing the technological imperative in computer animation', *Screen*, p. 297.
21. Ibid. p. 297.
22. Darnley, *Visual Digital Culture: Surface Play and Spectacle in New Media Genres*, pp. 85–6.
23. Lunenfeld, 'Introduction', in Lunenfeld, *The Digital Dialectic: New Essays on New Media*, p. xvi.
24. Power, 'Animated expressions: expressive style in 3D computer graphic narrative animation', *Animation: An Interdisciplinary Journal*, p. 117.
25. Ibid. p. 117.
26. Barker, *The Tactile Eye: Touch and the Cinematic Experience*, pp. 45–6.
27. Schaffer, 'The importance of being plastic: the feel of Pixar', *Animation Journal*, p. 85.
28. Ibid. p. 89.

29. Sobchack, 'Animation and automation, or, the incredible effortfulness of being', *Screen*, pp. 375–91.
30. Montgomery, 'Woody's Roundup and Wall-E's wunderkammer: technophilia and nostalgia in Pixar animation', *Animation Studies*.
31. Schaffer, 'The importance of being plastic: the feel of Pixar', *Animation Journal*, p. 72.
32. Ibid. p. 83.
33. Power, 'Animated expressions: expressive Style in 3D computer graphic narrative animation', *Animation: An Interdisciplinary Journal*, p. 117.
34. Sobchack, 'Animation and automation, or, the incredible effortfulness of being', *Screen*, p. 380.
35. Jacobs, *Framing Pictures: Film and the Visual Arts*, p. 163.

CHAPTER 4

Sighs and Sounds: the Materiality of the Voice-over

THE PLACE OF SOUND IN THE FICTION FILM

This chapter considers the material qualities of the voice-over in the feature-length fiction film. During the course of its writing, I experienced *Disorient*, a digital video installation by Fiona Tan exhibiting in the Gallery of Modern Art in Glasgow. This installation featured a voice-over of its own, provided by Michael Maloney reading extracts from Marco Polo's *The Travels*, written at the end of the thirteenth century. This emanated from four speakers arranged in a square, hanging from the ceiling in the middle of the gallery's large main exhibition space. About 30 feet (9 metres) from the top and bottom ends of the speakers stood two large screens on to which were projected two different films: one featuring lustrous tracking shots through an emporium, holding the kind of objects you might imagine Marco Polo hoarded from his travels to the east (an actor portraying Polo was occasionally seen inhabiting the space); the other consisting of footage of contemporary everyday life in the countries Polo explored, as well as shots documenting the construction of the emporium depicted on the other screen. The installation was completed by the presence of four more speakers, each mounted above head height on the gallery's pillars, which provided an architectural frame for the installation. Through these speakers could be heard environmental sounds, both human-made and natural, such as traffic noise and the sound of the sea. Also audible from these side speakers were the very few sounds that were directly tied to an on-screen action, namely the noises made by the Marco Polo figure on his occasional movements around the emporium.

The voice-over proceeded at a stately pace, and featured a number of pauses, the actor reading Polo's diaries precisely in a hushed tone. Captured digitally, the recorded quality of the voice was pristine and, standing directly under the central speakers facing the screen showing Polo's imagined emporium, I felt a complementarity in tone between the measured voice of the narrator and the smooth and slow movement of the camera past the emporium's various collected treasures. The vocal delivery and visual movement both seemed to represent seasoned explorers coolly taking the measure of sights that strike them as exotic.

Turning around to view the other screen, the voice-over suddenly seemed out of place, its consistent description of the indigenous eastern population as savage not tallying with scenes of people going about their everyday business. Its 'authentic' inventory of the sights of the east was also called into question by the behind-the-scenes footage that laid bare the artifice of the set depicted on the other screen. In addition, the evenly pristine quality of the voice-over sat uneasily with the rougher and more variable characteristics of some of the documentary footage. In this way, the material, as well as the expository, aspects of sound and image began to chafe against each other, rather than mutually enforce one another.

Even more strikingly, the perception of the voice-over's materiality changed when I moved away from my position beneath the central speakers. Standing instead by one of the pillars, my primary aural impression was provided by the environmental soundtrack. Standing centrally, while the actor was actually speaking, this soundtrack had been either extremely quiet or completely inaudible. During the relatively lengthy pauses between lines, the ambient noise had become more perceptible, in a way that provided a comforting bed of sound to ward off a potentially unsettling silence or the prospect that the gallery's own environmental sounds would become too distracting. In other words, the ambient sound helped to suture me into the world of the artwork while taking its place below voice in the sonic hierarchy, thereby exhibiting characteristics commonly associated with narrative cinema.[1] This hierarchy was upset when I moved position: 'background' noise was now at the fore of my sensory awareness while the voice-over had lost its authority, audible only as an indistinct collection of words, projecting comparatively weakly across the large exhibition space.

In my consumption of the installation, I became aware of my body and its sensory capacities in obvious ways: I was conscious of my ability to move within the artistic space and of the consequences this had on the auditory sensations I experienced at any given point. These sensations, in turn, affected the way I understood the relationships between the different aural and visual elements associated with the artwork that surrounded me.

In this chapter, I develop the notions that voice-overs have material qualities, that they are arranged in a hierarchy with other sounds that have their own materiality, and that these combinations of sound can be significant in terms of how the viewer[2] makes sense of the fictional world which the soundtrack helps to foster. In the fiction film, however, these sounds resonate in a viewing context that is quite different from the one allowed by the staging of *Disorient*. All the films discussed in this chapter gained their first exposure through cinema exhibition, and their soundtracks are constituted in relation to standards associated with this viewing context. One of these standards is the expectation that viewers inhabit a fixed position in relation to a single screen that stands before them and that, as a consequence, sound is also experienced from this perspective. This constitutes one of the conditions of the 'non-corporeal' spectatorial position described by Deborah Thomas in a passage quoted in Chapter 1.[3] It differs quite markedly from the mobility encouraged by the exhibition set-up for *Disorient* which made me aware of my own bodily movement and the effect this had on my sensory experience.

That said, even within this 'fixed' position, there *is* a difference between the way sound and image are perceived. Film images are 'naturally' two-dimensional whereas film sound has a propensity to be perceived as three-dimensional. This difference is explained by Edward Branigan:

> Light reveals its properties through the objects which reflect it whereas sound reveals its properties indirectly through a medium [of air] which moves and rubs against us . . .
>
> Sound thus achieves a greater 'intimacy' than light because it seems to put the spectator directly in touch with a nearby motion-event through a medium of air which traverses space, touching both spectator and represented event.
>
> The reproduction of sound in three dimensions contrasts with the reproduction of visual objects in two dimensions on a film screen. (Light from the projector, though moving through the three-dimensional space of the theater, represents that space by essentially illuminating only one surface – the screen – without disturbing the medium of air).[4]

Even 3D movies achieve their effect by illuminating a single surface so, following Branigan, the film image can never be three-dimensional in the manner of the soundtrack. According to the same reasoning, even monophonic sound technology causes vibrations in the air so the most 'primitive' soundtrack will still be three-dimensional.

The film image is perceived as being in front of us while sound is in the air all around us. This might indicate that the soundtrack impacts on the body in an intensive and immersive manner that is entirely distinct from the image but, while this may be true, it is clearly not the case that sound operates independently in the type of narrative cinema which is the focus of this book. A host of conventions have been developed to convince the viewer of the inextricable connection between sound and image even though both are contrived from separate technological processes and even though a film's sounds and sights are perceived differently from a sensory point of view.

Sound is so tied to image that the film sound theorist Michel Chion goes so far to state, polemically, that 'there is no soundtrack'. He argues that it is valid to refer to an 'image track' as this 'owes its being and its unity to the

presence of a frame, a space of the images in which the spectator is invested'.[5]
He continues:

> By stating that *there is no soundtrack* I mean first of all that the sounds of a film,
> taken separately from the image, do not form an internally coherent entity on
> equal footing with the image track. Second, I mean that each audio element
> enters into *simultaneous vertical relationship* with narrative elements contained
> in the image (characters, actions) and visual elements of texture and setting.[6]

So, despite film sound's all-encompassing qualities, perceptually speaking, the
image provides a powerful point of reference through which the sounds can,
nevertheless, be assigned a specific place. In narrative cinema, the magnetisa-
tion of sound to image has been encouraged by the development of a set of
conventions that implicate sound in the dramatic situations that the image
depicts. As Mark Kerins notes, even as technology has refined the experience
of film sound as an immersive one through the development of sophisticated
surround sound systems, a principle of adhering sound to narrative has
remained intact:

> [T]he digital surround style *emphasises* story. In the aural realm, the shifting
> ultrafield offers information about what is happening both on- and offscreen.
> The visual track, meanwhile, makes heavy use of close-ups to convey char-
> acter emotions or plot points. In short, the various elements of the digital
> surround style work to clarify or enhance a film's story, not to wrest the audi-
> ence's attentions *from* it. Indeed, every one of the film sound professionals I
> interviewed about the use of digital surround made a point to note that their
> sound design choices were driven by the *narrative*.[7]

THE BODY OF THE VOICE-OVER

The voice-over is an aspect of the soundtrack particularly associated with narrative. In her monograph on movie voice-overs, Sarah Kozloff initially makes
a distinction between voice-over *narration* and other forms of off-screen
voice, such as interior monologue ('a character's thoughts or feelings in his or
her own voice'), subjective sound (where 'we hear what the character "hears"
echoing in his or her mind'), the reading of a 'plot-turning letter or telegram',
and the rare occurrence of a voice-over conversation.[8] Her core definition
of voice-over narration is as follows: '"voice-over narration" can be formally
defined as "oral statements, conveying any portion of a narrative, spoken by
an unseen speaker situated in a space and time other than that simultaneously
being presented by the images on the screen"'.[9] Having made this tentative
distinction, however, Kozloff immediately qualifies it, stating that, in practice,
these categories of voice-over blur, so that, for example, 'interior monologue

may be so interlaced with narration that the blend is undefinable' or a 'read-aloud letter may itself relate a story'.[10] The suggestion here is that all types of voice-over are related to narrative and, defined in this way, the technique may appear as an aural element designed to counter the potentially 'unruly' operation of sound as a sensuous experience – the voice-over is a form of sound whose expository qualities are foregrounded over its material properties and effects, and this is what ties it to the screen.

Martin Shingler criticises the privileging of the voice-over in early academic writing on the film voice and, while he does not reference Kozloff specifically, her emphasis on the relationship of the voice to the image and her neglect of the voice's material values represent the type of bias and omission Shingler critiques. Considering how future work should develop, he argues there is

> . . . little necessity for such studies to remain fixated with the issue of voice-off and voice-over. Indeed, it would seem problematic for studies of the voice to continue to be dominated by this issue given that it is chiefly preoccupied with image rather than sound, i.e. the image (or lack of image) of the speaker. Film studies would surely gain more from an understanding of the qualities, uses and effects of the voice itself.[11]

This chapter *does* remain fixated on the voice-over, and, like Kozloff, centres on the question of how, in all its different forms, the voice-over functions as a type of dramatic narration. It also heeds Shingler's call to pay attention to the qualities of the voice itself, however. In keeping with the overall project of the book, the intention is to consider the significance of the material properties of the voice in fleshing out the film's fictional world. In accordance with the overall rationale for my film choices, I focus on examples where the qualities of an individual voice are tested extensively against other types of sound, possessed of their own materiality. All the films discussed in this chapter make the unusual move of utilising more than one voice-over narrator, and my readings of *All About Eve* (Mankiewicz, 1950) and *Gummo* (Korine, 1997) include a comparison between the sensuous qualities of different narrating voices. My accounts of moments from *Happy Together* (Kar-Wai, 1997) and *Magnolia* (Anderson, 1999) focus more on the relationship between the voice-over and diegetic sound: again, these moments are unusual, in the equal prominence they give to non-diegetic and diegetic sound, countering as they do the conventional practice of allowing the voice-over a protected space on the soundtrack when it is heard.

The question remains as to what qualities of the film voice will be privileged in a study that purports to focus on its material aspects. There are two elements to this: the first is the concentration on moments of vocal delivery where the body in the voice becomes particularly apparent. This body is often understood to be expressed through a voice's timbre which Jacob Smith, following an oft-referenced formulation by Roland Barthes, defines in the following way:

> The term *timbre* refers to the specific quality or resonance of a sound, as determined by its pattern of harmonic overtones. Timbre is that aspect of a sound which tends to be described by what Roland Barthes has called the 'poorest linguistic category: the adjective' (1985, 267). Thus the aspect of the voice that Barthes so famously characterised as its 'grain' is often described with words like 'raspy', 'clear', or 'reedy'.[12]

Mirroring the attention given to visual 'imperfections' in the previous chapter, I focus particularly on moments where speech falters and the grain of the voice comes especially to the fore. In attributing narrative significance to this faltering, I am following, in the specific case of the voice-over, the example set by Susan Smith in her reading of James Stewart's performance in *Mr Smith Goes to Washington* (Capra, 1938). The film ends with Stewart's idealistic congressman, Jeff Smith, exhausting himself through the delivery of an epic filibuster in the Senate chamber in an effort to expose the corruption of Senator Paine (Claude Rains). This eventually results in Paine's breakdown and confession, a development that has been criticised in terms of its plausibility (the breakdown is very sudden) and its contrivance (as an overly obvious way to bring the narrative to a close). Smith justifies the ending by finding dramatic significance in the material qualities of Mr Smith's voice:

> [F]or in the physical effort and struggle that Stewart's rasping, forced-through-the-throat style of delivery conveys, one could argue that much of the significance of the actor's performance lies in its ability to restore a sense of the *bodily* origins and integrity of the voice to the *discursive* realm of the senate chamber as Jeff proceeds to expose a congressman so habituated to using his own voice in the service of linguistic manipulation and cover-up to a more emotionally direct, visceral way of speaking and feeling.[13]

Here, Susan Smith claims that the distinctive material qualities of a character's voice, revealed particularly intensely as that voice comes under pressure, are crucial to the understanding of the film's central dramatic conflict.

Is it possible, though, to understand the voice-over as a voice under pressure or one that brings its body to the fore? There are two reasons this might be seen as unlikely. Firstly, as Kozloff states, many voice-overs occur from a position of temporal and spatial distance from the events being depicted on-screen (and via the diegetic soundtrack). These voices, then, like that heard in the *Disorient* installation, habitually register relatively unpressurised processes of recollection and reflection, making it unusual (though not impossible) for them to betray signs of stress. Secondly, voice-overs which occur in the present tense, such as the interior monologue, might often sound less com-posed than the 'distanced' voice-over but are also associated with a certain immateriality, presented as they are as expressions of a character's thoughts rather than their physical being.

These reasons, as well as the voice-over's particular association with exposition, may help to account for the lack of concern for the bodily quali-ties of the disembodied voice that is apparent in existing writing about the voice-over. Michel Chion, for example, distinguishes between three different types of speech in film. The category most associated with voice-over – what he terms 'textual speech' – is one which he sees as being centrally tied up with narration through its ability 'to make visible the images that it evokes through sound – that is, to change the setting, to call up a thing, moment, place, or characters at will'.[14] Chion's discussion is all about the storytelling authority the voice-over has over the image, and there is no mention of the material qualities of the voices that hold this power. By contrast, the other two categories, 'theatrical speech' (that is, synchronised dialogue, the most common way voices are heard in film)[15] and 'emanation speech' ('speech which is not necessarily heard and understood fully')[16] are considered in sen-suous terms: theatrical speech is recognised as having an 'affective function' as well as a 'dramatic' and 'informative' one;[17] emanation speech is charac-terised by its relative semantic unintelligibility, presented instead as part of a 'visual, rhythmic, gestural, and sensory totality'.[18] As part of this totality, speech becomes significant as a sign of the human body from which it is pro-jected (as an emanation) and due to its combination with other emanations rather than 'intimately tied to the heart of what might be called the narrative action'.[19]

Using Chion's terms, this chapter considers textual speech as an aural element that is usually relatively 'low-key', sensuously speaking: its displace-ment from the hurly-burly of the diegetic aspects of the film's fictional world is very often materialised by a vocal delivery characterised by a certain com-posure. This can mean, however, that any vocal 'disturbances' become more noticeable and worthy of comment; the voices are also rarely heard independ-ently, making them part of an aural 'sensory totality' composed of a variety of different textures. In other words, textual speech can be seen as a specific category with a particular power in terms of narration that, nevertheless, possesses qualities Chion associates with theatrical and emanation speech. The examples of voice-over that follow in this chapter are often particularly replete with the signs of emanation speech in a way that is, nevertheless, still 'intimately tied' to the narrative action.

As well as understanding the voice-over as a material emanation of charac-ter, I shall consider instances where the technology through which the voice is recorded and projected becomes evident as part of its material texture. This is in keeping with the attention I pay to technological mediation throughout the book, and also builds on insights provided by Andy Birtwistle in one of the very few studies devoted to the materiality of film sound. Birtwistle makes the claim that 'permeating every sound announced by a film is the audible trace of a meeting of technology and sound'.[20] Like much sensuous film scholarship, Birtwistle's attention to the materiality of sound is predicated on an attempt to go beyond what he calls the 'significatory paradigms' of 'narrative, identification and representation'.[21] This leaves space, however, to consider how certain films may purposefully make use of sound that lays bare its technological mediation for the kind of storytelling ends that are not Birtwistle's main focus of attention. Thus, at different points, my analysis focuses on moments where, to paraphrase Birtwistle, the viewer is encouraged to listen *to* the technology involved in mediating a voice-over rather than simply listening *through* it.[22]

There are fundamental differences between my experience of listening to the voice-over used in the *Disorient* video installation and the conditions of listening encouraged when voice-overs occur in the fiction film. In the *Disorient* example, I had a degree of freedom in 'composing' my own sound mix and in choosing what images to look at in combination with the soundtrack. This was enabled by my physical movement within the space of the artwork, the licence to move making me acutely aware of my own body and the various ways it experiences sound in different parts of a three-dimensional space.

The voice-over in the fiction film, like the rest of the soundtrack, also resounds around a three-dimensional space in a way the image does not. This sensation is only made sharper and more specific by advances in surround-sound technology. This sensory experience, however, takes place as part of a mode of viewing that is directed towards a specific point, the two-dimensional screen, and in the context of a practice of fictional world-building that arranges the film's different sounds in a fixed relationship to one another, according to conventions that encourage a dramatic connection between image and sound to be felt. In the analyses that follow, rather than considering these conditions as necessarily limiting ones, I understand them simply as the circumstances in which the material qualities of the voice-over can be expressive of dimensions of the fictional worlds of which they are a part.

THE TEXTURE OF TEXTUAL SPEECH: THE REVEALING VOCAL SLIPS OF ADDISON DEWITT IN *ALL ABOUT EVE*

All About Eve constitutes the most 'classical' of the examples chosen for this chapter. While it is unusual for a Hollywood film in its use of multiple voice-over narrators, it is otherwise typical in its presentation of voice-over as a kind of textual speech, to which the image responds, and in the effacement of the sound's technological mediation. Presented as the recollections of different characters who have had dealings with the film's title character, the voice-overs each delivers a 'portion of a narrative' in the manner identified by Kozloff. Kozloff, in fact, uses *All About Eve* as one of her case studies, and my reading of its opening passage of voice-over works in relation to hers. My intention is to bring a discussion of the materiality of sound into the analysis in a way Kozloff does not. By doing so, I suggest that even the most 'straightforward' instances of voice-over, which might seem to fall very squarely within the category of textual speech defined by Chion, possess a material quality that can assert some significance.

All About Eve features voice-over from three of the film's main characters, each of whom provides an account of their relationship with the rising-star actor, Eve Harrington (Anne Baxter). After the opening credits, the film moves straight into its first passage of voice-over, provided by the theatre critic, Addison DeWitt (George Sanders). Addison's voice-over is immediately set up as an authoritative one, fully possessed of the ability to 'make visible the images that it evokes through sound'[23] in the manner highlighted by Chion. He provides a cynical commentary on the ceremony he is attending in which Eve is given an award. He introduces all the film's main players, including himself, and provokes intrigue around Eve, indicating that she will be the central figure of fascination in the narrative to come. This, indeed, proves to be the case as the rest of the film discloses Eve's story from a number of perspectives and it is revealed how deviously she manipulates her way to stardom. Addison's fictional authority over what the viewer sees is such during this opening sequence that, just as Eve is about to receive her award, he is able to cause the image to freeze to allow him more time to bring the viewer up to date with what has happened.

Addison's authority established, the next character heard in voice-over is Karen Richards (Celeste Holm), a more modest narrator who begins to tell the viewer how she was responsible for introducing Eve to her friend, Margo Channing (Bette Davis), a famous actor whose star Eve ends up eclipsing. Karen's voice-over initiates a movement away from the present of the awards ceremony, which has been frozen in time, back to the point of her first verbal encounter with Eve some months previously. The voice-overs of both Karen and Addison return throughout the film, augmented by that of Margo, but it is this opening passage with which I am concerned.

Kozloff describes this scene in some detail, offering the following rationale for doing so:

My purpose in detailing the opening scene is to demonstrate that although Mankiewicz uses three character-narrators, they are not of equal status. Addison is the most powerful; he addresses us directly, provides necessary information, controls the camera and sound, and claims responsibility for the film. Furthermore, Addison elicits Karen's story; it is as if Karen begins to tell what she knows about Eve in answer to his unspoken command to reveal her secrets.[24]

Kozloff goes on to suggest that Addison's opening voice-over and, indeed, his representation through subsequent voice-overs and through his on-screen depiction is somewhat misleading. According to Kozloff, the film as a whole encourages the viewer to cherish Addison as an acerbic commentator who, by recognising the full extent of Eve's duplicity, gains our trust. Towards the end of the film, however, the extent of Addison's own self-interest is revealed as it turns out that 'he has uncovered all of Eve's deceptions not to expose or thwart her, but to blackmail her into becoming his sexual possession'.[25]

Kozloff suggests that Addison's sexual interest in Eve comes as a surprise, and that this leads to viewers realising they have been poor judges of character, just like the characters in the film who have been duped by Eve.[26] I would suggest that another hearing of the opening passage of voice-over, this time attuned to its different textures, contests this reading by revealing, from the start, a carnality in Addison's attitude towards Eve.

The immediate contrasting textures of the passage are provided by the interplay between the following materials: the relationship of the non-diegetic music to the voice-over it accompanies; the relationship between the voices of Addison and Karen; and the relationship between various passages of each voice-over, in terms of how the vocal delivery reveals different dimensions of the voice.

Addison's voice-over begins straight after the opening credits and pauses to allow the viewer to hear some of the 'tedious' speech made by the chairman of the society presenting its award to Eve. This passage of voice-over lasts for more than three minutes and its unusually long duration – in the context of Classical Hollywood – forms part of its relentless quality. This is also an effect of the style of vocal delivery which, with important exceptions, generally operates according to a principle of cold precision. The voice is heard as the product of a particularly self-controlled body, and the material signs of this are felt in the very first seconds. The first image after the opening credits is a medium close-up of the Sarah Siddons Award, the honour about to be conferred to Eve, whose name is clearly inscribed on it. Though Addison will emerge in this opening passage as a narrator who provides knowledge about the characters and their situations which would not otherwise be apparent to us, his first words are narratively redundant.

He simply repeats the words that are already visible to the viewer on the plaque that fronts the award: 'The Sarah Siddons Award for Distinguished Achievement'. Before the camera starts to crane back from the award, in a long movement that eventually reveals almost the entirety of the dining hall in which the ceremony is taking place, Addison has said the following: 'The Sarah Siddons Award for Distinguished Achievement is perhaps unknown to you. It has been spared the sensational and commercial publicity that attends such questionable honours as the Pulitzer Prize . . .' Addison is a theatre critic, accused on a number of occasions in the film of making speeches that will appear verbatim in his newspaper column the next day. Fittingly, the first words of his voice-over follow a 'script', repeating words that are legible to the viewer on the plaque. The intonation of the vocal delivery adds to the sense that a script is being given a very careful reading. The two instances of alliteration in this passage, 'Sarah Siddons' and 'Pulitzer Prize', are indicative of a voice produced through a process of physical restraint and economy. In each case, the alliterative letters are sounded out to make the alliteration felt: the 's's are appropriately sibilant and the 'p's pop lightly. The effort expended on each letter is evenly distributed to ensure the clarity of the alliteration. The 's's and 'p's are also not dwelt on excessively, however. Care is taken, for example, to allow for a light roll of the tongue that is heard in the 'r' of Sarah and to give space for each syllable of 'Pulitzer' to be sounded out in a flowing manner rather than being dominated by a popping 'p'.

The voice does provide evidence of a body producing it, therefore, but it is one that is highly disciplined: sensuously speaking, it does not give much of itself away even though, in an expository sense, it is promising to reveal all. Even the 'faltering' that follows shortly after this passage is a highly deliberate one: after the words 'Pulitzer Prize', Addison continues: '. . . and those awards presented annually by that, er, film society'. The 'er' here is heard not as an interruption of the flow of the sentence but, rather, as a strategically placed sound that provides a springboard for the words that follow. It marks the 'film society' as something Addison is too good for (he can hardly bear to say the words) rather than indicating a weakness in his oratorical style.

Overall in this passage, there is an evenness of spacing between words, a careful control of vocal pacing and clipped quality to the phrasing, which bear witness to a disciplined body working its vocal organs as economically as possible. The qualities evident here are ones that mark the 'default' delivery of Addison's voice-over throughout the film.

The voice-over is accompanied by non-diegetic music and this exhibits a sensitivity and delicacy that are not generally features of Addison's voice. Addison's introduction of the film's main characters and the theatrical milieu is, as I have indicated, relentless and precise, and these give it an overall quality of coldness. The music is complementary to the voice-over in the sense that its characteristics change as we are introduced to new players and/or situations in the fictional world. This helps to cement the authority of Addison as a narrator the viewer is relying on to guide them through this new environment: the music responds to Addison's promptings in a similar way to the image. The music, however, demonstrates a lightness of touch and ability to acquire different textures, as it responds to the different stages of Addison's narration, that are quite distinct from the remorseless sense of calculation embodied in Addison's voice.

The introduction of Margo provides an example of the contrast between the voice-over's (almost) one-note relentlessness and the music's nimbleness and textural variation. The film cuts to the first view of Margo as Addison begins to talk about her:

> Margo Channing is a star of the theatre. She made her first appearance at the age of four in *Midsummer Night's Dream*. She played a fairy and entered, quite unexpectedly, stark naked. She has been a star ever since.

While the voice-over here is delivered with characteristic precision and an evenness of tone, the music is composed of three distinct phases, each with its own pattern of rise and fall and combination of different kinds of sound. In the first phase, up until '*Midsummer Night's Dream*', a solitary woodwind figure, introduced on Margo's first appearance, is thickened by an array of swelling strings. The music changes quite abruptly as Addison discloses the details of her first stage appearance, through the line 'she played a fairy and entered, quite unexpectedly, stark naked'. This is accompanied by a short phase of twinkling percussion, with singular notes played on woodwind sounding out between. There is then a return to strings but these sound less tangled than before, a thinner high-pitched melody prominent over a muted but solid bank of strings.

The music is not antagonistic towards the content of the voice-over here. The introduction of strings provides a romantic swell that underlines that we are in the presence of a star, just as Addison tells us. The anecdote about her unusual debut as a child is marked by music that takes on child-like qualities of simplicity and brightness (sharp twinkles instead of romantic swells). The music, however, does strike a contrast to the timbre and inflection of Addison's voice. It displays a variation of texture and a sensitivity to the changing phases of the voice-over that are absent in the speech it accompanies which delivers each of its statements in a uniform manner. This may suggest that Addison's ability to command a broad authority over the representation of the depicted space comes at the cost of a more nuanced and sensitive responsiveness to his environment.

It is commonplace to understand non-diegetic music in a film as being able to provide sensations and to evoke feeling in a way that speech cannot. As Claudia Gorbman notes, it is music's 'freedom from the explicitness of language' that helps it perform its overarching semiotic and psychological roles.[27] As such, further evidence needs to be offered to demonstrate that a purposeful distinction between Addison's voice-over and the music is being proposed in this scene. This comes in the transition to Karen's voice-over which follows directly on from Addison's and which quickly leads to a change of scene as her recollection of her first verbal encounter with Eve is visualised.

Karen's voice-over is of a different nature from Addison's, rhetorically and materially. Whereas Addison's voice-over looks outwards, commenting on other characters and even acknowledging the presence of the film viewer (with the address to 'you'), Karen's offers an interior perspective. Her voice-over begins 'when was it? How long? It seems like a lifetime ago', indicating that her narration articulates the retrieval of personal memories rather than offering a more distanced overview of the situation like Addison's.

There is a natural difference between the material qualities of Addison's and Karen's voices, given that they are clearly the product of two distinct performers. Beyond this, the difference becomes a meaningful relationship within the fictional world because the voices are introduced side by side in circumstances that are similar (both are heard as non-diegetic narration) and unusual (Hollywood films – of any era – have very rarely begun with a relay of voice-overs). This foregrounding of their voices encourages a comparison to be made between them, and one result of this is that the viewer's experience of Karen's voice sharpens an appreciation of the distinctive qualities of Addison's. This works the other way, too, of course, but, for the purposes of this analysis, I am concentrating on Addison's characterisation.

Gender is an obvious marker of difference, and there is a sense that the contrasting mode of address in each voice-over is governed by familiar associations of men with public activity and women with the private sphere: Addison speaks on behalf of the characters around him at the awards ceremony whereas Karen's voice-over is framed as an intimate reflection on a private meeting. This does not mean, however, that the comparison between the two characters' voice-overs simply confirms the patriarchal authority of Addison. In fact, the contrast between the material qualities of the two passages of voice-over serves to undermine Addison's authority.

Karen's vocal delivery is much softer than Addison's and this allows a certain breathiness to be apparent as part of the voice's texture. This is indicated by the gentle trailing off of 'long', when she says 'how long?', and the open sound of 'now' when she says 'it's June now'. It is marked most clearly by the audible drawing of breath Karen makes before the line, 'Lloyd always said that in the theater a lifetime was a season and a season a lifetime'. This is a longer sentence than she has previously delivered and, through its repetition in reverse of a particular phrase, possesses a sing-song quality. Karen needs to enact a change of gear to tackle this line, and the viewer is allowed to hear the bodily sound that indicates that changing of gears. By contrast, as I have already observed, Addison's one moment of hesitation, the 'er' before 'film society', is presented as a calculated faltering for a sardonic effect. There is air around Karen's voice-over, and this brings into sharper focus the airlessness of Addison's.

The non-diegetic music that accompanies Karen's voice is attracted to the qualities of openness apparent in both the content and materiality of her voice-over (the voice reveals her thoughts and the air that pushes through her body). Whereas the music fidgets restlessly in the face of Addison's relentless vocal delivery, it is much more settled in relation to Karen. The movement to her voice-over is accompanied by the introduction of a simple seven-note woodwind melody, played lightly, which is repeated with minimal variation and then gives way to a more undulating melody, still played on the same instrumentation. When the image moves from a close up of Karen in reverie to the street scene she is remembering, the score is taken up by a swooning string melody that displays the same lightness of touch as the woodwind. The music is much more consistently in harmony with Karen's voice than it is with Addison's in both its dramatic application (it changes significantly only when the image changes) and its material qualities (both music and voice are 'airy').

The parting of the ways between Addison's voice-over and the non-diegetic score is made purposeful through its comparison with the harmony between music and Karen's voice-over that immediately succeeds it. The music responds organically to a voice that, through its breathiness, is also attributed organic qualities. By contrast, it achieves a certain distance from a voice that does not carry these markers of a living, breathing body and which is, instead, from the very first line, associated with the written word. The music might be said to back away from the inhuman calculation that is a feature of Addison's voice. In this way, the initial characterisation of Addison through music is a comparatively unflattering one, suggesting that the viewer may, like the music, want to keep its distance in terms of the belief he or she invests in his words.

In summary, the 'default' material quality of Addison's voice-over is its clipped precision which minimises the sense of a human body working to produce it. The dominant relationship between his voice and the non-diegetic music is one that plays off the music's nimble lightness of touch against Addison's relentless calculation. With these qualities and relationships established as a frame, any moments of deviation from this pattern become extremely significant.

The deviation comes on certain occasions when Addison mentions Eve's name. He does so nine times during the passage of voice-over under review and, in many of these instances, the vocal delivery is consistent with the voice-over's dominant clipped quality. For example, the first mention of her name accompanies a visual return to the award that is awaiting delivery to its winner. As the camera moves closer towards the plaque bearing her name, Addison says 'no brighter light has ever dazzled the eye than Eve Harrington', her name intoned with the utmost clarity, as if Addison were the master of ceremonies announcing the award. This 'clean' articulation of her name occurs whenever Addison is discussing, as here, the public face of Eve ('Eve the cover girl, the girl next door') or when he is promising the viewer that more information about her will be forthcoming ('but more about Eve later, all about Eve in fact').

There are also occasions, however, when Addison mentions her name without the pretext that he is doing so to inform the viewer about her. In fact, the first 'gratuitous' mention of her name immediately succeeds the precise 'reading' of her full name. Addison follows this with a much throatier 'Eve' that sounds out on its own rather than forming part of a new sentence. The same timbral quality is apparent when Addison's voice-over returns. This occurs after a passage of diegetic sound featuring the speech of the man who presents Eve with her award. Immediately before the return of the voice-over, the end of the speech triggers a sustained round of applause. The high-pitched, sharp quality of the clapping is suddenly silenced and replaced with Addison's low-pitched, relatively guttural intonation of 'Eve'. At the same time, the image goes into freeze-frame thereby exacerbating the sense that this is a sound to be savoured. This is a brief pause in Addison's relent-less vocal delivery, the dominant style of which is then reasserted for nearly twenty seconds, as the film cuts to a medium close-up of Addison that is used recurringly throughout the sequence. The return to the freeze-frame image, however, also involves another interruption of the dominant vocal style, again through a gratuitous, throaty rendition of Eve's name.

Three times in the opening passage of voice-over, then, Addison's voice provides evidence of an otherwise suppressed body. This suggests a carnality in Addison's attitude towards Eve that disturbs the dominant presentation of him as a sardonic and dispassionate chronicler of the events that led to her rise to fame. At least in the first two throaty iterations of her name, the music also exhibits a different relationship to Addison's voice-over than is apparent overall: Addison's first throaty 'Eve' is supported sincerely by rising strings, voice and music each 'swelling' as Addison's self-restraint momentarily slips; the second is also offered as a moment of vocal and musical swelling by virtue of the sudden replacement of shrill, diegetic noise (the applause) with fulsome, non-diegetic sound and by contrast of the 'movement' on the soundtrack to an image that has been abruptly stilled.

Kozloff suggests that Addison's sexual interest in Eve, and his potential untrustworthiness as a narrator, are revealed only towards the end of the film. She comments at one point that 'unfortunately, print cannot duplicate his distinctive tone and inflections'.[28] By attempting to apprehend these qualities, as well as considering Addison's voice within an overall soundscape, including its relationship to music and another voice-over, I am able to suggest that intimations of his carnal desires and his slipperiness as a narrator are present among the first words he speaks.

THE VOICE-OVER AND SOUNDS THAT DO NOT TELL STORIES IN *HAPPY TOGETHER*

The voice-overs in *All About Eve* are given a distinctive space in the film's soundscape, protected from diegetic sound and cushioned by non-diegetic music that never threatens to overwhelm the voice. This is one way textual speech can gain its authority, achieving an audible distance from the diegetic world provided by the images, in a manner that suggests the voice may be understood as measured commentary.

In the opening passage of *All About Eve*, diegetic and non-diegetic soundscapes are set up in opposition to one another but other films have intertwined them. This has the potential to challenge the authority of the voice-over, as other sounds vie for the viewer's attention, and also to affect the viewer's experience of the voice-over's materiality. This upsetting of the usual hierarchy between voice and other sounds was something I experienced by standing next to the side speakers during my visit to the *Disorient* video installation. A similar type of sonic disorientation is audible in the voice-over passages of Wong Kar-Wai's *Happy Together* but it is one that is patterned into the film's fictional world rather than created by the physical movement of the spectator.

The film follows Lai Yiu-Fai (Tony Leung), a Hong Kong resident who breaks up with his same-sex partner, Ho Po-Wing (Leslie Cheung) while on a road trip in Argentina. Fai is heard in voice-over on several occasions, ruminating on the state of his relationship and his current circumstances, pondering over a potential return to Hong Kong and offering comment on the sights and sounds around him. Over the course of the narrative, Fai forms a friendship with a co-worker Chang (Chen Chang) who is also heard, just three times, in voice-over. Despite the infrequency of Chang's voice-over, it is important in foregrounding the material quality of voice as a significant element of the film's world: in fact, all three passages of voice-over from Chang are explicitly about the properties of voice.

Chang functions as an aspirational figure for the restless Fai in terms of the stability he radiates (in Fai's eyes). Fai has come to Argentina in the midst of a relationship that clearly has major problems. His on-off relationship with Po-Wing is mirrored by his vacillations, expressed in voice-over as well as through his actions, over where to base himself, how to relate to his family and how best to live his life in general. Chang, by contrast, seems content in whatever he does and, when Fai visits Chang's family in Taipei on the way home to Hong Kong, he comes to a realisation, expressed in voice-over, as to why this may be:

> Finally, I could see why he's happy running around freely. He has a place where he can always return to. I wonder what will happen when I see my father. We'll see. I take a photo of Chang because I don't know when I'll see him again. What I do know is, if I want to see him I know where I can find him.

These constitute Fai's final words of the film and convey what he has learned from Chang: that he needs to work on his relationships at home if he is going to experience the type of inner freedom he envies in Chang.

Chang's inspirational qualities, in the eyes of the film's protagonist, make his voice-overs worth listening to, offering as they do a particularly intimate insight into an inner peace that Fai covets. In fact, these voice-overs are not just relevant as expressions of a mindset to which the lead character may aspire but also as expressions within the fictional world that advise the viewer on how the narration overall is meant to be read. As such, Chang's voice-overs function as 'rhetorical figures of narrational instruction'[29] in the manner I attributed to the recurring image of the two Hitchcocks in *Double Take*.

Chang does not appear until nearly halfway into the film and is heard before he is fully seen. A close-up of a pair of hands washing dishes is accompanied by a voice-over that begins, 'you can tell it's a kitchen by the sound'. The camera quickly pans up to reveal Chang's face but the fact that this line of voice-over is completed before the face is fully revealed suggests that the voice is particularly privileged in this film. When Chang's face is disclosed, it becomes clear that he has his eyes shut, a gesture that his voice-over intimates is designed to help him tune in more sensitively to the sounds around him: 'listen carefully', he says, 'some people are cooking and some people are arguing. Others are talking or washing up.' The exhortation to listen carefully, along with the closing of his eyes, suggest that the shutting down of one sense

Figure 4.1   *Wong Kar-Wai,* Happy Together *(1997)*

(in this case sight) allows a more concentrated experience of another (here sound).

Apart from the pan that takes up the beginning of the voice-over, the rest of the shot is a still one with Chang's face at its centre in close-up (Figure 4.1). Out of focus, behind his right shoulder, an argument is developing between a kitchen worker and a waiter, with a cook standing behind Chang's left shoulder having to chase after his colleague as he moves threateningly towards the waiter at the back of the frame. On the other side of the frame, also at the back, stands another cook, revealed through the next shot to be Fai talking to Po-Wing. There is a sound bridge between the two shots, with the film 'tuning' in to Fai's conversation ('what are you doing?') during the close up of Chang, thereby prompting a cut to the reverse perspective at the other end of the room, so that the viewer understands where the voice is coming from and to whom it is attached.

The shot of Chang's face is a striking one, playing off a central, focused image of serenity against an unfocused backdrop of bustling and aggressive activity. If Chang is to be viewed as a figure who offers narrational instruction to the viewer, what if his demonstration of listening carefully were to be taken literally, meaning that the viewer shut his or her eyes to tune into the sound? By doing so, the sensory effect of sound as a three-dimensional spatial experience becomes more sharply felt. *Happy Together* makes use of Dolby Digital stereo (2.0), and an array of sounds is spread across the stereo spectrum at this moment: Chang's voice is central and to the fore. It possesses a muffled quality, which suggests its capture within a tight space, and this contrasts with the room echo that is associated with the moment's other sounds. These consist of the clamorous tones of the men arguing, mixed slightly to the left and, just as Chang's voice-over pauses, the voice of Fai, heard, like Chang's, through the central channel but with a greater sense of existing within a diegetic space: it is quieter than the voice-over, pitched at a volume and with a room tone similar to those of the people arguing though also differentiated from them by its position in the stereo mix and its presence as a singular sound rather than one composed of entangling elements.

Completing the soundscape is the sound of crockery and cutlery clattering together as they are being washed, and this is heard as a series of sharp clinks, positioned at the right of the sound mix. These sounds are not dramatically significant in the way the other sounds are: they are not attached to the interiority of a character like Chang's voice-over; they are not the voice of Fai, a sound that has become familiar to the viewer by this point, so that he or she expects him to come into view once his voice is heard. By following Chang's advice to listen carefully, however, the sounds become more 'audible' and take their place as part of a sonic sensory experience which balances shrill human voices clashing with each other with high-pitched noises from inanimate objects that are also coming together. While the central channels *are* taken up by the voices of characters who provide the dramatic focus for the film, in a manner consistent with a vococentric aesthetic that has dominated all sorts of narrative cinema, these are surrounded by other sounds in which the viewer is also encouraged to take an interest: sounds that promise stories that are never told or sounds that have no story to tell in the first place. As such, the viewer is encouraged to understand the fictional world as one that has sights and sounds that are not all 'sucked in' by the centripetal force of narrative.

The coexistence of the characters' voices and voice-overs with other diegetic sounds is emphasised throughout the film. There are nineteen passages of voice-over from Fai and, in all cases, the voice-over is made to compete with diegetic sound. In the overwhelming majority of cases, Fai's voice is a singular, non-diegetic element within a complex diegetic soundscape that adheres to a particular principle of realism. That is to say, whatever the circumstances of their actual production and post-production, the diegetic sounds are presented as though they have simply been captured by a microphone as they spontaneously occurred. This provides a realist texture to the soundtrack that provides a very different context for the post-produced sound – that is, the voice-over – from the 'enclosed' sound world offered by the combination of non-diegetic voice and non-diegetic score in *All About Eve*.

Chang's first voice-over explicitly exhorts the viewer to listen in a particularly attuned manner at the same time as the soundtrack as a whole is organised to encourage a specific type of listening. The film shows it is 'listening to' Chang the next time he explicitly talks about sound, this time in a passage that also encompasses Fai's voice-over. This occurs about twenty minutes after Chang's first voice-over, by which time Fai has had another violent falling-out with Po-Wing and has struck up a friendship with Chang. A young woman comes into the kitchen in which they work to invite Chang out but he declines. When Fai asks him why he turned her down, Chang replies:

> I don't like her voice. I like women's voices to be deep and low. Actually, it depends. Anyway, what I mean is, voices that make my heart beat faster.

As Chang talks about preferring the voice to be deep and low, there is a cut from Fai to a sideshot of Chang which shows him closing his eyes and, as he says 'deep and low', drawing a breath and nodding his head forward. This gives the impression that he is searching for a way to express through his body a sound he cannot actually produce with his voice. This moment, along with his comment that he likes voices that have a physiological impact on him (make his heart beat faster) underline the impression that Chang has a peculiarly intense and physical relationship with sound. This is contrasted to Fai who, when asked by Chang what kind of voice he likes, looks vaguely uncomfortable and replies, 'I don't really care'.

Fai's discomfort can be accounted for in two ways. Earlier, we have seen him look uncomfortable when Chang picks up a phone in the kitchen that has Po-Wing on the other end of the line. We never see Fai talk to Chang about Po-Wing and it is possible that he does not want to disclose the nature of his relationship to him. It is also possible, however, that Fai simply does not really understand the question: he is not attuned to sound in the same intimate way Chang is.

Chang's superior sense of sound is further elaborated upon in the scene that follows immediately afterwards. Chang and Fai are in a noisy bar, a loud, tinny chatter and diegetic music providing an intrusive backdrop to their conversation, making it necessary for each of them to raise their voices. The discussion turns towards Chang's special sensory abilities after he correctly predicts that a fight is about to break out at the other end of the large bar simply by discerning the sound of voices rather than seeing the argument develop. Chang tells Fai that 'you "see" better with your ears. You can pretend to look happy but your voice reveals the truth. You can see everything by listening.'

Two different functions of listening are suggested in Chang's comment and both are encouraged in the viewer by the way sound is presented in this scene. One is narrative orientated: the secrets of a person can be unlocked by

paying attention to his or her voice. The second function is more purely perceptual. Chang suggests 'you can see everything by listening' and the soundtrack is organised as much to reveal a sensory totality through sound as it is to
enhance the viewer's understanding of dramatic situations. Throughout the
previous scene, the clinking of cutlery and cooking equipment, along with a
low buzz of room noise, fill out the stereo soundscape while Chang and Fai
talk. In the bar scene, the conversation which, in isolation, might appear to
articulate one of the film's themes in a rather leaden way, takes place within
a soundscape that appears to contain 'everything': traffic noise coming in
from the street outside; music whose acoustic properties reflect its playing
in a large space through a public-address system which sounds as if it is at
full volume; 'background' chatter that is more invasive than it would be in a
film that is more eager to privilege dialogue designed for a particular dramatic
purpose. In addition, both the music and chatter are subject to a rise and fall,
their course disturbed by the outbreak of the fight. In this way, environmental
sound provides a messy, ever-evolving texture that catches the ear alongside
the conversation between the two lead characters.

At the end of the bar scene, Fai challenges Chang to tell him what people
are saying at the other side of the bar. Though Chang says, 'I'll try' and he
rests his head in his hands as if really concentrating, the film pauses in the
space for some seconds without, however, waiting for Chang's answer. The
effect is to encourage the viewer to enjoy a moment of listening that takes in
'everything' rather than being directed towards a particular dramatic point.

The acceptance of a mode of listening that is as interested in the sensory
qualities of sound as well as the dramatic ones is articulated in Fai's voice-
over that immediately succeeds this moment. The film cuts from the bar to a
daytime scene in which Fai and Chang, among others, are playing football in
the street. The diegetic voices heard here are particularly 'bodily' ones, a player
'oohing' excitedly as he runs with the ball, and a goal provoking loud, ecstatic
cheering. Another layer of vocal noise is added to the soundtrack through the
diegetic presence of a portable radio which carries the tinny sound of what
appears to be the voice of a very excitable sports commentator.

Chang and Fai have a short conversation, with the sounds of the other
players and the radio still present and, while they are still talking, Fai's voice-
over begins. All these diegetic sounds continue to be heard as the voice-over
proceeds. In it, Fai says:

> Chang is the loudest out of all of us. You get hot playing football in the alley.
> This summer seems to be going by so fast.

Fai has been heard six times in voice-over before this moment and, on each
of those occasions, the voice-over had been focused on expository detail or

on the revelation of his feelings about his relationship with Po-Wing. Here, by contrast, the emphasis is on his sensory experience of sound, heat and even of time (attributing a sense of speed to his sensation of time passing). This occurs within a diegetic soundscape that retains its sensuous dimensions even as the voice-over is added to it.

The next voice-over, five minutes later in the film, has a similar emphasis on the sensory. It occurs as Fai says goodbye to Chang who is going off travelling. As they embrace, Fai comments in voice-over:

> Was it because we had become close? When I held him, all I could hear was my own heart beating.

It is as if contact with Chang releases a dormant potential in Fai to experience the world sensuously. Without Chang's physical presence, the rest of Fai's voice-overs revert to exposition and a self-analysis of his character. What his final voice-over reveals, however, is that Fai has learned from Chang that he needs to be 'grounded' to be happy: ('I could see why he's happy running around freely. He has a place where he can always return to'). That this grounding involves a sense of existing sensuously in the world, rather than simply knowing you have a home to go to, is suggested by the decision not to end the film at this point (which would have been a dramatically plausible open ending, leaving the viewer to imagine how Fai's reunion with his father would go). Instead, there is a coda which features a non-diegetic cover version of the 1960s pop song 'Happy Together', playing over speeded-up images of Taipei's travel network at night. The sequence eventually relocates Fai who is seated at the fore of a glass-fronted train (significantly, he is wearing headphones). He turns to look out the window, at which point the film switches to a point-of-view shot looking out from the train, showing the tracks disappearing as it speeds into a station.

This first-person shot is choreographed to the moment in the song where the singer abandons words and instead goes into a phase of 'ba-ba-bas'. This final moment can be interpreted in terms of character psychology: Fai, symbolically speaking, speeding towards the future rather than dwelling on his past with Po-Wing. It can also be considered much more ironically, particularly in the choice of an upbeat heterosexual love song to provide the finale to a film about the falling apart of a gay relationship. It is also, however, for Fai and viewer alike, a 'purely' sensational experience of exuberant sound, dazzling sights and excessive speed. These readings of the moment, I would suggest, are equally plausible and attest to the effect of ambiguity that David Bordwell sees as the hallmark of art cinema narration.[30]

As an English-language pop song in a film featuring Cantonese, Mandarin and Spanish speech, this moment also stands out, suggesting that a precise

Figure 4.2   *Wong Kar-Wai,* Happy Together *(1997)*

comprehension of the lyrics (which, in any case, culminate in the worldless but evocative ba-ba-bas) is less important than other musical qualities. Of the four films discussed in this chapter, only *Happy Together* is not primarily in English and the languages spoken are foreign to me. At one level, this makes my reading of *Happy Together* a rather different experience which does involve literally reading the English subtitles to help me make sense of the spoken word. This suggests a different kind of relationship between sound and image, with the spoken aspects of the soundtrack rendered visible. Figure 4.2 shows the way I experience *Happy Together*, demonstrating that the presence of voice in a particular moment can be indicated in visuals in a way that is not true of any other aspect of the sound discussed in this chapter. This also indicates the privileging of the expository function of voice and dialogue in narrative cinema.

The kind of analysis I develop here, however, is not entirely dependent on linguistic comprehension. Rather, it is about the relationships between different types of sound and their positioning within the fictional world. While Fai's voice-over remains disembodied, I am interested in the ways in which it rubs up against the materiality of diegetic voices which compete for attention in a densely populated soundscape – and more clearly suggest a relationship between voice and body (in their relative breathiness, volume and pace of delivery, for example). It is these relationships that lend a depth to the experience of the film, immersing the viewer (even a 'reading' viewer) in a sensuous film world, establishing a closeness to the characters in which the content of their speech is at times less significant than the effect of its delivery. In its passages of voice-over, the film offers a multilayered aural experience in which the sensory evocation of the sound of a place occurs alongside the use of sound for dramatic purposes. The sensuous presentation of environmental sound does not distract from the voice-over but, equally, it is not completely assimilated into a regime that mines sound for its dramatic significance. The increased sensory awareness of Fai is part of his character's development but the film's incorporation of the voice-over only as part of a three-dimensional soundscape is audible from the very start.

TECHNOLOGY AS TEXTURE: THE SOUND OF MECHANICAL REPRODUCTION IN THE VOICE-OVERS OF *GUMMO*

The inclusiveness of *Happy Together*'s soundtrack allows for the occasional presence of a type of sound usually excised, as far as possible, from the fiction film: that is to say, the noise that lays bare that what we are hearing is the result of an artificial process of recording. In *Happy Together*, this is indicated by the audible wind noise that is produced when capturing sound on location rather than in the controlled circumstances of the studio.

As Andy Birtwistle points out, all film sound carries the traces of the technology that produces and disseminates it:

> Every sound heard in a film bears the trace of technology's sonic signature. If we were to analogise the soundtrack of a film in terms of voice, then the sound of film technology also resides in what Roland Barthes describes as the 'grain' of that voice.[31]

By likening this sonic signature to the grain of the voice, Birtwistle is emphasising the materiality of technology, woven inextricably into the sounds it produces. Equally, however, he admits to the long-standing attempt on the part of the film industry to 'silence cinema's materiality'[32] which, in relation to sound, has taken the form of efforts to improve the 'fidelity' through which sounds are recorded and reproduced. Even in *Happy Together*, the voice-overs themselves are presented quite conventionally, recorded cleanly via close miking, mixed centrally on the stereo spectrum and reproduced in an internally consistent manner that does not carry overt signs of technological mediation. We know, of course, that these are voices that have been captured and reproduced mechanically but the film does not announce them as such. The purposeful augmentation around these 'natural' voices is provided by the other sounds that surround the voice-overs rather than the materiality of the technology being foregrounded within the space of the voice itself.

By contrast, in both my final examples, the technological materiality of the film voice is made audible in a purposeful manner. The analysis that follows, of a scene from *Gummo*, demonstrates how that materiality can help to serve characterisation in the context of a film that is not committed, overall, to principles of narrative coherence.

The systems of narration of *Gummo* are not immediately penetrable. In fact, a number of critics have either celebrated or bemoaned the film's lack of coherence: for example, Benjamin Halligan claims the film has 'no constant'[33] through which the viewer can understand its fidgeting between different types of film and video stock. Korine himself has laid claim to the movie's 'mistake-ist' aesthetic.[34] It is, indeed, the case that the film does not contain a strong narrative line and is wilfully eclectic in terms of the different types of images it uses and, more pertinently to this chapter, in the disconcerting shifts that occur on the soundtrack. The consistent narrative thread, such as it is, revolves around the two main characters, Tummler (Nick Sutton) and Solomon (Jacob Reynolds), who make money killing cats and selling them on to local traders. Their scenes are interspersed with a number of episodes featuring other members of the community.

A variety of film stocks are used in the film: conventional 35 mm, still photographs, scratchy 8 mm, digital video and VHS home video (often refilmed through a video monitor). The soundtrack is just as eclectic, featuring conventional film sound, balanced to ensure dialogue intelligibility, but also a much rougher type of location sound in the video footage in which the dialogue is often indistinct. In addition, non-diegetic music sometimes subdues the on-screen soundtrack entirely, and this music ranges from Buddy Holly and Roy Orbison to a number of death metal bands, as well as a cappella renditions of vernacular folk songs. On occasion there is also the insertion of brief snatches of non-musical sounds that do not emanate from any plausible on-screen source. Finally, there is also quite an extensive use of voice-over, almost exclusively from the two main characters.

Gummo's first sounds indicate two extremes in its treatment of its aural elements. With the company logo of the producers FineLine Features still on-screen, the soundtrack emerges, consisting of the Destroy All Monsters song, 'Mom's and Dad's Pussy'. This continues over the first collection of images, and features the sampling of a girl singing a taunting nursery rhyme. The rhyme starts with the refrain 'peanut butter motherfucker' and continues with the girl calling various people 'a pussy'. As provocative as this combination of child's voice, nursery rhyme singing and profanity may be, what also comes to the viewer's attention is the technology through which the sound is being mediated. The sound has been processed to produce a delay effect which multiples the voice so that it is heard simultaneously with different levels of echo around it saying the same words at different times. The effect is extremely messy rhythmically and also features sonic artefacts that would be avoided in more conventional circumstances: when the girl sings 'moth-erfucker' at its loudest, the voice becomes distorted and there is an audible echoey click elsewhere as if the microphone had been knocked and this had become part of the delay effect. In addition, an occasional murmuring of two male voices can be heard, giving a 'crossed line' effect.

After about thirty seconds, this gives way to a voice that is also evidently technologically treated but to a completely different sensory effect. This voice is produced through extremely sensitive close miking so that the speaker's hushed tones are felt with all their bodily force. Repetition is involved here, too, but it comes from the speaker's own reiteration of his first words, 'Xena, Ohio, Xena, Ohio', rather than through technological processing. The tech-nology is audible in the sense that it is heard to boost a whisper into a forceful aural presence but, in doing so, the technology amplifies, rather than detracts from, the voice's natural laconic properties: the viewer is left with the aural impression of words being dragged slowly up the speaker's throat before finally emerging.

This voice belongs to Solomon, one of the film's protagonists. The exces-sively close miking, audible in the non-diegetic appearances of the voice, gives the voice-over a special status in relation to this character. The other protago-nist, Tummler, is also heard in voice-over and, in these instances, his voice tends to carry the signs of technological interference rather than a technology that boosts its organic properties. In other words, Tummler's voice-over has more in common materially with the sound of the first seconds of the film than it does with Solomon's. The contrast between the two voice-overs is significant: they are heard side by side in one particular scene and it is on this that I shall concentrate.

The passage occurs about an hour into the film and features a collage of visual and aural elements that is in keeping with the film's chaotic aesthetic overall. It begins with Tummler reciting a suicidal monologue that begins: 'Dear world, I have confusion running in every direction from my brain. I've tried and tried to make it here in this fucking world, but I think it was a mistake that I was ever born.' This is spoken as synchronised speech, with the viewer shown a shaky close-up image of Tummler which appears to have been refilmed through a monitor. As the monologue continues in similarly suicidal vein, however, synchronisation is abandoned in favour of a montage of different close-ups of Tummler who is running his hands through his hair in a distressed way. Synchronised sound returns, suddenly and briefly, as a close-up shows Tummler with his finger pointed to his temple saying, 'I'll put a gun to my fucking head right now'.

The montage then moves to seemingly completely unrelated footage that mixes material culled from a video by the heavy metal band, Slayer, and other shots of what appears to be some kind of satanic ritual. This is accompanied non-diegetically by a ferocious track by black metal band, Mystifier. There is then another shift to refilmed (mainly) monochrome images of a group of men being interviewed, the subject of discussion again appearing to be something to do with the occult. Between the two snippets of interview that we are allowed to hear, the images of the men continue but are soundtracked by the voice of Solomon, who says: 'Life is beautiful, really it is. Full of beauty and illusions. Life is great. Without it, you'd be dead.'

On the face of it, it is difficult to credit the monologue/voice-over of Tummler and the voice-over proper of Solomon as emanations of their characters, a function conventionally attributed to the voice-over and evidenced, in different ways, in the examples from *All About Eve* and *Happy Together*. Tummler's monologue is reminiscent of an earlier passage featuring him delivering a similarly pessimistic and misanthropic speech, visualised through a similar quality of image and, in fact, making use of exactly the same shot on one occasion. Neither monologue, however, stems logically from what we have seen of his character in the more overtly narrative-driven segments of the film up to this point: that is to say, the 35 mm film sequences featuring Tummler and Solomon. In these, Tummler is not depicted as being suicidal. Similarly Solomon's voice-over does not fit what we have seen of his character on-screen: the eloquence and worldly wisdom of the monologue do not tally with the thirteen-year old boy – who says very little at all on-screen throughout the movie – we see in the 35 mm filmed sequences.

So, on the surface, the voice-over testimony cannot be trusted as a reliable indicator of the state of mind of the character speaking it. In addition, as I have observed, the focus of this extract intermittently shifts away from the main characters, with the insertion of images and sounds that are seemingly unrelated to the voice-overs.

Through the narrative irrelevance of the voice-overs and the interruption of other kinds of sound, the soundtrack can be seen to help the film slip away from any type of narrative centre – instead, it helps it construct what Benjamin Halligan calls a 'psycho-geographical' point of view whereby image and sound 'give in' to the environment being depicted.[35] Solomon's opening voice-over tells the viewer that the town in which it is set had been hit by a tornado and, under Halligan's reading, the extremely fragmented soundtrack and images are the debris from which the viewer has to reconstruct the shattered environment for themselves. So the severely scrambled nature of sound (including the voice-overs) and image is meaningful in terms of the mapping out of a certain wrecked milieu but not in relation to the twin disciplines of enlightening the viewer about the situations of the film's nominal lead characters or of supporting dramatic developments.

There is also a sense that the film is deliberately presenting a set of images and sounds that is simply too much for the viewer to take in. Caryl Flinn discusses the use of sound as a kind of 'shock' in the films of the New German Cinema, a shock that cannot be fully absorbed.[36] This seems to have some application to *Gummo*, which may not be surprising as Harmony Korine has consistently named New German Cinema director Werner Herzog as his major film-making influence.[37] In this sequence, there is a discernible excess of sound: Tummler's voice keeps detaching itself from its bodily source as it moves from a diegetic presence, to voice-over, and back to the diegesis again; the death metal track cuts brutally into the ambient soundtrack which has insinuated itself under Tummler's monologue but then suffers its own abrupt exit as the ambient track re-establishes itself under the video footage of two young men explaining away their involvement in some sort of satanic ritual. Here, then, sound is experienced as a kind of sensory overload of which the voice-over simply becomes another element. This differs from the example of *Happy Together* which consists of voice-overs that do have a discernible relationship to the dramatic situations of the characters who voice them and to the images they accompany, both in terms of the qualities of the voices and the content of their speech. The other aural elements which accompany the voice-overs in *Happy Together* make the soundscape more complex but the effect is of sensory abundance rather than overload.

In these ways, voice-over can be seen as part of a soundtrack that helps to map out a milieu more than it supports characterisation or story; and the voice-over also forms part of a 'shocking' aural experience marked by sensory excess rather than a refinement around particular dramatic situations. The voice-overs, however, are not completely inarticulate in terms of presenting Tummler and Solomon as distinct figures within a fictional world. There *is* some internal thematic continuity between the voice-overs of each character across the film. More importantly for the purposes of this chapter, characterisation is also supported by the development of the technological texture of the voices across the extract.

The voice-overs of each character are not evidently consistent with their on-screen behaviour in other parts of the film but they do have a sense of continuity and individuality in themselves. Tummler's voice-overs (of which there are seven) tend to stress their own sense of performance while Solomon's (of which there are five) are more reflective and less self-aggrandising. In the sequence under review, Tummler is shown looking down as he begins the monologue, suggesting that he is reading from a script. Solomon's voice-over is more hushed, and combines with images of other people, qualities shared with all his other voice-overs. Both monologues have a strained poetic quality to them and both can be seen as consistent with the attempts of performance or reflection on the part of Tummler and Solomon that occur regularly on the soundtrack in the film, and which are only allowed fleeting expression in the more story-oriented episodes in which they feature.

In this way, the voice-overs can be interpreted as acts of imagination on the part of the main two characters. This is a way of understanding the voice-overs as revealing another side to the characters rather than considering them as deliberately estranged from what we know about them. In this interpretation, the insertion of 'outside' video footage between these voice-overs represents something of the cultural milieu in which their imaginations are stimulated. The extent to which their imaginations are subject to external mediation is also made apparent at the material level of the sound through the way even their 'inner voices' acquire technological textures.

Two types of technological noise are associated with Tummler's voice: it sounds unnaturally tinny, missing the bassier tones you would expect to experience were you to encounter the voice in real life. This could be a product of the original recording process of the voice, of its re-recording through the refilming process, of post-production tinkering, or a combination of all three. In any case, the end result is a voice that bears the markers of its mechanical reproduction rather than trying to efface them. The second noise is a continuous hiss which, like the tinniness, could have been produced in a number of different ways, the key point being that it is deliberately not filtered out by the film's Dolby Digital stereo process even though Dolby was invented precisely to reduce this kind of noise.

The interruption of the monologue/voice-over with the death metal track by Mystifier leads to these technological textures disappearing from the soundtrack, the song existing in a non-diegetic soundscape that does not draw attention to the materiality of the sound's recording or reproduction processes. The hiss re-emerges briefly upon the introduction of the documentary footage of a young man being interviewed but is conspicuously faded down when Solomon's voice-over begins. At this point, the extreme close-miking effect, apparent for all of Solomon's voice-overs, amplifies the material qualities of his voice so that the viewer hears the breath he takes between each clause as well as the words themselves. Whereas the sonic signature of technology seems to rob Tummler's voice of some of its natural properties, Solomon's undergoes a process of technological enhancement, with the technology appearing to dissolve into the voice, giving it a special power.

The aural montage of this sequence moves from a position where the addition of technological textures to the mix produces an impoverished voice, in terms of its human characteristics, to one where the technology is felt as an enhancement of the voice's body. Mediating between the two texturally different types of voice-over is the death metal track, a piece of culture that is, like the voice-overs, made possible through the mechanical recording and reproduction of sound. This track is presented neutrally in the sense that the technology involved in repurposing its sound for this particular moment is effaced. As such, it becomes, in its technological texture as well as its musical content, part of the 'natural' material that constructs the culture which inspires these characters' imaginative lives. Benjamin Halligan observes that *Gummo*'s 'characters are defined by the commercial categories of "difference" that are on offer; they are products of the cultural assimilation of the left-of-field'.[38]

The definition of the characters through a technologically mediated consumer culture is so ingrained that technology finds expression in their physical beings, including their voices: understood in this way, the different kinds of sonic signature audible in Tummler's and Solomon's voice-overs distinguish them as characters existing within this culture, both influenced by it but responding in different ways. In this sense, this signature resonates as a 'shock' that *is* absorbed, registered as part of the sound that each body produces.

Andy Birtwistle suggests that the drone-like quality of film or video ground noise ('undesirable noise inherent in reproduced sound')[39] has the following properties: 'This sound of technology is non-directional, and non-narrative, in the sense that it neither supports narrative nor demonstrates any internal development.'[40]

Heard on its own, this is undoubtedly true but *Gummo* provides an example where the 'drone', here associated with Tummler's monologue/voice-over, is placed alongside other technological textures in a manner that does express something of the place of characters within a fictional world, even if it is not a world that supports a linearly constructed narrative.

THE HEAVENLY 'ACOUSMATIC' VOICE-OVER AND THE EARTHY EMANATIONS OF THE DIEGETIC VOICE: THE SINGING OF 'WISE UP' IN *MAGNOLIA*

The final example of this chapter brings together a number of the concerns that have been addressed in the preceding analyses. P. T. Anderson's multi-strand narrative *Magnolia* features a very unusual moment (at least in a non-musical, feature-length fiction film) in which all the major characters, despite being in separate locations, sing along to the song 'Wise Up', by Aimee Mann, which can be heard playing non-diegetically throughout the sequence. As I shall suggest, Mann acts as a voice-over narrator here, as she does when her songs are heard in other parts of the film (in fact, P. T. Anderson claims that various narrative situations in the film were inspired by Mann's songs which pre-existed the writing of the script).[41] Never given an on-screen source, Mann's voice is, to use Michel Chion's oft-cited term, an acousmatic one. Chion bestows mysterious powers upon the acousmatic voice which distinguish it from the voice-over of characters who are represented on-screen (as has been the case in the three previous examples):

> A sound or voice that remains acousmatic creates a mystery of the nature of its source, its properties and its powers, given that causal listening cannot supply complete information about the sound's nature and the events taking place.[42]

The exercising of power on the part of Mann's voice is evidenced by its partial 'possession' of the on-screen characters who seem compelled to try to match up to her singing. The purpose of my analysis is to consider the significance of the gap between the characters' vocal performances and Mann's. In so doing, I pay particular attention to the material qualities of each voice, to the moments where sound as an emanation of body becomes key to understanding the weighting of different elements within the film's fictional world.

The film follows the stories of nine characters through the course of a day in the San Fernando Valley. The lives of these characters intertwine at various points without coalescing around one particular narrative event. The 'Wise Up' montage occurs more than two hours into the three-hour movie. It shows the characters each taking stock of their situation which has reached a traumatic pitch for them all and acts as a moment of reflection before the film moves to its closing stages. Figures 4.3–4.11 summarise the state of play for each character as the 'Wise Up' sequence begins.

In a sprawling, multicharacter narrative like *Magnolia*, it might seem necessary to have moments like these where the situations of all the different characters are encompassed within a single sequence to suggest the resonances between them. Indeed, all the scenes featuring voice-over in *Magnolia*, musical or not, work to establish thematic parallels between the disparate episodes. For example, the film is bookended by a voice-of-God narrator relating a series of events that revolve around unlikely connections, a theme that is then pursued in the main body of the narrative. In the 'Wise Up' sequence, there is something about the synchronisation of the dramatic temperature in each character's story that suggests a connection between them: all of them have just suffered personal crises and are preparing themselves for further traumas to come. There is also a number of shared camera movements and similarities in the organisation of *mise en scène* in each episode that suggest links between the characters. For the purpose of this chapter, however, the most significant resonances occur between the song and each character's attempts to sing his or her allocated section of it.

Figure 4.3   *Paul Thomas Anderson,* Magnolia *(1999):* Claudia

Sung Line: [Aimee Mann only: It's not what]. . . you thought, when you first began it, you got what you want, but you can hardly stand it though, but now you know, it's not going to stop

Situation: Tortured by relationship with sexually abusive father (quiz show host Jimmy); shredded with nerves at prospect of date with cop Jim.

Figure 4.4   *Paul Thomas Anderson,* Magnolia *(1999):* Jim

Sung line: It's not going to stop, it's not going to stop, 'til you wise . . . [Aimee Mann only: up]

Situation: At crisis point in job as cop after losing gun in a chase.

Figure 4.5   *Paul Thomas Anderson,* Magnolia *(1999):* Jimmy

Sung line: You're sure there's a cure, and you have finally found it

Situation: Back home after collapsing on his last appearance as quiz show host; recently diagnosed with terminal cancer.

Figure 4.6 *Paul Thomas Anderson,* Magnolia *(1999): Donnie*

Sung Line: You think one drink will shrink you 'til you're underground and living down, but it's not going to stop

Situation: Scarred in adult life by being known as the child prodigy who won the quiz show Jimmy hosts years back; preparing to raid the safe at the workplace from which he has just been fired.

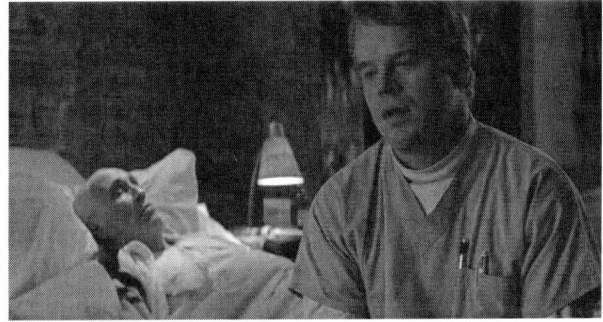

Figure 4.7 *Paul Thomas Anderson,* Magnolia *(1999): Phil*

Sung line: It's not going to stop, it's not going to stop [with Earl also audible on second line]

Situation: Just administered a fatal dose of morphine to the terminally ill Earl.

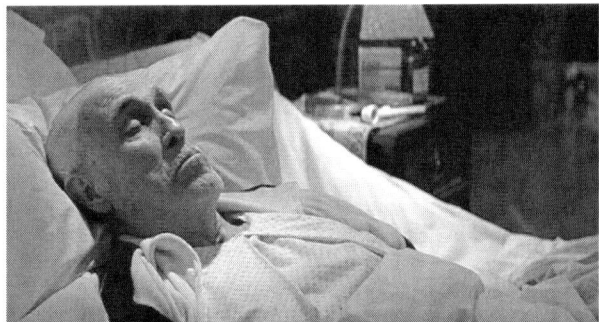

Figure 4.8 *Paul Thomas Anderson,* Magnolia *(1999): Earl*

Sung line: 'Til you wise up

Situation: About to die after a long emotional speech full of regrets for the mistakes he has made through his life.

Figure 4.9   *Paul Thomas Anderson,* Magnolia *(1999): Linda*

Sung Line: Prepare a list for what you need, before you sign away the deed, 'cos it's not going to stop

Situation: Just taken overdose, knowing that her husband Earl is about to die.

Figure 4.10   *Paul Thomas Anderson,* Magnolia *(1999): Frank*

Sung line: It's not going to stop, it's not going to stop 'til you wise up, no it's not going to stop, 'til you wise up, no it's not going to stop

Situation: About to meet long-estranged father Earl on his death bed.

Figure 4.11   *Paul Thomas Anderson,* Magnolia *(1999): Stanley*

Sung line: So just give up

Situation: Seeking solace in the public library after humiliating himself on the quiz show hosted by Jimmy.

The song begins and the characters find themselves singing along as if they have no other choice but to do so. This very notion, that the characters 'fall in helplessly' to the melody and words of the song, sets Mann up as a kind of guide for the characters. This casts Mann as a particularly intervening voice-over narrator: the characters sing only because she prompts them to do so. There is a sense that the characters are being lifted out of their immediate situations and allowed to gain an understanding of their lives which can be sustained only at the moment of their singing. They may claim, through the song, to know that each needs to 'wise up' but the wisdom is only borrowed momentarily from the singer who is feeding them the words: after this sequence each character plunges into the various crises that form the climax of the film, as if the 'lesson' Mann has taught them has been forgotten.

A particularly distinctive aspect of the scene is the way the characters' voices attempt a more and more accurate impersonation of Mann's as the sequence develops. Mann's voice exhibits a 'polish' that is a sign of her professionalism as an experienced singer. Its pristine quality is also an indicator of a technological treatment of voice designed to showcase, as effectively and unobtrusively as possible, her handling of the lyric.

Initially, by contrast, the characters' voices sound much less composed: the bodily grain in each voice, the hesitations or the 'mistakes' with vocal phrasing all register each character's lack of musical professionalism but also a general absence of poise – understandable, considering their traumatised states at this point in the narrative. In this way, the film makes use of the expressive possibilities of 'artless singing' which Claudia Gorbman claims is often marked by

> the imperfections in the voice – breathiness, faltering and quavering, false notes, singing out of comfortable range, pauses, forgotten or mistaken lyrics – that equate amateurishness with authenticity, and that make of the singing a natural and sincere expression of the character.[43]

In truth, of course, as performers in a film, the actors' voices are as subject to careful recording and technological rendering as Mann's but, within the economy of the film's fictional world, a contrast between the measured, smooth vocals of Mann and the more rough-edged, bodily delivery of the characters is both suggested and made significant.

In the singing of the first six characters, at least, the distinction between the 'professional' voice-over and 'artless' on-screen voice is kept apparent. Claudia (Melora Walters) has to catch up with the words and melody after snorting a line of coke through its first phrases; Jim's (John C. Reilly) lower male voice immediately suggests a difference from Mann's higher female voice and the difference is accentuated when Jim fails to sing 'up', the last word of the chorus. Jimmy (Philip Baker Hall) follows with a brusque and gravelly rendition of his lines which fall out of sync with the guiding voice on the soundtrack; Donnie (William H. Macy) makes a better stab at following the melody which has reached a more undulating phase (the line 'you're underground and living down') but his delivery is mumbled: he is hunched over the kitchen table in a pose not conducive to clear vocal performance. The discrepancy between on-screen vocal performance and off-screen voices reaches its high point in the singing of Phil (Philip Seymour Hoffman), the nurse, and Earl (Jason Robards), the dying man: here Aimee Mann's vocals are augmented by soothing backing harmonies but this is contrasted with the movement from Phil to Earl who, just as the backing emerges, offers the most *croaky* on-screen performance thus far.

Up to this point, then, the on-screen voices interact with the off-screen voice in two ways simultaneously: on the one hand, the on-screen performers' attempts to reproduce the words and melody of the song are highly stylised and suggest a momentary disruption of their characters' realist integrity. To this extent, the performances do not fit with Gorbman's conception of artless singing, instances of which are 'perceived as integral parts of the "realistic" diegetic world'.[44] Instead, by singing along, the characters are lifted towards the same distanced commentary position as Mann's narrator. At the same time, however, this aural process of stepping out of the role is not completed: the mistakes each performer makes in their act of imitation differentiates them from both each other and from Mann's guiding voice, allowing their characters to retain a sense of individual personality. Despite the potential Brechtian distance that might be suggested in this moment – a non-musical in which the characters suddenly burst into synchronised song – there remains a sense that the performers are still being true to their fictional roles: these characters are too immersed in their own situations to be completely abandoned in the impersonation of the song.

In the final phase of this sequence, however, the professional voice of Mann and the relatively artless voices of the characters come much closer together. In terms of its proximity to Mann's singing, Linda (Julianne Moore) produces the 'purest' rendition of the song: her voice is closest in terms of pitch and she follows the melody precisely. Frank (Tom Cruise) clearly does not possess the same similarity of vocal tone but there is a clarity of attack and synchronisation of melody with Mann's rendition that is not apparent in the more hesitant performances we have heard before Linda. Finally, the coda of the song, which deflates the positive message of the title by suggesting we should 'just give up' rather than 'wise up', is covered by the child character, Stanley (Jeremy Blackman): his young, high-pitched voice approximates Mann's more closely than do the voices of the other male characters in the scene. In addition, Stanley's slightly off-key rendition of the final 'just' before 'give up' is not an indication of his voice's frailty compared to Mann's off-screen voice, as is the case with the 'mistakes' made by the on-screen singers earlier on. In fact, Stanley is simply attempting to match the faltering of Mann's own performance at this point which can be taken as a deliberate cracking of the singer's poise as the attempts to remain positive enacted by the song – there might be hope if you wise up – give way to pessimism: you might just as well give up.

The 'Wise Up' sequence presents an ordered interaction between Mann's voice-over and the on-screen voices of the characters who find themselves singing along with her. The overall effect of the scene is highly stylised: the characters react to the music rather than the music reacting to the on-screen action as is more normally expected of the relationship between film music and on-screen events outside the musical. Within this stylised situation, however, the interaction between off-screen and on-screen voices undergoes a deliberate progression: an initial stage where the individual qualities of each character still fight for attention through their voices which only partially succumb to the off-screen voice that begins to possess them; by the end of the sequence, however, the characters' voices have become less individuated, with the bum note from Stanley an attempted replica of the one already performed by Mann. The professional voice of the trained singer and artless voice of the child character imitate each other, both faltering vocally as the song runs out of any optimism it may have had. By the end of the scene, Stanley has become a pessimistic observer of his own situation, sharing the commentary role adopted by Mann. Stanley's voice loses its status as an emanation of individual character, becoming absorbed instead into a voice marked by the control associated with textual speech at its most poised: a voice existing in a 'closed' non-diegetic soundscape, cushioned by music and revealing of its body in only the most deliberate ways (Mann's final faltering is a knowing twist on a line and melody that we have already heard her sing a number of times before).

In this sequence, the different categories of speech identified by Chion – textual, theatrical and emanation – are intermingled. The textual speech, in the particularly powerful form of Mann's acousmatic voice, exerts its authority by calling up characters at will and 'commanding' them to sing along to her tune. The physical stillness with which the characters sing along, however, concentrates attention on to their vocal performances, thereby transforming their singing into a kind of theatrical speech: as monologue that has a 'dramatic, psychological, informative, and affective function'.[45] Furthermore, though the delivery of the song may be wholly intelligible, like theatrical speech, this is accompanied by different kinds of faltering which function as emanations of the body of the voice being heard. It is in these moments of emanation that the distinctiveness of the characters remains intact, even as they are all being brought under the umbrella of Mann's musical narration.

This sequence from *Magnolia* works as a kind of tableau. A melodramatic form, Jacob Smith defines the tableau in the following way:

> The tableau was the moment when characters on the stage would freeze, arranging themselves in a composition meant to highlight the emotional and moral dimensions of the action, in the process creating a 'visual summary of the emotional situation' and a 'resolution of meaning'.[46]

Relating this observation to sound, specifically through the example of early twentieth-century phonograph parodies of stage melodrama, Smith notes: 'The goal of the tableau, to make inner moral and character essentials evident in a particularly vivid manner, is achieved on these records through freezing the voice in terms of tone and timbre.'[47]

In the example from *Magnolia*, the tone and timbre of voices are also made central to the summarising of the emotional situation but the frozen voice, which can be equated to Mann's non-diegetic vocals, is made to interact with voices that reveal themselves through their capacity for unpredictable movement, sometimes resembling Mann's guide vocals but just as often not. As such, the material frailty of the 'readings' of Mann's song is just as, if not more, significant in revealing character in *Magnolia* than what is being sung. In this way, my approach towards the sequence is different from Pauline Reay's who considers the relevance to a character's dramatic situation of the particular line they are given to vocalise.[48] While this is, of course, a legitimate area of focus, the driver behind the analyses in this chapter has been to make meaning of the quality of voices rather than the facts of the words they deliver.

In addition, I have stressed the need to consider the voice-over in relation to other soundtrack elements rather than in isolation. In fact, the evolving nature of the relationship between diegetic and non-diegetic voices in the 'Wise Up' sequence calls into question the appropriateness of using the term 'voice-over' to describe Mann's singing. The 'over' suggests a fixedness of positioning and dominance to her voice that is not sufficient in describing the dynamic way it weaves through the on-screen characters' voices. The term is descriptive of an audio-visual relationship (the voice *is* heard over the images) but proves inadequate when considering the relationship between the disembodied voice and other sounds. Heard from this perspective, Addison's and Karen's voices at the start of *All About Eve* do resonate as voice-overs, heard on top of other soundtrack elements, whereas Mann's is heard as a 'voice-under', providing a guide track for the diegetic characters' voices. The disembodied voices of *Happy Together* are neither under nor over other sounds but, rather, in the midst of them. The weave of sound between the voice-overs and other aural elements in *Gummo* varies from moment to moment but one constant is the inextricable entwining of each voice with its technologically produced sonic signature.

One proposal resulting from the preceding analyses is that it would be desirable for the image-centric term 'voice-over' to be overhauled so that it is used only in the context of an investigation of voice that is sensitive to a film's total soundscape: were it to be repurposed in this way, it would be just one of a number of possible descriptions to indicate how a disembodied voice contributes to the sonic texture of a moment. It is as part of the overall sonic texture that the individual characteristics of a voice are felt. In the fiction film, the sound design is fixed in a way that distinguishes it as an aural sensory experience from an installation like *Disorient* in which aural texture and the positioning of the voice within the soundscape are subject to a good deal of control from the perceiver. It is precisely the deliberateness, however, with which one sound is oriented to another (as well as to particular aspects of the image) that makes it possible for the viewer to discern the significance of those sounds in relation to the situations and characters of the film's fictional world.

Notes

1. For a 'classic' academic discussion of cinema's vococentrism, see Doane, 'Ideology and the practices of sound editing and mixing', in Belton and Weis (eds), *Film Sound: Theory and Practice*, pp. 54–62.
2. Writing specifically about sound highlights the visual bias inherent in the term 'viewer'. I retain the term purely as a matter of convention, in keeping with many other critics who have written about film sound (or, for that matter, film as a multidimensional sensory experience). Given the nature of this chapter, it should be self-evident that I understand listening as an integral part of film viewing, even on those rare occasions where it is silence that is being listened to.
3. Thomas, *Reading Hollywood: Spaces and Meanings in American Film*, pp. 111–12.
4. Branigan, 'Sound and epistemology in film', *The Journal of Aesthetics and Art Criticism*, p. 313.
5. Chion, *Audio-Vision: Sound on Screen*, p. 39.
6. Ibid. p. 40.
7. Kerins, *Beyond Dolby (Stereo): Cinema in the Digital Sound Age*, pp. 117–18.
8. Kozloff, *Invisible Storytellers: Voice-Over Narration in the American Fiction Film*, p. 5.
9. Ibid. p. 5.
10. Ibid. p. 6.
11. Shingler, 'Fasten your seatbelts and prick up your ears: the dramatic human voice in film', *Scope*.

12. Smith, *Vocal Tracks: Performance and Sound Media*, p. 82.
13. Smith, 'Voice in film' in Gibbs and Pye (eds), *Close-Up 2*, p. 205.
14. Chion, *Audio-Vision*, p. 172.
15. Ibid. p. 171.
16. Ibid. p. 177.
17. Ibid. p. 171.
18. Ibid. p. 178.
19. Ibid. p. 177.
20. Birtwistle, *Cinesonica: sounding film and video*, pp. 93–4.
21. Ibid. p. 8.
22. Discussing the dominant understanding of the sound of technology, Birtwistle writes: 'The assumption is that the sound of technology is something that is listened *through* rather than listened *to*.' Ibid. p. 88.
23. Chion, *Audio-Vision*, p. 172.
24. Kozloff, *Invisible Storytellers*, p. 68.
25. Ibid. p. 70.
26. Ibid. p. 70.
27. Gorbman, *Unheard Melodies: Narrative Film Music*, p. 55.
28. Ibid. p. 69.
29. Wilson, *Narration in Light: Studies in Cinematic Point of View*, p. 49.
30. Bordwell, *Narration in the Fiction Film*, p. 212.
31. Birtwistle, *Cinesonica*, p. 93.
32. Ibid. p. 90.
33. Halligan, 'What is the neo-underground and what isn't: a first consideration of Harmony Korine', in Xavier Mendik and Steven Jay Schneider (eds), *Underground U.S.A.: Filmmaking Beyond the Hollywood Canon*, p. 156.
34. Kelley, 'Mike Kelley interviews Harmony Korine', *FilmMaker*.
35. Halligan, 'What is the neo-underground', p. 159.
36. Flinn, *The New German Cinema: Music, History, and the Matter of Style*, pp. 70–106.
37. Apart from statements in interviews, evidence of Korine's admiration of Herzog is indicated by his casting of the director in two of his films, *Julien-Donkey Boy* (1999) and *Mister Lonely* (2007)
38. Halligan, 'What is the neo-underground', p. 155.
39. Birtwistle, *Cinesonica.*, p. 85.
40. Ibid. p. 104.
41. Among other places, this claim is made by Anderson on the liner notes for the *Magnolia* CD (1999)
42. Chion, *Audio-Vision*, p. 72.
43. Gorbman, 'Artless singing', *Music, Sound and the Moving Image*, p. 159.
44. Ibid. p. 157.
45. Chion, p. 71.
46. Smith, *Vocal Tracks*, p. 97.
47. Ibid. p. 99.
48. Reay, *Music in Film: Soundtracks and Synergy*, p. 65.

CHAPTER 5

The Dramatic Affect of Multiple Casting

INTRODUCTION

The book's cover image shows two Hitchcocks, the same actor/director playing different roles some years apart. In my discussion of this image in the introduction, I emphasised how its visible 'joins' create meaning. In Chapter 3 I also alluded to different physical manifestations of 'Hitchcock' in *Double Take* more broadly, including the impersonator Ron Burrage. The film therefore offers both one figure embodying multiple roles and multiple figures embodying the same 'character' or, at least, aspects of that character. It is this latter phenomenon that I will investigate more closely in this chapter, focusing on a practice I will refer to as visible 'multiple casting', following Nicole Choolun.[1] I consider, in particular, the dramatic significance of the actual moments of collision between different physical presences who inhabit the same role. I identify two types of visible multiple casting: 'motivated' visible casting in which the joins between the performers are justified by an overt fictional premise [the identity-crisis psychological drama *Don't Look Back* (De Van, 2009) and fantastical *The Imaginarium of Doctor Parnassus* (Gilliam, 2009) provide the case studies here]; and 'unmotivated' visible casting in which multiple performers portray the same character without an obvious narrative explanation [*Palindromes* (Solondz, 2004) and *I'm Not There* (Haynes, 2007) are presented as two contrasting examples of this phenomenon].

   The focus of my analysis is on the physical presence (or absence) of the different performing bodies at the moment the character is 'handed' from one actor to another: this involves considering the work each body is seen to do (or not do) and the relative weight (in a physical sense) attributed to each performer at the moment of transference. It also involves thinking about the materiality (or immateriality) of aspects of film style, in particular editing, at those moments when more than one performer lays claim to the body of a single fictional character.

   Despite the idiosyncratic nature of the examples I shall consider, certain types of multiple casting are exceedingly common – indeed, industrially routine – in the commercial fiction film. As James Naremore notes:

> [M]ovies are the only medium in which several actors are *typically* used to play
> one role: a voice is dubbed, a body double represents a torso, a hand model
> manipulates objects in close-up, a stunt man performs dangerous action in
> long shot, etc. All these different figures are merged in the editing and mixing,
> appearing on the screen as a single characterisation, an 'object' of fascination
> tied together by the name of a character and the face of a star.[2]

The key characteristic of these forms of multiple casting is that they are not
intended to be noticed, the performances arranged in a hierarchy whereby
only one actor is openly acknowledged. This might be for fear that the
exposure of multiple performers would take the viewer out of the story.
The premise that a viewer should be sutured into the fictional world of the
narrative film is a long-standing one (both in industry rhetoric and critical
accounts) and it is, therefore, not surprising that 'visible' multiple casting,
at least of the unmotivated kind, is a marginal practice even within non-
mainstream, feature-length, fiction films. Those films that *do* make multiple
casting apparent, however, can access an expressive possibility that invisible
casting disallows: namely the potential to apprehend the differing physical
properties of the separate performers and to juxtapose them in a dramatically
meaningful way. In these cases, the precise moment of juxtaposition can
become foregrounded, rather than glossed over, and it is on those moments
that my subsequent analyses will linger.

'MOTIVATED' VISIBLE MULTIPLE CASTING (1): EFFORTLESS MORPHING AND LABOURING BODIES IN *DON'T LOOK BACK*

Before moving on to examples where the difference between performers
playing the same character is asserted rather than erased, it should be noted
that the proposal of sameness between performers can still be a determining
principle even when different bodies are visibly being associated with the portrayal of a single character. Vivian Sobchack suggests that this is a particular
feature of digital morphing, a process whereby one body can transform into
another and back again with an ease that is distinctly inhuman:

> . . . with its end in its beginning (and vice versa), digital morphing transforms
> the very grounds of a cinematic temporality tethered to – if not completely
> bound by – gravity: gravity as a value of photographic indexicality to a spatial
> and material world, to the visibility of particular human and representational
> labors marked by change in space and time, and to human mortality.[3]

Sobchack's claim that the morph escapes the laws of gravity is suggestive in
the context of a sensuous investigation of film. The characterisation attributes
to the morph a weightlessness that is both spatial and temporal. The morph

involves a smooth sliding from one body to another that appears impossibly fluid visually. It also seems entirely disconnected to linear concepts of time, operating instead to a principle of reversibility: the body can just as easily morph back to a previous form as move on to another one. Sobchack contrasts this movement to the use of cuts and dissolves to transform bodies [for example, in a werewolf movie such as *The Wolf Man* (Waggner, 1941)], formal techniques of moving from one image to another that suggest ellipsis and, therefore, the forward flow of time.

These qualities of weightlessness and reversibility are made use of in the storytelling of *Don't Look Back* (de Van, 2009), a psychological drama that charts the breakdown of a woman who is haunted by the feeling that she is living someone else's life. Rather than confirming these spatial and temporal qualities as ones inherent to the digital morph, however, the effortless, reversible morph finds significance within a fictional world where much messier, weighed-down and truncated moments of morphing are also shown to be possible.

The film begins with Sophie Marceau portraying Jeanne (Figure 5.1), a writer who has no memory of her childhood. She starts to experience episodes whereby her surroundings suddenly seem unfamiliar to her and this crisis of identity develops into one where she senses her physical appearance changing. The film registers Jeanne's subjective point of view, with the result that the viewer sees her body change as she experiences it changing. This means that in the latter part of the film, Jeanne is portrayed by a different actor, Monica Bellucci (Figure 5.2), but there is a significant stretch whereby the transition between the two actors remains incomplete and the struggle to move from the inhabitation of one body to another is registered visually. This results in a morphing effect that has 'got stuck', presenting a hybrid face in which the particular features of Marceau and Bellucci are hard to discern (Figure 5.3). In fact, it is most often impossible to tell whether the effect of a face stuck in transition is created by a digital morphing of the two stars' features, the distortion via CGI of a single face (rather than the merging of two), or by physical effects (for example, make up). In addition, other signs of body trauma provide a mess around the facial morphing that inhibits any understanding of the transformation as a smooth or effortless one. In short, rather than escaping the laws of gravity and linear time, the attempted morph here is conspicuously weighed down by the labour of moving from one body to another.

The unwieldiness of the morph is indicated by the demonstration of effort evident at two key moments of transformation: the point when Marceau's face appears sustainedly, rather than fleetingly, changed; and the scene, about fifteen minutes later, which results in Bellucci's features finally becoming obviously apparent.

Figure 5.1   *Marina de Van,* Don't Look Back *(2009)*

Figure 5.2   *Marina de Van,* Don't Look Back *(2009)*

Figure 5.3   *Marina de Van,* Don't Look Back *(2009)*

In the first scene, Jeanne has returned to her apartment to find everything different from how she remembered it. In addition, her husband's face is becoming more unfamiliar and, as a final blow, her two children also look different. Distraught, Jeanne retires to her bedroom to change but her clothes suddenly seem too small. A disquieting rolling sound accompanies a close-up of Jeanne turning her head and looking down, whereupon a shot of her hands show her spreading her fingers and pulling her rings off them in response to feeling her hands expand. The rolling sound continues, augmented by creaks, as the camera pans down her legs, which have come out in bruises, towards her feet, the toes of which are tensed as if these are also growing uncontrollably. The experience of bodily transformation at this point is constructed through sound effects and the tensing of the body rather than through facial morphing. The figure of the morph is apparent immediately after this, however, as Jeanne pulls over the mirror door of her wardrobe and a cut to her reflection shows that her face has suddenly changed (Figure 5.4): one side is fuller with darker and longer hair, a blackened eye and fuller lips, while the other retains the dimensions of Marceau's face as the viewer has got used to it in the film.

This image lasts just a few seconds and is returned to very briefly soon after. It does stand out from the shots that surround it, exhibiting a posed, painterly quality which is not apparent in the more naturalistically rendered action (visually speaking) that surrounds it: the interior colour scheme is suddenly much more subdued, the sky outside and 'natural' lighting coming in from the window behind Jeanne appears digitally composited, there is an airbrushed quality to Jeanne's skin tone, and the split between the two sides of the face is exactly symmetrical. The uncanny symmetry is much less apparent in subsequent shots where Jeanne is less statically posed, as she is always moving about and covering her face, especially when her husband enters the room.

The key point about the appearance of the morph is that it is presented as a static image, disconnected in many ways to the images that surround it – images that present bodily transformation as a bruising, tortuous process (the sound effects and the tensing of the body give the impression that Jeanne's bones are in danger of breaking out of her skin). As such, the image is robbed of the effortless fluidity attributed to the morph by Sobchack, characterised instead by spatial and temporal stasis (existing as an ill-fitting pause in the frenetic action that surrounds it).

The brief insertion of the two shots where the facial morph is obviously digitally composed intimates a smooth process of bodily transformation that does not actually occur. Jeanne's face does, indeed, remain stuck in its transitional state as hospital investigations do not provide an immediate

Figure 5.4   *Marina de Van,* Don't Look Back *(2009)*

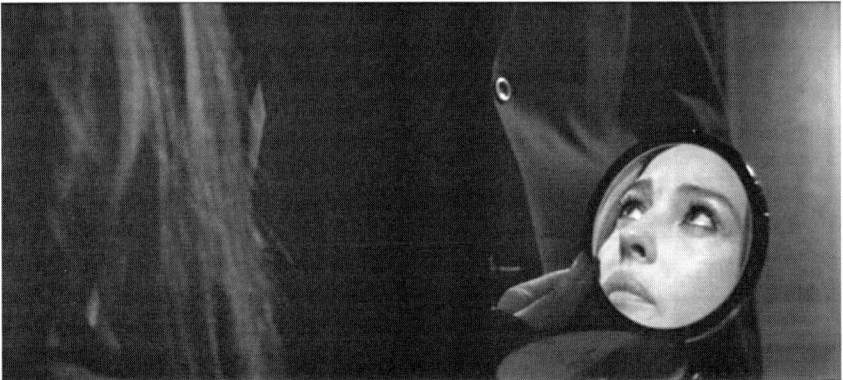

Figure 5.5   *Marina de Van,* Don't Look Back *(2009)*

explanation for her identity crisis. The morph from Marceau's face to Bellucci's is completed only while Jeanne waits for her mother to finish a game of cards at her club. Whereas the previous (half)-transformation was represented as a laboursome visceral process in which the airbrushed quality of the image of the morph appeared incongruous, here, digital effects are used in a way that resists the potential for the morphing process to be depicted as a weightless and effortless one.

   This instance of morphing is depicted in a single shot, lasting over a minute, which begins with Jeanne framed centrally in medium close-up and continues with the camera slowly circling towards one side of her face before retracing its steps and then moving around to the other side. During its final stages, the attack Jeanne has felt on her body appears to have abated (signalled by a quietening of her body movement and by the winding down of the tense, high-pitched strings that have accompanied the scene). At this point,

Jeanne takes out a make-up mirror to see what she now looks like, and the camera is in position to catch her reflection, showing Bellucci's face (Figure 5.5). This identity remains stable right until the film's climax in which the mystery around Jeanne's identity is solved: this revelation involves a further bodily transformation that will be analysed presently.

The moment of morphing depicted here is experienced as a long one, causing immense strain on Jeanne's body. The episode begins with an already agitated Jeanne bridling as she tips her head back and starts to breath very heavily. This breathing achieves a prominence on the soundtrack, its bodily qualities emphasised by contrast to the very high-pitched, screechy strings that have appeared on the non-diegetic soundtrack. As the camera moves around to her left side, her facial features begin to contort in unnatural ways. For example, the bridge of her nose flattens only then to expand beyond its previous limits, as if it is somehow being deflated and inflated. At the same time, Jeanne reaches her hands towards her cheeks in an effort to feel, and to physically arrest, the contortions over which she evidently has no control.

When the camera starts to swing back towards a face-on position, the digital effects become ever more obvious, the contortions displaying an inhuman elasticity. At this point, a rolling, guttural sound, which has provided another texture to the soundtrack throughout the transformation scene, becomes more prominent through its choreography with the palpitating stretching of Jeanne's face, given full exposure by having her in the centre of the frame at this moment. As soon as the camera has moved beyond this central point, the palpitations calm, and it is at this juncture that Jeanne reaches into her bag to retrieve the make-up mirror. Jeanne's face is in a state of tension to the extent that, while it is clear that a facial transformation has taken place, it is not obvious that it is Bellucci's face which we now see: Jeanne has her mouth open and is looking down in distress towards her bag, and these gestures elongate her face, making it difficult to recognise one of the most striking differences between Marceau and Bellucci, namely the latter's fuller face. It is only as Jeanne steadies herself to look in the mirror, towards the end of the movement of the camera, which settles in a position just behind her right shoulder, that the fuller nature of her right cheek is apparent. The reflection of Jeanne's eyes and nose in the mirror provides further evidence that Jeanne is now being embodied by Bellucci but this is finally confirmed only as she tips her head up to acknowledge an oncoming employee of the club and more of Bellucci's face appears in the mirror.

While this transformation does possess some of the impossible elasticity characteristic of the digital morph, a number of factors contribute to burden the moment with weight. The soundtrack is marked by the noise of physical labour, in both Jeanne's breathing and in the guttural non-diegetic sound that starts off resembling a heartbeat, and then palpitates along to the most extreme of Jeanne's facial contortions. These contortions *are* ones that seem impossible according to the viewer's understanding of human physiology. They are also based on recognisable gestures of physical distress, however (a scrunching of the nose, a flexing of the cheeks, a drawing in and out of the lips and a baring of teeth), and these are framed by signifiers of suffering that are ordinarily human (that is, Jeanne's throwing back of her head and heavy breathing at the start of the transformation and her distressed look down-wards at the end of it). Furthermore, the 'everyday' gesture of distress at the end of the episode involves a 'natural' distortion of the face (its elongation) that makes the outcome of the morphing process indistinct. At all stages, then, the digital morphing process is connected to, and mediated through, the performance of a struggling human body.

As such, this transformation scene has much in common with that of *Dr Jekyll and Mr Hyde* (1941), a sequence Sobchack cites to establish the differ-ence between non-digital and digital metamorphoses. Using the sequence to make a case for the non-reversible nature of the non-digital morph, she claims:

> Spencer Tracy 'becomes' Dr. Jekyll in front of the camera and our eyes, not through an elided process involving unseen applications of makeup and pros-thetic devices but through the visible labor and duration of the actor's per-formance in its uninterrupted metamorphosis . . . the transformations in time effected by [this presents itself] as the consequence of temporal and physical *labor* – . . . of characters and objects in the phenomenal world encounter-ing and overcoming obstacles as they endure and change according to the demands of what is perceived by a physically embodied and mortal spectator as 'real' existential time.[4]

Jeanne's transformation here is, like the one described above, posed as one taking place in real linear time. The laboured quality of the performance is one aspect of this, and the linear trajectory of the transformation is also signalled in the confirmation of the newly formed identity in the make-up mirror. This indi-cates that the morphing process has now stopped and that the body has settled on a shape that can be captured in reflection, just like any other kind of physical object or mortal being. Indeed, Jeanne retains the face and body of Bellucci for a consistent stretch thereafter, as she follows a lead that takes her to Italy and a reunion with what turns out to be her biological mother. It is as the fact of her genealogy becomes clear that the final morphing process takes place, this time involving Jeanne's transformation into herself as a young girl (played by Vittoria Meneganti), at the age at which she was taken away from her natural mother.

The actual moment of regressive morphing is prepared for by a long and gradual transformation scene in which Jeanne wanders around the old family home and finds her body shrinking. For the majority of the scene the transformation is relayed through canted camera angles, expressionistic lighting schemes and – I suspect – the uncredited use of body doubles of smaller height than Bellucci. Jeanne is shown feeling her legs uncomprehendingly, struggling to keep an even stride as she climbs up steps and staggers along a corridor while her legs grow shorter. The qualities of suffering and labour associated with the other moments of transformation are also evident here. In an interview included in the film's press kit, director Marina de Van discusses the significance of the emphasis on the suffering body:

> [R]upture was vital. The return to childhood is always represented visually as an attractive rejuvenation, in images where the damage wrought by aging is erased at high speed. But if you think about it, to transform an adult into a child quickly would require the breaking of bones, the extraction of flesh, trying to cram a body into a box far too small for it! . . . This painful, broken aspect is illustrated in the film by the shrunken, limping woman; by Jeanne's deformed body in Italy.[5]

This expresses the general effort made in the film to offer a 'realistically' visceral representation of a fantastical process. Unlike the two previous transformation scenes, however, the emphasis on the labour and physical difficulty of the movement between bodies *does* give way to a moment of digital morphing possessed of the qualities of weightlessness and reversibility identified by Sobchack.

After staggering through corridors, Jeanne enters a bedroom on whose walls hang a lot of old photographs of a young girl. Presumably, this is Jeanne's childhood room, or at least a room that has been made into a shrine for her. Whatever the trigger, entry into this room appears to be the moment where Jeanne confirms to herself her long-held feeling that this is the place of her birth. In the first obvious CGI shots of the sequence, we see Jeanne looking scared as she shrinks further, causing the furniture around her to appear to grow. This moment is accompanied by a crescendo of screeching strings, rumbles and stabbing horns but this quietens as Jeanne continues to make her way around the room, now dwarfed by the furniture. As she reaches a dressing table, she sees an ornate glass bottle on top of it and her expression now registers an excited recognition rather than fear, as if her memories are flooding back. She lifts herself up so that she can see what else lies on the dressing table and, as she does so, there is a cut to a shot that reveals her reflection in the mirror: moving slowly up to a standing position, Jeanne morphs smoothly into her childhood self so that, by the time she is fully standing, her features are completely transformed.

The lightness of this transformation, in comparison to the labour of the previous ones, is indicated in a number of ways. The morphing effect is represented as a process whereby one body dissolves smoothly into another rather than as something that subjects an unwilling body to traumatic transformation; the soundtrack is dominated by flowing, sumptuous strings rather than by the combination of screeches, guttural rumblings and laboured breathing evident in the previous morphing scenes. Jeanne gives the impression of floating during the morph, a result of her rising upwards with a fluency that contrasts strongly with her cumbersome movement immediately prior to the transformation (where the shrinking of her legs had made it impossible for her to walk properly at all).

Temporally, the transformation operates on a principle of reversibility rather than forward-moving linearity. This is indicated most obviously by Jeanne's reversal back to her childhood state but also by the *growth* apparent in the transformation from the shrinking body that has beset Jeanne just before the morph to a body that stretches up with ease. Here, then, the morph both reverses 'human' time by turning an adult face into a child's one, as well as the 'fantastical' time of a traumatic transformation, which had been subjecting the body to a seemingly unstoppable de-ageing process (which puts it in danger of disappearing completely) but which is reversed through the morph just enough so that the transformation of both face and body is established on an even keel. The reversibility is also suggested in the very ease with which one body and face transforms into another, suggesting an easy passage between one state and another that, as Sobchack suggests, implies a potential for a reversibility even if it is not actually depicted.[6]

Transported, in her imagination, back to her childhood, Jeanne goes through a process of memory retrieval that solves the mystery of her identity: it becomes clear that she had originally been named Rose Maria but had been taken away from her biological mother and adopted into another family. When her newly adopted sister, Jeanne, was killed in a car crash, Rose Maria assumed Jeanne's identity, the trauma erasing the memory of her previous existence.

Don't Look Back presents three different types of digital morphing of Jeanne's body, each possessing different levels of viscerality and each suggesting a different type of effort from, and damage to, her body. Only in the third instance does the morph take on the weightless and timeless qualities indicated by Sobchack. It should be acknowledged that Sobchack, too, discusses other possibilities in the digital morphing of one body to another: the paradigm of the morph working against the laws of gravity and forward-moving linear time is established as a kind of phenomenological baseline against which deviations might be judged. Sobchack's examples are all culled from different audio-visual works, however, whereas the example of *Don't Look Back* demonstrates how alternative ways of moving from one performer to another can be tied to the story arc of a particular character within a single fictional world. It is significant that the morph from one performer to another becomes effortless only in this final instance, when Jeanne is on the cusp of solving the mystery of her identity. The mental effort of retrieving a memory is given bodily expression throughout the movie, and the differences in the morphing scenes are a sign of the – eventually successful – struggle involved in this process. Jeanne's final transformation is a non-morphological one. She moves from child to adult (initially in the form of Sophie Marceau) in the controlled and self-willed act of changing into adult-size clothes in the train back from Italy. The final scene features all four performers involved in the characterisation of Jeanne/Rose Maria (Marceau, Bellucci, Meneganti and Francesca Melucci, the girl who plays the 'real' Jeanne, killed in the car crash). They appear as clearly separated bodies, acknowledging each other's existences, rather than as presences in the process of merging with each other. This signals Jeanne's acceptance of her identity and her ability now to manage the multiple facets that contribute to her sense of self. This acts as an end point in the characterisation of Jeanne, the painful lead up to which is expressed through the material messiness of the earlier morphing scenes.

That said, the trajectory of *Don't Look Back* is one that works towards a difference between bodies that is expressed alongside an asserted continuity: a continuity vouchsafed by the knowledge that these bodies represent different facets of the same character; and by aspects of performance and *mise en scène* that undercut the presentation of the performers as different (for example, at the end Marceau and Bellucci are wearing identical clothes and are brought into a position whereby their profiles overlap each other by the time the film cuts to its credits, due to the movement of the camera). This assertion of continuity within difference is symptomatic of films that link performers together around the same character through 'logical' premises, that is to say, via a psychological rationale that is made clear to the viewer (as in *Don't Look Back*), a fantastical justification that is presented as plausible within the context of a particular fictional world, or through a generational pretext whereby different performers play the same character at different ages.

'MOTIVATED' VISIBLE MULTIPLE CASTING (2): THE UNIQUE WEIGHTINESS OF HEATH LEDGER IN *THE IMAGINARIUM OF DR PARNASSUS*

Literal co-presence within the space of a shot (as evidenced by the mor-phing scenes and proliferation of actors within the frame in the final scene of *Don't Look Back*) is not a prerequisite of asserting continuity within difference in these instances. Even when the transition from one perfor-mance to another is made via a hard cut, the effect need not be jarring. The combination of different performances of the same character through the principle of collision is, in fact, the exceptional aesthetic, existing as such in relation to a much more conventional effort to stress continuities across the performances.

In terms of films that use fantastical premises to license multiple casting, *The Imaginarium of Dr Parnassus* provides an interesting test of the assertion of continuity within difference. The film revolves around a travelling theatre troupe that acts as a portal to another dimension in which the dreams of the people who enter it become a reality. Its star, Heath Ledger, playing the morally ambivalent conman, Tony, died mid-production, apparently after completing his scenes set in the real world but before working on the sequences taking place in the Imaginarium. Filming was completed after three other star actors (Johnny Depp, Colin Farrell and Jude Law) took on the role of Tony in separate episodes set in the fantastical world, the conceit being that each represents a different dream version of Tony within the magical sphere of the Imaginarium.

The conceit is supported by having the bodies of other characters change when they enter the Imaginarium. This helps the transformation of Tony appear as a phenomenon within the film's fictional world rather than only an acknowledgement of a situation that has arisen extratextually. The broad continuity with the logic established in the fictional world is augmented by physical continuities between the Tonys. These are ones that both exploit the biological make-up of the actors as well as make use of a consistent 'dress-ing' of the character to establish the connections between the performances. At the most basic level, all four actors playing Tony are white men; any significant differences in the physique, age or facial make-up of the actors are subdued within the performances rather than accentuated. This is achieved primarily by the character being repeatedly seen dressed in a white suit that hides the body, by the sharing of a hairstyle (hair brushed back into a ponytail) and by the adoption of a goatee beard (Figures 5.6, 5.7, 5.8 and 5.9). The look of each actor is not completely uniform and is subject to the narrative situ-ation but there is a common code of representation that strives to minimise

Figure 5.6   *Terry Gilliam,* The Imaginarium of Doctor Parnassus *(2009)*

Figure 5.7   *Terry Gilliam,* The Imaginarium of Doctor Parnassus *(2009)*

the difference in the physical appearances of the actors without going to the extent of making those differences disappear completely.

There is, nevertheless, an insistence on the separateness of Ledger's incarnation of Tony in its association with a particular dimension of the fictional world uninhabited by the others. Ledger's Tony exists, almost exclusively, in the 'real' world, according to the film's fictional premise, whereas the other versions are completely contained within the Imaginarium. This gives Ledger's Tony a physical intractability that is not granted to other bodies in

Figure 5.8   *Terry Gilliam,* The Imaginarium of Doctor Parnassus *(2009)*

Figure 5.9   *Terry Gilliam,* The Imaginarium of Doctor Parnassus *(2009)*

the film. Other characters are seen either to undergo a transformation within the depths of the Imaginarium itself or to present themselves as unaltered in either dimension. For example, the premise of the Imaginarium's transformative potential is introduced near the start of the film when a drunken yob, named Martin (Richard Riddell), chases Parnassus's daughter Valentina (Lily Cole) into the Imaginarium which has taken on the appearance of a fairytale forest, complete with cardboard cut-out trees. Once inside, he trips and falls flat on his face into a pile of mud. The moment of impact is registered in a close-up of his face, its sensation accentuated by a swell in the orchestral score that gives way to a loud squelch at the moment he hits the ground. Even through the mud and movement of the fall, it is immediately apparent to the viewer that Martin's face is different, indicating he is now being played by a different performer (Bruce Crawford). This is also somehow immediately evident to the character, an intuition causing him to touch his face in panic even before seeing he has changed through a reflection in a muddy pool of water beside him.

The Imaginarium constitutes a world where the physical laws governing the real world and the natural properties of objects are challenged. In this particular sequence, the setting appears firstly much more two-dimensional than the real world, comprised of cardboard cut-out trees, carefully positioned 'stage' mud and a pool of water. After Martin's transformation, however, an impossibly sweeping, craning camera movement away from him reveals a landscape that is unbelievably expansive and 'three-dimensional', the camerawork revealing that Martin now finds himself in a large pit in the forest, surrounded by huge gnarly trees. A further revealing of expansive space is made possible when a disembodied green hand grabs Martin's shoulder and lifts him so high into the sky that Earth below looks as it would from outer space. Even though Martin is now ostensibly in space, giant jellyfish float around him. The green hand lets him go whereupon Martin falls an indefinable but huge distance, hurtling towards a cloud-laden landscape whose barrenness seems to stretch indefinitely. The only object on the ground is a giant drawing pin on to which Martin narrowly escapes falling. The placing of objects and their proportion to one another clearly overturn the relationships the same objects would have in real life.

In the same way, the material qualities of the Imaginarium are entirely distinct from those associated with the real world. Beginning as a world which is materially impoverished (composed of two-dimensional trees and a dollop of mud that is just sufficient to provide a landing mat for Martin's face and no more), it turns into a landscape which is entirely exaggerated, either in terms of abundance (huge, translucent, glowing jellyfish entangling with one another in orbit around the Earth) or apocalyptic barrenness (plumes of low cloud pressing down upon a fiery sky hovering over entirely infertile terrain). In its exaggerated form, the landscape takes on an entirely virtual dimension, clearly generated by CGI effects whose painterly qualities are flaunted rather than any attempt being made to hide them.

The human figure is a vulnerable one in this landscape. Martin has no control over the physical changes that envelop him, and the early intuition of his own transformation (rather than discovering it first through his reflection in the water) discloses the horror of realising too late that a change has taken place. The stumble into the mud is the first physical sign that Martin cannot make a stand in the Imaginarium and, after his transformation, he is thrown around helplessly within a world possessed of an entirely unpredictable elasticity. In this context, his body becomes light enough to be carried up into space by a disembodied hand and small enough to be dwarfed by a drawing pin.

Heath Ledger's version of Tony is never subjected to physical 'attack' within the Imaginarium in the same way, and this gives his performance a unique sense of an intractable human weight. It might be argued that this is an obvious consequence of Ledger having only participated in the filming of the real-world sections: this automatically makes impossible the appearance of his version of Tony in the Imaginarium. This assumption needs to be qualified quite heavily in two ways, however: firstly, Ledger *does* appear, albeit very briefly, in the Imaginarium scenes; and secondly, a deliberate choice is made to embody characters differently from Tony, in terms of how they are changed by the Imaginarium, even though their transformation could have been represented in a way that brought it into line with what was now possible in relation to Tony, given Ledger's sudden death.

Tony first enters the Imaginarium after his showman skills have persuaded a woman to enter before him. Following her in through a foil curtain on Parnassus's mobile stage set, he pauses as soon as he is through the other side, taking in the spectacular view (a moment that captures Tony in medium close-up). Tony is wearing a white mask that covers his eyes, most of his forehead and features a long 'beaky' nose (this is all part of his stage costume). This means that part of his face is obscured but it is, nevertheless, still apparent that this is Ledger (Figure 5.10). Behind his shoulder lies evidence of a world possessed of the same impossible proportionality and sense of gravity as the previous incarnations of the Imaginarium. In this case, a gleaming giant string of pearls floats to and fro gently in front of the stems of giant lily pads, the tops of which can be seen apparently lying on the surface of the water at the top of the frame. The texture and colour of the backdrop are openly cartoonish and clearly digitally generated.

A shot from Tony's point of view reveals the territory further and captures the woman standing on a lily pad on a lower water surface, looking about in amazement at the collection of shining, gigantic, high-heeled shoes around her. A further crane back, much like the one that had revealed the huge proportions of the Imaginarium in its first incarnation, discloses assorted baubles, jewellery and even a golden Buddha floating about the space, its dimensions made to seem even grander by the reflections of objects in the water. The textures and scale of the environment are utterly fantastical and the woman is

Figure 5.10 *Terry Gilliam,* The Imaginarium of Doctor Parnassus *(2009)*

seen to transform fantastically in response. She looks into a bejewelled mirror and sees a much younger version of herself, dressed in the same outfit, but engaged in an entirely different pose. Unlike the transformation of Martin in the earlier scene, the alter ego here is presented as a wish-fulfilling apparition rather than as an entity that possesses the character entirely. Both moments, however, involve the spectacle of someone recognising a bodily transformation, over which they have no control, at the point of change.

Tony, meanwhile, has started to hop across to the woman via the lily pads that line the way. The *mise en scène* in which Tony moves is fantastical but his movements are not: he makes small, deft jumps between the lily pads to reach the woman. The same is true of Tony's subsequent appearance in the Imaginarium just before he becomes embodied by Jude Law. In this case, Ledger is seen climbing, in a 'normal' way, a gigantic ladder: the proportions of the ladder are unconventional but his movements are not. In the earlier sequence, Tony's hopping across the lily pads is represented through the craning shot that reveals the wider space and, as such, the understanding of Tony as being embodied by Ledger at this point can only be assumed. His identity is reconfirmed, however, as he approaches the woman just in time to catch her as she falls backwards. As Tony moves her around to ensure she does not fall from the lily pad, there is a cut that brings him closer to the camera, and it is clear that this is still Ledger's face. It is only after the woman has turned around to look at him and started to lift his mask that a cut accompanies the revelation that Tony is now embodied by Johnny Depp. There is an exchange between Tony and the woman, and it is then that he catches himself in the mirror and realises he looks different. Unlike the other two characters who undergo bodily transformation in the Imaginarium, Tony experiences the change only after the fact, the belated recognition also being registered when he is embodied by Jude Law and Colin Farrell. This preserves the sense of Ledger existing as the 'real world' Tony even within the space of the Imaginarium. At the moment when its magical influence on Tony's body becomes clear, Ledger is nowhere to be seen.

Ledger's enduringly 'real' physical qualities are also registered through the way he exits the Imaginarium. Tony is a character who does not have a pre-existing relationship with, or knowledge of, the Imaginarium and, as such, it is in relation to the reaction of other characters in the same situation that his own reaction should be judged. All the other characters in this category are propelled out of the Imaginarium in a way that suggests it has exerted an intense physical hold on them that has lifted them off their feet: a boy who wanders into the Imaginarium is rolled out of it wrapped up in a big rug; other than Valentina, the first woman who enters flies out of it into a pile of bin bags on the roadside (the Imaginarium is in transit at the time); the other women whom Tony lures into the Imaginarium through his showmanship emerge looking deliriously happy, seated on a floral-bedecked swing.

Tony, embodied by Ledger, by contrast, literally keeps his feet on the ground when he exits the Imaginarium. He tumbles, rather than flies, out through the curtain after his first visit. Later, he attempts to enter the Imaginarium but, for reasons that are not explained, it is not 'working', meaning that Tony lands with a thump on the other side of the curtain. The effect is to show that Tony, in the form of Ledger, is capable of exhibiting an entirely unaltered human sense of weight, even in the supposedly magical realm of the Imaginarium.

The exception to this display of weightiness occurs during Tony's second exit from the Imaginarium after he has been embodied by Jude Law. Here, the entire *mise en scène* on to which Tony looks magically turns into a 'curtain' through which he can return to the real world. Stepping through this threshold, his presence back in the everyday world is registered only by his voice. It is at this point that the real-life absence of Heath Ledger halfway through the production of the film is most noticeable: evidently, there was simply no footage of Ledger that could have been plausibly used to cover this particular exit. This highlights the contingency involved in representing the character of Tony, given Ledger's untimely death, and, as a whole, his relationship with the Imaginarium does not follow the logic through which that relationship is represented in terms of other characters. Indeed, his bodily disappearance during this particular exit fits as uneasily with the logic of the exits of other characters as the one in which Tony *retains* a proportional human weight: for the other characters, the experience is embodied as a *more* physical one than they are used to, rather than one that dematerialises them, subjected as they are to a force that propels them through the air.

The general retention of human weight around the threshold between the real world and the Imaginarium also does not tally with the introduction of Tony as a character who seems to have defied human laws of gravity: he is first seen hanging with a noose around his neck under a bridge, yet he is not dead even though the weight of his body should really have guaranteed this (the key to his survival apparently lies in his possession of a magical flute though the mystical properties of this are never explained). The overall representation of Ledger's performance as one that is distinctly human is supported by the way he is seen to move between the real world and the Imaginarium; it is also evidenced by the 'roughness' of certain close-ups involving Ledger in the real-world sequences which have presumably been retained in the absence of alternatives. On the other hand, there are equally moments in the real-world sections where Tony's movements are represented without seeing Ledger's face, the suspicion being that a body double has been used to ensure continuity between the footage of Ledger available to the film-makers. The entire absence of Tony's body in the short passage of dialogue that succeeds his exit from the Imaginarium is the extreme manifestation of Ledger's actual absence of which the sometimes awkward use of body doubles is another result.

Nevertheless, the moments when Ledger's body and face *are* present on-screen are ones that emphasise a sense of human weight as a quality of his performance. As such, the framing of the film as a celebration of Ledger's presence in the world (it is billed as 'A Film from Heath Ledger and Friends') becomes a more important value motivating the film's representational strategies than adherence to the premises it otherwise establishes for its fictional world.

'UNMOTIVATED' VISIBLE MULTIPLE CASTING: CRITICAL EXPLANATIONS

The Imaginarium of Dr Parnassus motivates the performance of the same character by more than one actor through a defined fictional premise. The celebration of Heath Ledger's weight as a performer, however, brings a level of incoherence into the way that premise is played out. A premise is, nevertheless, indicated by the film whereas that is not the case for the final examples which offer no overt motivation for sharing out the performance of a character among different actors. The lack of narrative clarity around these instances opens up the potential for a collision of different bodies in the portrayal of the same characters in which the material qualities of those bodies and the materiality of the moment of impact between them assume a particular importance (in the absence of any explanation as to why the bodies are coming together, the physical spectacle of this collision becomes a potentially more foregrounded aspect of the moment). This does not mean that such collisions can have no storytelling significance at all, as my examples will demonstrate.

A small number of writers have commented on the phenomenon of 'unmotivated' visible multiple casting. For the majority of these, the critical impulse has been to discover a 'hidden' driver to the casting whether that be on a narrative or thematic level or in pursuit of self-reflexive formal play. Choolun, for example, argues that the use of multiple casting for 'provocative purposes'[7] in *I'm Not There* allows the film to portray its subject, Bob Dylan, through a series of performances 'rich with emotional expressivity'.[8] According to Choolun, the combination of these performances heightens, rather than detracts from '[t]he spectator's capacity for observation and critique by inviting him or her to attend more closely to the performances themselves as a route to engagement with character'.[9]

Choolun is responding to an assertion by Murray Smith that unmotivated multiple casting undercuts the viewer's ability to recognise a character, recognition being the basic condition upon which emotional engagement with a character rests.[10] It should be noted, however, that Smith – with due caveats about overgeneralising – suggests that this disruption of emotional engagement through multiple casting is most often achieved for the purposes of social critique. He states that films using multiple casting '[c]an be seen to share a strategy of characterisation which attempts to cut away the physical ground of bodily continuity and discreteness in order to reveal both the common and conflicting interests in a society more clearly'.[11]

Whether claiming a narrative (the understanding of character) or thematic (the understanding of society) rationale for multiple casting, both Choolun and Smith concentrate on the global significance of the phenomenon rather than on the bodily details of the multiple performances. Choolun argues that the viewer's investment is in the overall portrait of a particular character while Smith asserts that the cutting away of 'the physical ground' through which a character is usually recognised leads to a more abstract appreciation of the character's function rather than to a concentration on the physical ground of bodily *discontinuities* with which the viewer is now confronted. In short, both Choolun and Smith avoid paying attention to the different physicalities of the performers even though this is the premise on which multiple casting is based.

James Naremore interprets the use of multiple casting differently, viewing it as a practice that encourages the viewer to step out of his or her immersion in a particular fictional world and, instead, to become aware of the constructed, rather than organic, nature of a single screen performance, a contrivance that routinely involves multiple bodies (in the form of body doubles, hand models, stunt performers, etc.) as well as the overtly visible star. Commenting particularly on *That Obscure Object of Desire* (Buñuel, 1977), the most discussed film to make use of multiple casting, Naremore asserts:

> Buñuel's device is empty of the usual narrative significance, but it is neverthe-less meaningful, commenting on the arbitrary, fetishistic structure of desire and at the same time exposing a technique [of invisible multiple casting] by which classical cinema usually supports that structure . . . By reminding us of such a phenomenon, Buñuel playfully attacks the very foundation of 'organic', Stanislavskian aesthetics.[12]

Once again, the emphasis is diverted from the details of the physicalities of the different performers and how those are combined in the performance of a single character, this time on to a notion that the film lays bare a practice that is normally kept hidden. For Naremore, the significance of the visible multiple casting is in its exposure of the invisibility of multiple casting in other films, rather than on the material facts of the visibility itself.

Kristen M. Daly also suggests that unmotivated multiple casting lifts the viewer away from his or her immersion within a film's fictional world, not by exposing the fiction's essential artifice but, rather, by evoking a range of extratextual references through each performance:

> In these examples [of multiple casting], the discourse is multiple and not unilateral or totalising. The filmmaker cannot control the references and connections, which the viewer will make. Each actor and aesthetic style in *I'm Not There* conjures different references. The filmmaker chooses to simply set up the design and let it run, allowing the outside influences of different storylines, contemporary media influences, and outside references to inter-penetrate and distort any unified and totalising text.[13]

Under this conception, there is no question that the particular nature of the combination of different physical presences embodying the same character *within* a fictional world will be addressed as the practice is seen to lead to the explosion of the very notion of a film as a world of its own.

The views outlined thus far represent two extremes in the understanding of unmotivated multiple casting. Choolun and Smith find ways to discover motivation where there might seem to be none and, in both cases, these are what Johannes Riis terms 'intra-fictional justification[s]',[14] either to do with characterisation or theme. Daly and Naremore, by contrast, offer 'extra-fictional justification[s]',[15] whereby the practice of multiple casting functions as a rhetorical point of narration that redirects the viewer's attention to other media texts or to the industrial practices that served to create the illusion of a filmed fictional world. What connects these polarised accounts, however, is their lack of attention to the sensuous detail of each performance involved in unmotivated multiple casting and the precise ways the performances are joined. For all these writers, this materiality is, figuratively speaking, immaterial as the multiple casting is always seen to be at the service of another purpose.

Elena del Rio offers a way to think about the materiality and sensuality of screen bodies in her Deleuzian account of film performance. Her study is subtitled *Powers of Affection*, and this indicates an understanding of performance as forceful and sensuous, a matter of bodies in motion. As she explains:

> Performance is the bringing forth of the power of bodies, in sum, the mobilisation of the body's affects. Performance is the actualisation of the body's potential through specific thoughts, actions, displacements, combinations, realignments – all of which can be seen as different degrees of intensity, distinct relations of movement and rest. Thus, the body's expressivity coincides with its continually transformative activity in its relations with other bodily assemblages, human or otherwise.[16]

This understanding of screen performance is helpful in two ways in developing my own line of enquiry. Firstly, it focuses on the specifics of the bodily activity that contributes to a performance rather than bypassing this stage of the process in favour of attention to the effect this exertion is perceived to have. This activity is assessed by del Rio in terms of its differing degrees of intensity, and I hope my previous analyses of *Don't Look Back* and *The Imaginarium of Dr Parnassus* has made clear my interest in understanding screen performance in this way: in the former case, I concentrated on the different levels of labour evident in the performances during the morphing scenes, while, in the latter, I discussed the special sense of weight attributed to Ledger's performance.

Secondly, del Rio stresses that one body's expressivity is experienced only in relation to other bodies. Again, this has already been a central theme of this chapter but del Rio supports a notion that has only been intimated, rather than demonstrated through analysis, thus far: namely, that the affective power of a performance may be especially enhanced at moments where bodies possessing markedly different material qualities are juxtaposed. This is only implicit in the statement of del Rio's cited above but is expanded upon in other passages of her book. For example, she claims:

> Affective displacements and inventions often occur through the juxtaposition of incongruent affections. In Sirk's melodramas, a violent and trans-

formative energy is felt through an affective montage that forces together the speeds and rhythms of contiguous disparate scenes or of disparate bodies within a single scene.[17]

In a footnote, del Rio suggests that 'composite bodies', which would include those of a character played by more than one performer, hold a particular power: 'Instances of composite bodies such as are found in some of the films I discuss in this book ... evoke the Spinozist/Deleuzian idea of bodies forming alliances with each other in the interest of composing a more powerful body.'[18] Key examples of this phenomenon, discussed in del Rio's book, are the 'multi-form and multiple'[19] bodies apparent in *Mulholland Drive* (Lynch, 2001). *Mulholland Drive* is not obviously an example of multiple casting but, rather, makes use of a casting strategy that is multiple casting's counterpart: namely, the use of the same actor to play multiple roles (Naomi Watts portrays characters named Betty and Diane while Laura Harring plays characters named Rita and Camilla). The dream logic of the film is so pervasive, however, that, as del Rio argues, it becomes possible to understand all these roles as ones that are passed between the performers:

> Betty and Rita are thus constantly 'passing into one another', metamorphosing into each other. Betty is Diane's ideal version of herself, but Rita, in her blonde wig, is also Betty and Diane. Rita suffers from a constant state of sleepiness and amnesia, an extension of Diane's own sleep and dreaming.[20]

Del Rio's itemisation of the 'linkages and unlinkages between bodies and attributes'[21] goes on, and this conveys effectively the extreme slipperiness of the film's acts of characterisation. For del Rio, this serves to destabilise the notion of Betty/Diane/Rita/Camilla as identifiably autonomous characters, with the result that the affective charges of the performances associated with them are dislocated from their conventional moorings:

> Dismantling the classical hierarchy where subject originates affect, the affect here [in a set-piece scene set in Club Silencio] becomes somewhat detached from character and stands on its own, non-subjective, ground. Rather than one subject owning the affect, it dwells in and passes through a multiplicity of bodies.[22]

In general, del Rio is most interested in moments of 'pure' affect which work as moments of 'performative eruption'[23] that lead to the temporary cessation of narrative. The radical deconstruction of the autonomy of the character in *Mulholland Drive*, partly an effect of multiple casting, allows for a particularly powerful and sustained barrage of affective moments that, 'unable to lean upon [their] usual crutches [of association with characters/ dramatic situations], engag[e] evermore intensely in a state of creative frenzy'.[24]

Not all films employing unmotivated multiple casting deconstruct the notion of character to the extent of *Mulholland Drive*. In the final examples of this chapter, I want to explore the notion that the performative eruptions caused by the collision of different actors' takes on the same character can still be usefully understood in relation to the dramatic situations presented within a film's fictional world. As such, my approach returns to the preoccupation with narrative or thematic 'meaning' apparent in the writing of Choolun and Smith but does so through an engagement with the potentially explosive friction between the materially different performances that compose a character in films that use multiple casting. This materiality is partly to do with the physical bearing of the performer, in terms of 'organic' attributes such as height, build, voice, movement, and so on. These attributes, however, are never apprehended by the viewer without the mediation of film style, and my final two examples, *Palindromes* and *I'm Not There*, contrast in the way the former evens out the physical differences of its performers through its aesthetic choices while the latter showcases each body through a sensuously distinctive stylistic register.

THE WILFUL IGNORANCE OF PHYSICAL DIFFERENCE IN *PALINDROMES*

Aviva, the protagonist of *Palindromes*, is a teenage girl who goes through a series of traumatic episodes throughout the film. Opening before the main time frame of the narrative, with Aviva at this point a little girl, the film begins with the funeral of Aviva's cousin, Dawn, the protagonist of Solondz's debut movie, *Welcome to the Dollhouse* (1995). Dawn has committed suicide and, in her first scene, Aviva discloses to her mother that she had been told this is because she was subjected to a date rape from which she had become pregnant. Aviva expresses a desire to have lots of children of her own and the film then moves forward 'some years' (according to a caption). Through the course of the narrative, Aviva gets pregnant after having sex with Judah, a boy of a similar age, is pressurised into having an abortion by her parents, runs away, meets up with and has sex with, an older man named Bob, and gets taken in by a religious group that turns out to house a group of pro-life extremists, one of whom is Bob. She witnesses Bob attempting to kill the doctor who had carried out her abortion, accidentally murdering the doctor's daughter instead. She then holes up with him in a motel room where he is shot dead by police. Aviva returns to her family and meets up again with Judah who has renamed himself Otto. The film ends with the two of them having sex in the woods, after which Aviva announces that she thinks this encounter might have made her pregnant.

This plot synopsis reveals nothing of the film's use of multiple casting but this is, in itself, significant in terms of establishing the apparent lack of motivation in utilising the technique. There is a clear narrative line, overloaded with controversial content, that at no point licenses, within its fictional premises, the embodiment of the protagonist by different performers. One of the most provocative tensions of the film is between the continuous, linear unfolding of shocking events and the unexplained discontinuities between the different bodies used throughout the film to depict Aviva. It is in the film's final scene that the tension between narrative continuity and the physical discontinuity of on-screen bodies becomes most acute as it is only at this point that all eight performers portraying Aviva are shown within the space of a single scene.

In the main body of the film, the appearance of each Aviva is prefaced by a title card featuring a name that relates to the unfolding dramatic situation (so, for example, Aviva as a little girl is 'Dawn' Aviva because of the film's opening during her cousin's funeral). This does at least place a marker between different components of narrative action. In the final sequence, there is no such forewarning. The scene begins with the final version of Aviva, 'Mark' (played by Jennifer Jason Leigh), featured in long shot getting in to Judah's car. She begins to pull the seatbelt across her whereupon there is a cut to a side-profile close-up of her face which makes it clear that another performer has now taken Leigh's place (it is now 'Bob' Aviva, played by Shayna Levine). Following a conversation in the car, there is a cut to a long shot detailing Judah pulling up in a car park in the woods. As Aviva gets out of the car, it is apparent that she is now incarnated by 'Mama Sunshine' Aviva, played by Sharon Wilkins. The couple walk into the woods and sit by a stream. Judah loosens his trousers and moves to climb on top of Aviva. Before his back blocks the camera entirely, we have seen Aviva also undo her jeans and start to lie back. This means that the following cut, to a close up of 'Huckleberry' Aviva (Will Denton), her head just moving back to rest on the ground, functions as another example of the scene's strict observance of the principles of continuity editing (for example, cutting on action in a seamless manner). In this section of the scene, the disconcerting clash between the film's overall commitment to continuous narrative and its discontinuous casting policy is felt more intensely at a shot-by-shot level. The collection of bodies portraying Aviva displays a variety of physical attributes: 'Mark' Aviva is blonde, skinny and clearly much older than most of the other Avivas (Jennifer Jason Leigh was in her early forties at the time of production); 'Bob' is fuller faced, has black curly hair and is of a similar age to that attributed to Aviva; 'Mama

Figure 5.11   *Todd Solondz,* Palindromes *(2004)*

Figure 5.12   *Todd Solondz,* Palindromes *(2004)*

Sunshine' is very large (compared to the other Avivas), African American and clearly an adult (though younger than 'Mark' Aviva); 'Huckleberry' is a young teenager, white, androgynous (actually played by a boy) and has a neat bob of hair (Figures 5.11, 5.12, 5.13 and 5.14).

While the editing asserts the continuity between these performers, their bodies express extreme differences. Three of the incarnations of Aviva do resemble each other more closely than the others but these ('Bob', 'Judah'

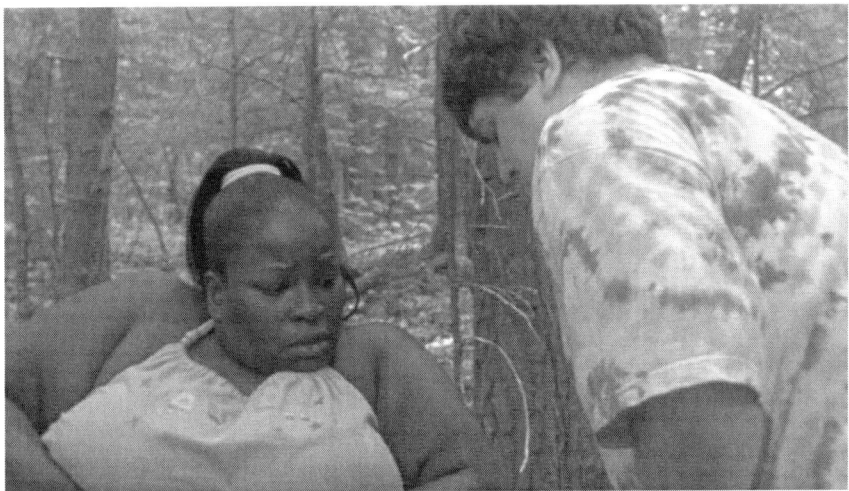

Figure 5.13   *Todd Solondz,* Palindromes *(2004)*

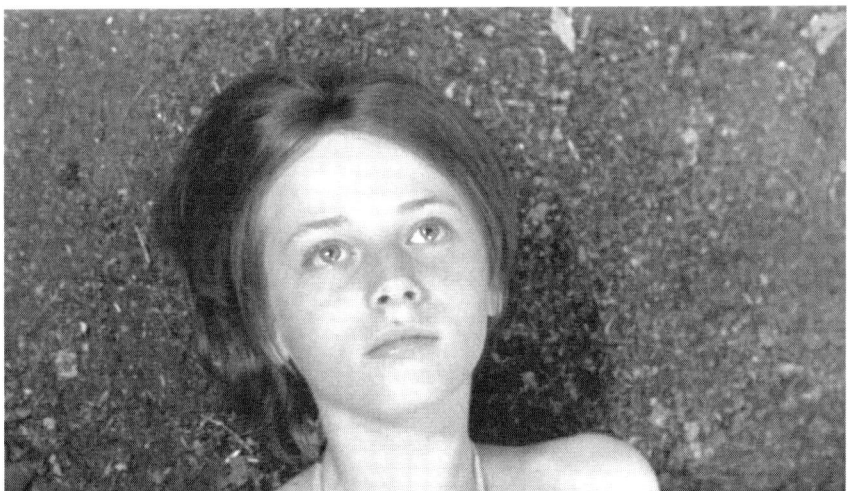

Figure 5.14   *Todd Solondz,* Palindromes *(2004)*

and 'Henrietta') are not set side by side in the sequence, suggesting that the sequencing of bodies is deliberately designed to create friction between their different physical features. In fact, the Avivas are presented in the reverse order from their sequencing in the main body of the film so the final scene could be said to enact an intensive colliding effect between different bodies that is latent in the rest of the film but remains unfulfilled owing to the separation of each Aviva into an individually captioned episode.

While I would suggest that this is a friction that the viewer cannot fail to notice, it is not registered at all in the film's formal operations. In this way, the film's narrational style is proposed as a radically *unsensuous* one, demonstrating a complete unresponsiveness to the changing corporeality of its protagonist. Whereas many of the examples in this book have demonstrated the possibility for films to evoke tactile qualities, the editing here is entirely dispassionate and unevocative, failing to acknowledge the changes in the physical representation of a character even though it is the cutting from one shot to another that makes these changes apparent.

The sequence up until this point displays the bodies of Aviva in a way that is not absorbed into her characterisation or the specifics of the dramatic situation. This makes the performers' physical differences between one another an issue in and of itself and this may lead the viewer to ponder a number of ethical questions. For example, what are the politics of a film that engineers a taboo-breaking storyline about child sexuality, sexual abuse and the morality of abortion, but uses it to engage in an apparently purely formal investigation whereby the central character becomes the vehicle for an arbitrary set of performances that, in turn, are simply 'fodder' to demonstrate the power of continuity editing? What are the ethics of spectatorship involved when the attachments of a performer to a character are suspended so that the voyeuristic nature of watching the physical attributes of another human being on-screen is exposed? The prompting of these questions suggests that the sequence deliberately takes the viewer out of his or her immersion within the fictional world to hold up to critical light conventions of casting and viewing. As such, the use of multiple casting could be seen to serve the self-reflexive extrafictional purposes identified by James Naremore. This is certainly part of the effect of multiple casting in this scene and it is one that is predicated on a split between the viewer's awareness of the corporeality of the bodies on view and the film's seeming indifference to them.

The split between the sensuous apprehension of material on the part of the viewer and the wilful ignorance of the same on the part of the film continues to be registered, even more uncomfortably, as the sexual activity of the scene begins. While the point at which Aviva begins to lie down, preparing herself for sex, is portrayed by an adult performer, the moments of actual sexual contact are covered by three young teenage Avivas: 'Huckleberry', 'Henrietta' (Rachel Corr) and 'Henry' (Hannah Freiman). The formal continuities between their representation are now registered, not through continuity editing but rather through repetitions in framing (Figures 5.15, 5.16 and 5.17) and coverage by the same non-diegetic music. The head and shoulders of all three Avivas are shown in close-up taken from above as they lie on the

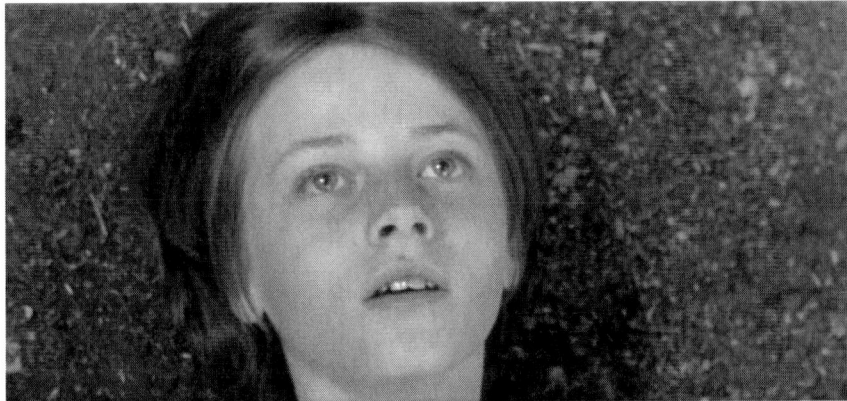

Figure 5.15   *Todd Solondz,* Palindromes *(2004)*

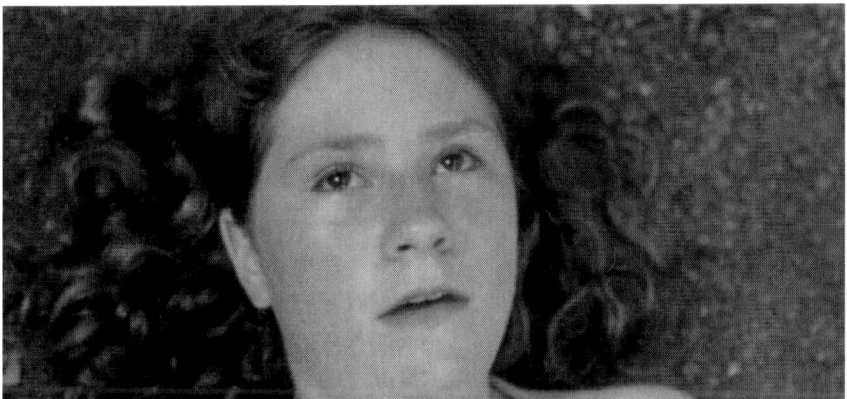

Figure 5.16   *Todd Solondz,* Palindromes *(2004)*

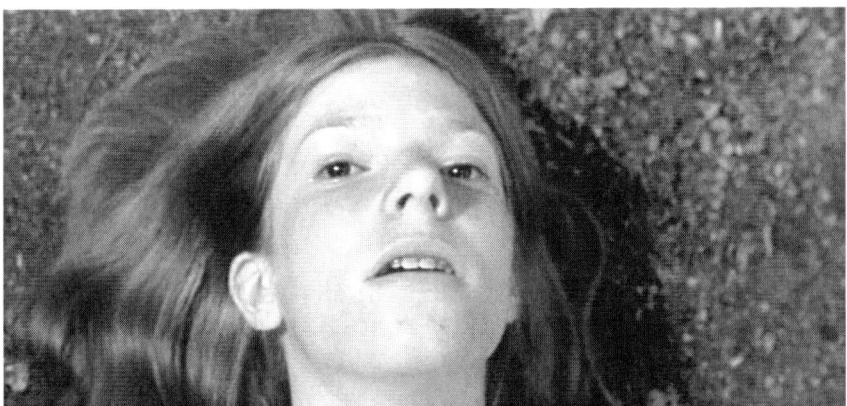

Figure 5.17   *Todd Solondz,* Palindromes *(2004)*

ground. In each case, the performers' eyes are rolled back and their lips are parted, each caught in a pose that has, in cinema, conventionally signalled that the female character on-screen is losing herself in sexual pleasure. Their heads and shoulders also slide gently back and forth along the ground, registering that Aviva's bodies are being moved by the thrusts of Judah on top of her. The appreciation of the movement as a gentle one is encouraged by the use of slow motion in these shots which lends the motion a gliding quality. This works against the intimation of the sexual encounter as a hurried one which had been indicated by the functional manner in which each character had loosened their trousers and the way Judah had climbed on top of Aviva without any foreplay.

The weight of Mama Sunshine is her most unique physical feature, in terms of her comparison to the other incarnations of Aviva. In this scene, Aviva is wearing a sleeveless top that also exposes her back, and the shots involving Mama Sunshine have revealed, from front and from back views, how her body bulges around the top. The decision to use her as the switching point between the preparation for sex and the actual sexual contact exacerbates the apprehension of the bodies of Aviva that follow as slight ones. Within the sex scene itself, the Avivas' facial gestures register a 'loosening' of the body that lends it a softness, and the slow motion exacerbates the impression of their bodies' relative weightlessness. The overhead view of the camera also serves to 'flatten' their physical features. In addition, the absenting of diegetic sound and the use of a musical soundtrack that consists of an airy, female vocal 'la, la, la-ing' increase the sense of lightness associated with their bodies at this point. The transformation of Aviva into such a physically insubstantial figure is sealed by the representation of Judah during the sex scene. The actor (John Gemberling) playing this character at this point is different from the performer (Robert Agri) who portrayed him in the 'Judah' section earlier in the film. Judah is larger in this final scene than previously. The views of the three Avivas during the sex scene are interspersed with face-on close-ups of Judah's head and shoulders as he thrusts into Aviva. These shots are in real time, rather than in slow motion, and he is clearly expending a lot of effort – physical and mental – to penetrate Aviva in what he views the 'proper' way (he prefaces the loosening of his trousers by promising Aviva that he has matured a lot since the last time he saw her). His face is scrunched up in con- centration, he is sweating and he bobs up and down *and* thrusts forwards and back, allowing the camera to capture different dimensions of his face as his position to it changes. He exhibits a hefty, laboursome, voluminous human presence that contrasts with the representation of Aviva as slight, weightless and two-dimensional, a figure who is simply being pushed back and forth by Judah's thrusting.

These representational strategies combine to suggest that all the strength has been drained from Aviva's body, making any attempt at physical resistance or self-controlled expression on her part impossible. This is an extremely disquieting spectacle for the viewer. Narratively, the sexual encounter is presented as a consensual one between two teens who are of similar ages (meaning, under the state law of New Jersey where the film is set, the encounter is also legal). Formally, however, the film enacts an extreme aestheticisation of the body of Aviva, provoking the viewer to respond to images that depict three young teenagers (two girls and a boy) in a pose that is both eroticised and defenceless. As with the earlier part of the scene, the formal strategies of Aviva's representation confront the viewer with an ethical dilemma, this time in terms of their acceptance of watching images of children that, in another context (and, for some, no doubt in this one), would be deemed abusive.

Thus far, my argument about the sensuous qualities of multiple casting in the scene has been directed towards the kind of extrafictional considerations identified by James Naremore. I want to hold on to the sense that the casting technique is also significant in 'intra-fictional' terms, however, that is to say, that the use of multiple performers to represent Aviva allows for an enhanced understanding of her character. To make this case, it is necessary first to review the significance of Judah being played by different performers in the film.

At first sight, the replacement of one actor with another in this final scene could be seen to be of a piece with the self-reflexive practices associated with the multiple casting for Aviva, as already noted. The use of this technique in relation to another character might be seen to reinforce the notion that the deployment of different actors to portray Aviva is defiantly non-psychological. The interchanging of performers is no longer tied to only her character, making it less tempting to understand the performer changes connected with Aviva in terms of the representation of her psyche (that is, to discourage a reading that sees each performer as representing different sides of Aviva's personality).

The casting of Judah, however, *can* also be seen to be motivated by the psychology of the character. Differently from Aviva, Judah's transformation is noted by another character. In the car, Aviva tells him 'you look a little different' and this is when he reveals that he has actually changed his name and now calls himself Otto. Later in the scene Judah repeats that he feels he has really changed and this exacerbates the sense that, though the physical difference between the two performers portraying Judah is arbitrary, the fact of the difference is given a justification narratively (it represents Judah's effort to transform himself).

A specific narrative significance is attributed to the timing at which 'Judah' Aviva reappears and this encourages a more character-based understanding of the earlier changes of performers in relation to Aviva, as well as of the final transformation that succeeds it. The non-diegetic music and highly aestheticised framing of the Avivas ceases abruptly as a side view of Judah sees him pulling himself away from Aviva and swearing exasperatedly, evidently displeased with his sexual performance. There is then a cut to 'Judah' Aviva (Valerie Shusterov), the performer who had portrayed the character in the original episode in which she and Judah had had sex. Like the immediately preceding shots of her character, she is lying on the ground but the framing has lost its aestheticised qualities. Aviva now cuts across the screen, rather than being viewed head-on, and more of her upper body is visible, her chest heaving as she tries to catch her breath. The soundtrack registers her panting and her breathless attempt to reassure Judah that she had enjoyed the encounter. Aviva has suddenly become reanimated with ordinarily human properties, producing sounds and exhibiting movement that indicate a 'working' body rather than one that demonstrates an inhuman floatiness.

The return to this Aviva, at this point, realigns her representation with the film's dramatic developments. As Aviva stands up and continues to reassure Judah, her physical appearance is once again made to matter, a flesh-and-blood reminder of the couple's sexual history rather than abstract material for the film's experiments with editing and framing. Appropriately, at this point, the couple have a debate about the extent to which Judah managed to penetrate Aviva, the awkwardness of the conversation revealing a messy and unidealised conjoining of bodies that registers the everyday physicality of the characters.

The final change of performer, from 'Judah' to 'Dawn' Aviva (Emani Sledge), may appear to reassert the arbitrariness of the physical differences between the Avivas as well as resume the scene's wilfully provocative mode of address. In close-up, the youngest of the Avivas says 'I have a feeling, though it's just a feeling, that this time, I'm going to be a mum'. Towards the end of this line, Aviva turns to face the camera so that the phrase 'I'm going to be a mum' is addressed directly to the viewer. The shot lingers as the little girl breaks into a contented and sustained smile.

This is a disconcerting 'happy' ending that uses a child performer to pass judgement on a sexual encounter and to voice a belief that the character is about to go through a biological process that the performer herself is clearly far too young for. Ethical questions of casting and spectating once more come to the forefront of the viewing experience, as the physical signifiers of childhood (registered in the performer's lisping, stilted vocal delivery as well as her visual appearance) clash with the adult nature of the scenario. The use of direct address exacerbates the sense that the viewer is being subjected to a deliberate provocation at this point.

The representation of 'Judah' Aviva, however, as a substantial, rather than arbitrary and abstract, body in the scene offers a reference point for the body of 'Dawn' Aviva and, indeed, all the other Avivas that is connected with character psychology and experience. In terms of her age, the casting of a young girl (rather than teenager) as 'Dawn' Aviva is not arbitrary: she first appears in an episode which is explicitly marked as taking place some years before the main time frame of the film. As such, her reappearance here takes the viewer back to the origins of Aviva's character as we have got to know her. From the very beginning Aviva has been characterised as a girl for whom sex is haunted by the spectre of abuse: in 'Dawn' Aviva's case this was signalled by her telling her mother she knows that her cousin killed herself because she had become pregnant after a date rape. In other incarnations Aviva is subject to statutory rape by a man who turns out to be a known paedophile; she is pressurised by her parents into having an abortion she does not want; and she is medically examined, without her knowledge, by the pro-life extremists with whom she finds shelter who are looking for evidence that she has gone through a termination. In this light, the 'flicking' back, in the reverse order of their original appearance, through all the Avivas can be seen to imply that this history of abuse cannot be forgotten even at moments when the sexual contact is consensual and desired. Furthermore, the coldly formalist manner by which the film moves between the Avivas can be seen not just as a provocation towards the viewer but also as a registering of the way the body of Aviva, as a character, has been subjected to examinations and violations over which she has not been able to exert any control.

SYNAESTHETIC CHARACTERISATION THROUGH MULTIPLE CASTING IN *I'M NOT THERE*

While the reappearance of 'Judah' Aviva in this final scene lends a character-based significance to the movement between performances, this does not alter the perception of the sequence's editing strategies as overwhelmingly clinical. This is of a piece with the neat lining up of performances across the film, with each version of Aviva confined, until the end, to a particular episode, sectioned off from the others by a title card. By contrast, my final example, the Bob Dylan biopic, *I'm Not There*, features a juxtaposition of different bodies performing the same character, the joins between which are marked by an unusual sensuousness. While I shall first offer some commentary on the material aspects of the different performances themselves, my focus will also be on the sensory aspects of the editing processes that move the viewer from one body to another. These possess an unusual 'body' of their own in a way that suggests that all aspects of the fictional world, including its most seemingly functional narrational devices, are suffused with sensuous qualities, providing a portrait of its biographical subject that works primarily through the senses.

The attitude of *I'm Not There* to its bodies and to their organisation is entirely distinct from that displayed by *Palindromes*. In the latter, the over-whelming indifference demonstrated to the physical differences of the per-formers playing Aviva is expressed, in part, by the film's relentless linearity: the suffering of Aviva continues remorselessly as different performers come and go. By contrast, the various performances of Dylan in *I'm Not There* are allowed to cross-pollinate with one another, encouraging resonances from one version to chime with another. Furthermore, each version of Dylan is also disclosed through a specific visual and aural aesthetic that gives them a distinctive sensuous quality even as they are set aside one another and, on occasion, intermingled. Nicole Choolun notes the unique 'emotional expressivity'[25] of each surrogate Dylan and this is accompanied by an equally distinctive material expressivity. Rapid cross-cutting between the Dylans is not common though I shall focus on the most intensive gathering of the performers in my subsequent analysis. The insistence, however, with which a particular aesthetic is associated with a specific Dylan does produce an accumulative effect in which the sensuous qualities of each characterisation become familiar to the viewer so that a material frisson between episodes is both felt and experienced as dramatically significant.

Six performers offer seven different takes on Bob Dylan in the film. In another contrast to *Palindromes*, each take is represented as a distinct char-acterisation, complete with an individual story arc, rather than, as is the case with the versions of Aviva, a continuation of the same character involved in the same dramatic situation. While this might seem to prohibit *I'm Not There*'s inclusion in a discussion of multiple casting, it is clear that each character is intended to contribute to a kaleidoscopic portrait of the famous singer. This was not just an idea promoted in the publicity for the film and the critical discourse around it but also in the 'coincidence' of all the characters possess-ing attributes and inhabiting dramatic situations that are linked to knowledge about Dylan circulating in the public domain. The sense that each character helps to build a composite fictionalisation of Dylan is cemented in the final shot of the film in which the 'real' Bob Dylan is finally (in a visual sense) revealed: this is the figure whose disclosure the fictional characterisations have been working towards.

Nevertheless, the presentation of different versions of Dylan under dif-ferent aliases does mean that the film avoids becoming straightforwardly biographical. Instead, *I'm Not There* combines narrative details, reworkings of his music, quotations from Dylan's interviews, excerpts from work that inspired Dylan, and allusions to other artworks and events that have not been previously connected to Dylan. All of this offers a more impressionistic view of Dylan than would be allowed in a conventional biopic, and part of this impression is gained through the imparting of a particular 'feeling' of Dylan through each characterisation: the non-literal representation and non-linear ordering of Dylan's life and work give the film licence to foreground experiential qualities.

The broad sensuous attributes of the different Dylans can be summarised in the following way: Jude (Cate Blanchett) represents Dylan in his 'electric' phase in the mid/late 1960s at the point where he was seen to 'abandon' the folk movement and take the lead in constructing the phenomenon of the 'rock star'. In terms of bodily matters, this Dylan is the most physically vulnerable, introduced fleetingly near the start of the film as a corpse on an autopsy table and subsequently connected with expressionistic images and sounds associated with physical collapse (for example, he is reintroduced to the film undergoing medical attention, the amplified sounds of a heartbeat intimating a body under stress and/or subject to medical monitoring). Furthermore, Jude is characterised by a physical jitteriness that indicates a body that is sleep deprived and artificially stimulated. The sense of artificial stimulation is exacerbated by the monochrome cinematography associated with the character's representation which provides a stripped-down colour palette among which the white lights that are directed towards Jude (often in the form of flashlights from journalists' cameras) take on a more aggressive appearance than they would have done in a more naturalistic colour scheme. This is also the character represented through the most hyperactive visual style, with the use of time-lapse photography, speeded-up footage and artificial back projections.

The young African American incarnation of Dylan, Woody (Marcus Carl Franklin), in contrast to Jude, is represented through a bucolic aesthetic, dominated by a pastoral yellowy green visual palette. Referring to the earliest stage of Dylan's musical development and his initial self-styling on the folk singer Woody Guthrie, Woody is defined by his 'organic' relationship with his music, expressed most forcefully by the image of him clutching his guitar even as he sleeps. He is also depicted as having particularly close contact with natural elements, getting thrown into mud and appearing to drown in a dream sequence.

As a contrast to Woody's self-consciously organic connection to his music and the natural world, the depiction of Robbie (Heath Ledger) is essayed with a greater sense of cool detachment. This is a Dylan whose romantic relationships have been compromised by his rise to stardom (though Robbie is a famous actor rather than singer). The physical performance of Robbie is more guarded than other incarnations, Ledger adopting an habitual hunched pose, the character most often wearing shades, a bulky jacket and sometimes sporting a beard. He is also subject to a more formal and less tactile regime of framing than some of the other characters, as if this is a character who is always slightly distanced. Even though the first shot of Robbie actually exposes his naked body, this is glimpsed through a reflection in a mirror and it sets the tone for a series of views that keeps Robbie at one remove. The default framing of him is not a close-up, which would disclose his emotions, but rather one that depicts him in long shot alone, in frames that contains lots of decor, that also commands the viewer's visual attention.

Jack (Christian Bale) represents the early 1960s Dylan, as he became the leading light of the burgeoning New York folk movement and gained international fame as a protest singer. Bale's physical movement is characterised by an introspective intensity. Like Robbie, Jack's posture is habitually hunched; like Woody, he seems tied to his acoustic guitar and this also has a bearing on his overall posture (for example, in an excerpt from a television interview, he sits hunched over his guitar, as if the instrument offers him some form of protection); like Jude, the media interest in his body becomes a substantial aspect of how that body is presented to the viewer. Jack's story is presented in the style of an 1980s-era television documentary about the singer and this licenses the repeated use of mock archive footage and stills to represent him, each with a mediated quality conventional to that particular format (for example, glossy album covers, *vérité*-style performance footage, fuzzy black-and-white television footage). The variety of visual textures used to represent Jack's body gives the impression of his 'true' self getting lost amid the media representations of him.

Jack undergoes a spiritual transformation, which is also registered physically, when he becomes a born-again Christian (as Dylan did in the late 1970s) and reinvents himself as Father John (also played by Bale). Whereas the 'natural' movement of Jack always appears to be shackled by the mediated and commercial packaging of his body, Father John's body is presented as one unconcerned with stylisation. This is indicated through physical attributes, such as his unkempt frizzy hair, wispy stubble and slouched demeanour, and also through an unfussy overall visual style (the documentary footage at this point settles into a consistent aesthetic characterised by evenly textured televisual colour). During a performance of 'Pressing On' to his congregation, Father John's body becomes noticeably more animated and the camerawork more expressive, cutting to close-ups that detail different aspects of the performance and featuring *vérité*-style shots of the congregation and of Father John from the diegetic audience's point of view. This heightened expressivity is represented as being driven by the spiritual zeal Father John feels inside rather than being grafted on to an unwilling body artificially, as is suggested in relation to Jack.

Billy (Richard Gere) represents the most fantastical version of Dylan offered by the film, the singer portrayed as Billy the Kid living in a surreal version of a Wild West town populated by characters sung about by Dylan in *The Basement Tapes*, a series of recordings that had circulated as bootlegs before their official release in the mid 1970s. Billy the Kid is in hiding, and this alter ego represents Dylan in his most enigmatic, subterranean form: Billy is a keeper of secrets and this lends him a mysterious power. That power is registered in relation to the senses by his particularly acute ability to see: like Jude and Robbie, Billy wears glasses but, whereas the former pair sport rock star shades that obscure their natural vision, Billy wears spectacles designed to enhance it. The first view of Billy, in the film's opening moments, is an extreme close-up of his eyes and this is all we see of him for another forty-five minutes (and, in fact, his second appearance offers only a fleeting glimpse of him). This opening shot only finds a narrative context over an hour later as it initiates a scene in which Billy rises from his bed and steps outside his hideaway in the middle of a forest. Billy's first act as he rises from his pillow is to reach for his glasses and put them on.

Extended passages of Billy riding towards, and into, the town of Riddle feature many instances of Billy looking around him, and there are key moments when filmic techniques express an intensive form of seeing. For example, after leaving his forest hideaway, Billy rides through the woods before coming to a halt. A series of close-ups, zooming closer each time to his face, register that he is looking out on to the hilly landscape concentratedly, while the corresponding point-of-view shots indicate the intensity and activity of his gaze (the first features a fast pan across the landscape, the second a slow zoom into the space, the third a further zoom that jitters slightly). The fourth point-of-view shot, another zoom, is very abruptly interspersed with zoomed-in archive footage featuring explosions which turns out to be part of a television news report on the Vietnam War being watched by Robbie's wife, Claire.

The visceral, collisive quality of the montage here is exacerbated by the unsettling rumble that enters the soundtrack in time with the point-of-view shots and which builds towards the rendition of an excoriating version of 'All Along the Watchtower' by Pearl Jam. At the same time as Billy is trying to keep himself out of sight, he demonstrates an ability to see far beyond the limits of normal everyday vision (he 'sees' Vietnam from a remote American hilltop).

In his final scene, Billy has escaped from gaol after being caught by Pat Garrett's henchmen and has hopped on to the empty carriage of a train. The scene begins, in keeping with the established pattern, with a close-up of his face as he wakes up and puts on his glasses. He then discovers a guitar, however, (the same one carried on to a train by Woody near the start of the film) which he dusts off and, in his final shot (the last image of a Dylan alter ego in the film), he is viewed in long shot, sitting in the opening of the carriage, strumming on the guitar. The implication is that Billy's special sensory ability, which had been expressed through his powers of sight, is now being expressed through a different sensuous medium associated with sound, namely music. In this way, the film ends with the spectacle of a Dylan alter ego expressing his sensuous gifts through music, thereby directing the disparate fictionalisations of the singer towards the medium associated with its real-life subject, the musical talents of whom are then more directly represented in the archive footage of Dylan himself performing, the only occasion on which Dylan is actually seen in the film.

The fictional versions of Dylan are given distinct sensuous profiles that are in keeping with the particular aspect of the singer's public career or private life they represent. For example, Jude represents Dylan's electric phase, and the tenor of the aesthetic (including Cate Blanchett's performing style) in his episodes is suitably wired; Jack represents the saturation point in the media attention that accompanied Dylan's first ascent to international fame, and so the images of him take on the texture of a range of commercially mediated visual styles.

Of all the Dylan alter egos, the one with the most restricted field for physical expression, and represented through the most austere visual aesthetic, is Arthur (Ben Wishaw), the only surrogate I have not yet mentioned. Named after the French poet, Arthur Rimbaud, an acknowledged influence on Dylan's writing style from the mid 1960s, this is the only Dylan alter ego not to be involved in an eventful narrative: he is introduced sitting down at a table in some sort of courtroom just after a shot of his interrogators behind their desks. The first time the film cuts back to Arthur, an interrogator's voice is heard but the purpose of the questioning is never made clear and, subsequently, Arthur appears completely alone, with no attempt made to reveal what the trial might have been about or how it may have developed and been resolved.

Arthur is also the only Dylan surrogate not to be associated with particular events from the singer's musical career or private life. Instead, the courtroom setting is, according to Todd Haynes in his DVD commentary, a reference to Rimbaud's involvement in the trial of his lover Paul Verlaine. The words Arthur speaks *are* attributable to Dylan, culled from interviews he gave during the mid 1960s, but this makes him a surrogate for a *disembodied* version of the singer, one represented through quotations in the written press rather than through his musical performances or deeds in his public or private life that would require a physical presence.

As such, Arthur represents the creative mind of Dylan rather than any physical impression he may have made in the world. Of all the alter egos, he is the one given the least screen time and, when he is seen, he is always framed in the same way (Figure 5.19): in monochrome, addressing the camera directly in medium close-up, set against a completely blank backdrop. The static nature of the set-up is varied, to some extent, by the fidgety actions of the performer but, given he does not leave his chair, this is the most stilled physical performance associated with any of the Dylan surrogates and it is the one delivered with the least complex and/or sumptuous visual aesthetic. The sense of him existing as the only Dylan alter ego who is not embodied in physical activity is reinforced by the fact that he is the only one whose framing remains unchanged from the photofit montage of all the Dylans that appears three times during the film, presenting still versions of the figures who are seen to 'come to life' in their particular episodes (Figures 5.18 and 5.19).

Arthur, however, is also the character most likely to exert a presence within episodes otherwise dedicated to another Dylan or to provide the continuing strand in passages that bring a number of the surrogates together. At various points, he is interspersed, visually, within episodes concentrating on Woody, Jude and Robbie and, on a number of occasions, his monologues are used as non-diegetic voice-over to provide the soundtrack for the transition to another Dylan or to tie together a montage featuring several Dylans. As such, despite the static framing and stripped-down visual aesthetic associated with his representation, he is, in fact, fundamental within the film's fictional world to the collision of sensuously different bodies all referencing the same subject (that is, the 'real' Bob Dylan).

The most extensive coming together of the surrogates is tied to the monologue in which Arthur lists the 'seven simple rules for a life in hiding'. Hiding here is clearly meant in the sense of avoiding creative risk, the rules prescribing a cautious approach to life and art (the final rule is that you should never create anything) that runs directly counter to the prevalent image of Dylan as a risk-taking creative genius (as such, the advice is delivered with a heavy sense of irony).

In this montage, Arthur is visualised intermittently but is mostly heard over episodes featuring all the other Dylans. This allows for an intensive gathering of the bodies of the six different performers, as well as the markedly different visual aesthetics associated with them. The sensuous impact of this

Figure 5.18   *Todd Haynes,* I'm Not There *(2007)*

Figure 5.19   *Todd Haynes,* I'm Not There *(2007)*

combination is most keenly felt at the end of the montage by which point Arthur's monologue has become accompanied by an instrumental passage from the Dylan song 'Cold Irons Bound' which is used as dramatic score on a number of occasions. This draws attention to the 'musicality' of Arthur's words and vocal delivery, lifting them into a different sensory register. Together, the words and music form a portentous and fulsome soundtrack that subdues all other sound (previously in the sequence, sound from the episodes being visualised could be heard). This allows for an increased concentration on the purely visual presence of the different Dylans (Jude, Arthur, Jack, Robbie and Woody) who follow each other in quick succession. The combination of music, voice and bodies, all possessed of particular sensuous attributes, provides a particularly potent example of an aesthetic assumption that the film promotes as a whole: that is to say, that Dylan is an artist of such creativity and complexity that a whole slew of artistic approaches, each with its own sensory charge, are necessary to attempt a portrait of him.

The notion that the multistranded sensuous energy of the film's aesthetic is inspired by its real-life subject is implied even during the edit points between the Dylan surrogates in this montage sequence. I argued that a characteristic of much of the editing in the final sequence of *Palindromes* is its invisibility, a seamlessness that chafes against the clear physical differences between the performers whose bodies are being joined together. By contrast, the editing of this sequence in *I'm Not There* is given a distinct material vitality so that the generative powers of the film's biographical subject are seen to encourage a dynamism in the sensuous qualities of the gaps between the different bodies of the performers as well as in the performances themselves.

The editing in this sequence has a tangible 'snap' and this is manifested in various ways. After the shot of Arthur announcing the theme of the ensuing montage ('seven simple rules for a life in hiding'), there is a cut to wooden blinds being closed and then a door being shut and its lock turned. These actions are accompanied with appropriately sharp diegetic sounds (the 'whish' of the blinds, the snap of a door being pushed to and the click of the lock). The transition to the Robbie section is ushered in by a shot of a small black-and-white television which clicks as it is turned on by remote control (we see Robbie's wife Claire holding the control in the following shot). The viscerality of the cut to Billy is made literal, heralded by a shot of a slab of meat being thrown on to a pile, landing with a fleshy slap. The movement to Jude, like the one to Robbie/Claire, is also heralded by a shot of a black-and-white television set, this time being switched manually (with an accompanying click) from one channel to another.

Towards the end of this montage, 'soundless' editing allows for a rapid rifling through the materially different versions of Dylan presented in the film. Before that, a 'noisy' editing practice provides a discernible punch to the more leisurely transitions between the different performers. Both techniques – the rapidity of visual turnover between performers and the equipping of editing with a dynamic sonic dimension – are represented in the film's motivic photofit montage of all six performers. This works as a figure of narrational instruction in the same way as the repeated shot of the two Hitchcocks passing each other in *Double Take*. Here, each transition between one fleeting photofit image and the next is accompanied by the sound of a single gunshot. The explosive quality this lends the editing demonstrates how the film carries a material charge *between* the performances of the different Dylans as well as imbuing each with a distinctive sensuous energy. Multiple casting in *I'm Not There* takes its place within an aesthetic which produces a fictional world that is sensuously loaded in all its aspects. This amounts to a particularly pervasive type of synaesthetic effect whereby one sensuous form, namely Bob Dylan's music, finds material expression in other sensory registers. As such, the film offers an especially 'full-bodied' final example for this chapter, providing a fictional experience of Dylan that is premised on sensuous specificities to such an extent that even the joins between the performances are made materially resonant. It also functions as an appropriately fully realised final case study for the book as a whole, manufacturing as it does a multitextured portrait of a character that is reliant on the material difference between multiple, sensuously diverse components.

Notes

1. Choolun, '"Think smart": multiple casting, critical engagement and the contemporary film spectator', *Refractory: A Journal of Entertainment Media*.
2. Naremore, *Acting in the Cinema*, p. 79.
3. Sobchack, '"At the still point of the turning world": meta-morphing and meta-stasis', in Vivian Sobchack (ed.), *Meta-Morphing: Visual Transformation and the Culture of Quick-Change*, p. 137.
4. Ibid. p. 134.
5. De Van, '*Don't Look Back* press kit', pp. 9–10.
6. Sobchack, op. cit., p. 44.
7. Choolun, op. cit.
8. Ibid.
9. Ibid.
10. Ibid.
11. Smith, *Engaging Characters: Fiction, Emotion, and the Cinema*, p. 26.
12. Naremore, op. cit., p. 79.
13. Daly, 'Cinema 3.0: the interactive-Image', *Cinema Journal*, pp. 93–4.
14. Riis, 'Implications of paradoxical characters for our models and conceptualisations', in Jens Eder, Fotis Jannidis and Ralf Schneider (eds), *Characters in Fictional Worlds: Understanding Imaginary Beings in Literature, Film, and Other Media*, p. 262.
15. Ibid. p. 262.
16. Del Rio, *Deleuze and the Cinemas of Performance: Powers of Affection*, p. 9.
17. Ibid. p. 47.
18. Ibid. pp. 111–12.
19. Ibid. p. 111.
20. Ibid. p. 198.
21. Ibid. p.198.
22. Ibid. p. 185.
23. Ibid. p. 25.
24. Ibid. p. 188.
25. Choolun, 'Think Smart'.

Conclusion

The crash scenes of *Amores Perros* provided a thematically apt starting point for the extended analyses in this book, given the insistence with which I have focused on the aesthetics of collision. Of course, this is not the only way a sensuous investigation of storytelling in film may be approached. For example, Lucy Fife Donaldson has recently published work on screen performance that is attentive to sensuous detail but with a focus on the singularities of a performing body rather than on the moment of impact between different ones. She considers the connection between the effort apparent in a performance and the 'kinesthetic empathy'[1] this might inspire in the viewer. Her conceptualisation of this relationship reveals an understanding of the embodied experience of film viewing that is similar to mine:

> The spectator I refer to (apart from my own personal responses) is the one implied by the formal presentation of people and events on-screen; I understand perception and response to be invited through the observable details of the film. When watching a film, the perceived effort, or qualities of movement within a particular performance are directly shaped by its formal placement; the decisions relating to its staging for the camera, as well as editing choices.[2]

Donaldson acknowledges that the human body on-screen is perceived as 'corporeal, sensory and moving'[3] by viewers who, in their response, remain aware of their own sensory capacities. She views the formal placement of the body on-screen, however, as a crucial determinant in the kind of response that a performance will elicit. At certain points, a viewer may be encouraged to feel (emotionally and sensorially) what a character feels but this type of engagement is only one option among many.[4] No matter how close the physical alignment between viewer and character may be, the framed quality of the performance will never disappear. The invitation to 'feel' a performance is always accompanied by the opportunity to 'interpret and evaluate it'.[5]

Donaldson's interest in the feel of a performance is connected with her wider research on texture in film, which apprehends the affective qualities of film, embodied in its fine material details, in relation to 'character, narrative and theme'.[6] Donaldson defines texture as: 'the combination of small-scale detail which holds the structure together. Texture has an important sensory dimension, it expresses the feel (in terms of perception and touch) of something and thus evokes response from the viewer/listener/reader.[7] The textures of images and sounds and the significance of these in articulating a fictional world have been among the key concerns of this book. When drafting the different analyses, I sometimes found it difficult to avoid getting lost in the small-scale details that create texture. This was especially true in relation to my attempts to account for *Double Take*, a film composed of so many different textures, often associated with the same object (for example, the bowler hat). There is a danger that paying attention to such fine details becomes an end in itself: the result can be that the analysis becomes overly myopic and thereby non-communicative; it might run the risk of ascribing an ineffable 'mystical' power to tactile qualities; or it might get embroiled in finding words to describe sensory experience for its own sake. The potential gains and pitfalls of this kind of analysis are summarised well by Elsaesser and Hagener:

> If we really want to gain access to things, their intrinsic qualities and inherent attributes, we need to practice a genuinely open examination of what the camera reveals and discloses. On the other hand, the haptic turn and other body-based approaches to the cinematic experience are sometimes in danger of celebrating a big-tent, inclusive feel-good-theory of sensory empowerment.[8]

It is to be hoped that the discipline of relating texture to specific developments in a film's fictional world mitigates against a form of criticism that comes across as unfocusedly 'touchy-feely'. A commitment to apprehending only the fictional aspects of this world, however, could be seen as an evasion of critical responsibility in itself. The cultural, historical and political significance and/or origins of the sensuous details I have considered have not been at the forefront of my analysis. I implied this was an issue when I discussed my lack of attention to the specifics of language in *Happy Together*. There would be numerous other opportunities, however, to criticise my approach as one that privileges aesthetics over the politics of representation. For example, I have said nothing about the racial and gender dynamics between the Dylan alter egos in *I'm Not There*. Four of the performers are white males, like Dylan, but one is an African American boy (Marcus Carl Franklin) and one is a white woman (Cate Blanchett). The last two performances have attracted the most commentary, and this includes a very critical account of the casting by Zelie Asava. Asava connects the multiple casting of *I'm Not There* with the phenomenon of morphing, sharing with me a reference point in her use of Sobchack's work on the morph. Asava insists on the racism of casting Franklin as 'an

African-American stereotype, a travelling hobo storyteller with a guitar',[9] arguing he is 'denied subjectivity or a world of his own'.[10] The evidence provided to support this statement is all on the level of the basic dramatic situations in which Woody is placed, and on the simple fact of the casting of an African American boy in this role. I would venture that this reading would be complicated, or its plausibility enhanced, through attention to the moment-by-moment detail of the performance, including its sensuous distinctiveness, as well as through a recognition of its combination with other performances. To the extent that the characters are all feeding into a multitextured portrait of a single biographical subject, *all* of them are denied a world of their own, so the discrimination against Woody would need to be assessed in that context.

These comments are not intended to devalue a more overtly politicised reading of the film than I have made but rather to suggest the potential for such forms of analysis to benefit from attention to small-scale detail and the textural interweaving of different elements. In terms of the case studies in this book, my commentary on the editing between, and framing of, the multiple Avivas in *Palindromes* does indicate the possibility of a sensuous study that is attentive to the operations of a fictional world *and* the real-world ethics of spectatorship and representation.

My hope is that the form of analysis I have pursued across this book will encourage readers to be alert to the sensorial details of films, recognising their real-world stimulating effects but also perceiving them as invitations to engage with the fictional aspects of the film world. This world is defined by certain boundaries, the screen providing access to it but also functioning as a barrier that keeps the viewer at a certain distance. Technological developments certainly have the potential to change the fundamental conditions through which fictional cinema engages the viewer. For example, the iCinema centre in the University of New South Wales has hosted a number of experiments in interactive and immersive storytelling, including *Scenario*, a 360-degree, 3D cinematic installation in which the audience develops a narrative in collaboration with CGI-created characters.[11] This provides a sensory experience for the user akin to entering Dr Parnassus's Imaginarium, the real human body moving in, and physically engaging with, an all-encompassing, sensuously detailed, virtually created environment.

This type of fictional world requires a different conceptualisation of the relationship between the senses and storytelling in film from the one I have developed in this book. I embarked on this study, however, because of my perception that there were aspects of the viewer's sensuous engagement with traditional forms of the fiction film that have not been fully addressed. In this context, the conditions of film spectatorship visualised in Truchet's 1896 poster for *Arrival of the Train* (Figure 1.1), remain pertinent. The women watching the film are represented as being sensorially captivated by the on-screen movement of the train but are also set at one remove. This understanding of the film–viewer relationship has underpinned the approach taken in this book: fiction films engage viewers sensuously but also keep them at a productive distance, one that facilitates an evaluation of the materials of their worlds.

Notes

1. Donaldson, 'Effort and empathy: engaging with film performance', in Dee Reynolds and Matthew Reason (eds), *Kinesthetic Empathy in Creative and Cultural Practices*, p. 161.
2. Ibid. p. 160.
3. Ibid. p. 159.
4. Ibid. p. 161.
5. Ibid. p. 159.
6. Donaldson, 'Texture in film', paper delivered at University of Hertfordshire, 7 December 2011.
7. Ibid.
8. Elsaesser and Hagener, *Film Theory: An Introduction Through the Senses*, pp. 127–8.
9. Asava, 'Multiculturalism and morphing in *I'm Not There*', *Wide Screen*, p. 3.
10. Ibid. p. 3.
11. For an account of *Scenario* and other innovations of the iCinema Research Centre, see Barker, 'Images and eventfulness: expanded cinema and experimental research at the University of New South Wales', *Studies in Australasian Cinema* (forthcoming as this book went to press).

Bibliography

Arthur, Paul, 'The status of found footage', *Spectator*, 20, 1, 1999, pp. 57–69.

Asava, Zélie, 'Multiculturalism and morphing in *I'm Not There*', *Wide Screen*, 2, 1, 2010, http://widescreenjournal.org/index.php/journal/article/view/44 accessed 1 October 2012.

Barker, Jennifer M., *The Tactile Eye: Touch and the Cinematic Experience* (Berkeley: University of California Press, 2009).

Barker, Timothy, 'Images and eventfulness: expanded cinema and experimental research at the University of New South Wales', *Studies in Australasian Cinema*, 2013 (forthcoming as this book went to press).

Bazin, André, *What is Cinema?*, trans. Hugh Gray (Berkeley: University of California Press, 1967), vol. 1.

Bazin, André, *What is Cinema?*, trans. Hugh Gray (Berkeley: University of California Press, 1971), vol. 2.

Beckman, Karen, 'Crash aesthetics: *Amores Perros* and the dream of cinematic mobility', in Karen Beckman and Jean Ma (eds), *Still Moving: Between Cinema and Photography* (Durham: Duke University Press, 2008), pp. 134–57.

Beugnet, Martine, *Cinema and Sensation: French Film and the Art of Transgression* (Edinburgh: Edinburgh University Press, 2007).

Birtwistle, Andy, *Cinesonica: Sounding Film and Video* (Manchester: Manchester University Press, 2010).

Bordwell, David *The Way Hollywood Tells It: Story and Style in Modern Movies* (Berkeley and London: University of California Press, 2006).

Bordwell, David, Janet Staiger and Kristin Thompson, *The Classical Hollywood CInema: Film Style & Mode of Production to 1960* (London: Routledge & Kegan Paul, 1985).

Bordwell, David and Kristin Thompson, *Film Art*: ninth edition (New York: McGraw-Hill, 2010).

Branigan, Edward, 'Sound and epistemology in film', *Journal of Aesthetics and Art Criticism*, 47, 4, 1989, pp. 311–24.

Cavell, Stanley, *The World Viewed: Reflections on the Ontology of Film* (Cambridge, MA and London: Harvard University Press, 1979).

Chion, Michel, *Audio-Vision: Sound on Screen*, trans. Claudia Gorbman (New York: Columbia University Press, 1994).

Choolun, Nicole, '"Think Smart": multiple casting, critical engagement and the contemporary film spectator', *Refractory: A Journal of Entertainment Media*, 18, 2011, http://refractory.unimelb.edu.au/2011/05/06/think-smart-multiple-casting-critical-engagement-and-the-contemporary-film-spectator-nicole-choolun/ accessed 1 October 2012.

Daley, Kristen M., 'Cinema 3.0: The Interactive-Image', *Cinema Journal*, 50, 1, 2010, pp. 81–98.

Darnley, Andrew, *Visual Digital Culture: Surface Play and Spectacle in New Media Genres* (London: Routledge, 2000).

Doane, Mary Ann, 'Ideology and the practices of sound editing and mixing', in Elisabeth Weis and John Belton (eds), *Film Sound: Theory and Practice* (New York: Columbia University Press, 1985), pp. 54–62.

Donaldson, Lucy Fife 'Texture in film', paper delivered at University of Hertfordshire, 7 December 2011.

Donaldson, Lucy Fife, 'Effort and empathy: engaging with film performance', in Dee Reynolds and Matthew Reason (eds), *Kinesthetic Empathy in Creative and Cultural Practices* (Bristol: Intellect, 2012), pp. 157–74.

Eisenstein, Sergei, *Film Form: Essays in Film Theory,* trans. Jay Leyda (London: Dobson, 1951).

Elsaesser, Thomas and Malte Hagener, *Film Theory: an introduction through the senses* (New York and London: Routledge, 2010).

Flinn, Caryl, *The New German Cinema: Music, History, and the Matter of Style* (Berkeley: University of California Press, 2004).

Gidal, Peter, 'Theory and definition of structural/materialist film', in Peter Gidal (ed.), *Structural Film Anthology* (London: BFI, 1976), pp. 1–21.

Gorbman, Claudia, *Unheard Melodies: Narrative Film Music* (London: BFI, 1987).

Gorbman, Claudia, 'Artless singing', *Music, Sound and the Moving Image*, 5, 2, 2011, pp. 157–71.

Halligan, Benjamin, 'What is the neo-underground and what isn't: a first consideration of Harmony Korine', in Xavier Mendik and Steven Jay Schneider (eds), *Underground USA: Filmmaking Beyond the Hollywood Canon* (London: Wallflower, 2002), pp. 150–60.

Jacobs, Steven, *Framing Pictures: Film and the Visual Arts* (Edinburgh: Edinburgh University Press, 2011).

Kelley, Mike, 'Mike Kelley Interviews Harmony Korine', *FilmMaker*, 1997, http://www.film makermagazine.com/news/2012/02/from-the-archives-mike-kelley-interviews-harmony-korine/ accessed 1 October 2012.

Kerins, Mark, *Beyond Dolby (Stereo): Cinema in the Digital Sound Age* (Bloomington: Indiana University Press, 2011).

Kim, Ji-hoon, 'The post-medium condition and the explosion of cinema', *Screen*, 50, 1, 2009, pp. 114–23.

Kozloff, Sarah, *Invisible Storytellers: Voice-Over Narration in American Fiction Film* (Berkeley: University of California Press, 1988).

Krauss, Rosalind, *A Voyage on the North Sea: Art in the Age of the Post-Medium Condition* (London: Thames & Hudson, 2000).

Kubelka, Peter, 'The theory of metrical film', in P. Adams Sitney (ed.), *The Avant-Garde Film: A Reader of Theory and Criticism* (New York: New York University Press, 1978), pp. 139–59.

Loiperdinger, Martin, trans. Bernd Elzer, 'Lumière's *Arrival of the Train*: cinema's founding myth', *The Moving Image*, 4, 3, 2004, pp. 89–118.

Lunenfeld, Peter, 'Introduction: screen grabs: the digital aesthetic and new media theory', in Peter Lunenfeld (ed.), *The Digital Dialectic: New Essays on New Media* (Cambridge, MA/ London: MIT Press, 2000), pp. xiv–xxi.

Manovich, Lev, 'What is digital cinema?' (1995) http://www.manovich.net/TEXT/digital-cinema.html accessed 1 October 2012.

Marks, Laura, U., *The Skin of the Film: Intercultural Cinema, Embodiment and the Senses* (Durham, NC and London: Duke University Press, 2000).

Montgomery, Colleen, 'Woody's Roundup and Wall-E's wunderkammer: Technophilia and nostalgia in Pixar animation', *Animation Studies Online Journal*, 6, 2 September 2011, http://journal.animationstudies.org/colleen-montgomery-woodys-roundup-and-walles-wu nderkammer/ accessed 1 October 2012.

Moskowicz, Julia, 'To infinity and beyond: assessing the technological imperative in computer animation', *Screen*, 43, 3, 2002, pp. 293–314.

Naremore, James, *Acting in the Cinema* (Berkeley: University of California Press, 1990).

Perkins, Victor, 'Where is the world? The horizon of events in movie fiction', in John Gibbs and Doug Pye (eds), *Style and Meaning: Studies in the Detailed Analysis of Film* (Manchester and New York: Manchester University Press, 2005), pp. 16–41.

Peucker, Brigitte, *The Material Image: Art and the Real in Film* (Stanford: Stanford University Press, 2007).

Pierson, Michele, 'Special effects in Martin Arnold's and Peter Tscherkassky's cinema of mind', *Discourse: Journal for Theoretical Studies in Media and Culture*, 28, 2–3, pp. 28–50.

Power, Pat, 'Animated expressions: expressive style in 3D computer graphic narrative animation', *Animation An Interdisciplinary Journal*, 4, 2, 2009, pp. 107–29.

Pye, Doug, 'Movies and tone' in Doug Pye and John Gibbs (eds) *Close Up 2* (London: Wallflower), pp. 1–80.

Reay, Pauline, *Music in Film: Soundtracks and Synergy* (London: Wallflower, 2004).

Riis, Johannes, 'Implications of paradoxical characters for our models and conceptualisations', in Jens Eder, Fotis Jannidis and Ralf Schneider (eds), *Characters in Fictional Worlds: Understanding Imaginary Beings in Literature, Film, and Other Media* (New York: De Gruyter, 2010), pp. 259–75.

del Rio, Elena, *Deleuze and the Cinemas of Performance: Powers of Affection* (Edinburgh: Edinburgh University Press, 2008).

Schaffer, William, 'The importance of being plastic: the feel of Pixar', *Animation Journal*, 12, 2004, pp. 72–95.

Shaviro, Steven, *The Cinematic Body* (Minneapolis and London: University of Minnesota Press, 1993).

Shingler, Martin, 'Fasten your seatbelts and prick up your ears: The dramatic human voice in film', *Scope*, 5, 2006, http://www.scope.nottingham.ac.uk/article.php?issue=5&id=128 accessed 1 October 2012.

Smith, Jacob, *Vocal Tracks: Performance and Sound Media* (Berkeley and London: University of California Press, 2008).

Smith, Murray, *Engaging Characters: Fiction, Emotion, and the Cinema* (London: Clarendon Press, 1995).

Smith, Paul Julian, *Amores Perros* (London: BFI, 2003).

Smith, Susan, 'Voice in film', in Doug Pye and John Gibbs (eds) *Close Up 2* (London: Wallflower, 2007), pp. 159–238.

Sobchack, Vivian, *The Address of the Eye: A Phenomenology of Film Experience* (Princeton: Princeton University Press, 1991).

Sobchack, Vivian, '"At the still point of the turning world": meta-morphing and meta-stasis', in Vivian Sobchack (ed.), *Meta-Morphing: Visual Transformation and the Culture of Quick-Change* (Minneapolis: University of Minnesota Press, 2000), pp. 131–58.

Sobchack, Vivian, *Carnal Thoughts: Embodiment and Moving Image Culture* (Berkeley: University of California Press, 2004).

Sobchack, Vivian, 'Animation and automation, or, the incredible effortfulness of being', *Screen* 50, 4, 2009, pp. 375–91.

Stoller, Paul, *Sensuous Scholarship* (Philadelphia: University of Pennsylvania Press, 1997).

Thomas, Deborah, *Reading Hollywood: Spaces and Meanings in American Films* (London: Wallflower, 2001).

Trotter, David, 'Lynne Ramsay's *Ratcatcher*: towards a theory of haptic narrative', *Paragraph*, 31, 2, 2008, pp. 138–58.

de Van, Marina, '*Don't Look Back* press kit', http://medias.unifrance.org/medias/103/164/42087/presse/don-t-look-back-2009-press-kit-french-2.pdf accessed 1 October 2012.

Wilson, George M., *Narration in Light: Studies in Cinematic Point of View* (Baltimore and London: Johns Hopkins University Press, 1986).

Index